# PHILOSOPH

"I enjoyed reading this book immensely and think very highly indeed of it both as a student text and as a serious work of philosophy. It is well-organized, well-informed, up to date, comprehensive in scope, and written in an extremely clear and accessible style."

E. J. Lowe, *University of Durham*

"Well-written, fair and comprehensive. There are good examples and positions are explained well. John Heil's book will be useful for almost any undergraduate course in the philosophy of mind."

Fred Dretske, *Stanford University*

What exactly is the mind? One popular view is that minds are just brains. Another is that minds are software routines running on neurological hardware. If you are tempted by either of these views, you are faced with the task of reconciling familiar characteristics of conscious experiences with the apparently very different features of brains and their operations. John Heil offers an alternative conception of the mind grounded in a metaphysical account of the contents of the world. On the way, he gives a guided tour of the most prominent accounts of the nature of the mind, including dualist, materialist, behaviorist, functionalist, interpretationist, and eliminativist accounts of the nature of mind, along with a critical assessment of recent trends in the subject.

*Philosophy of Mind* is written in an engaging way and designed to be understandable to readers with little or no background in philosophy. It includes material of interest to philosophers as well as to psychologists and neuroscientists and is supported by clear and practical examples.

**John Heil** is Professor of Philosophy at Davidson College, North Carolina. He is the author of *The Nature of True Minds* (1992) and *First-Order Logic: A Concise Introduction* (1994).

## Routledge Contemporary Introductions to Philosophy

### Series Editor:
*Paul K. Moser,*
*Loyola University of Chicago*

This innovative, well-structured series is for students who have already done an introductory course in philosophy. Each book introduces a core general subject in contemporary philosophy and offers students an accessible but substantial transition from introductory to higher-level college work in that subject. The series is accessible to nonspecialists and each book clearly motivates and expounds the problems and positions introduced. An orientating chapter briefly introduces its topic and reminds readers of any crucial material they need to have retained from a typical introductory course. Considerable attention is given to explaining the central philosophical problems of a subject and the main competing solutions and arguments for those solutions. The primary aim is to educate students in the main problems, positions and arguments of contemporary philosophy rather than to convince students of a single position. The initial eight central books in the series are written by experienced authors and teachers, and treat topics essential to a well-rounded philosophy curriculum.

*Epistemology*
Robert Audi

*Ethics*
Harry Gensler

*Metaphysics*
Michael J. Loux

*Philosophy of Art*
Noel Carroll

*Philosophy of Language*
William G. Lycan

*Philosophy of Mind*
John Heil

*Philosophy of Religion*
Keith E. Yandell

*Philosophy of Science*
Alexander Rosenberg

# PHILOSOPHY OF MIND

## A contemporary introduction

*John Heil*

London and New York

First published 1998
by Routledge
11 New Fetter Lane, London EC4P 4EE

Simultaneously published in the USA and Canada
by Routledge
29 West 35th Street, New York, NY 10001

Typeset in Aldus Roman by RefineCatch Limited, Bungay, Suffolk
Printed and bound in Great Britain by
TJ International Ltd, Padstow, Cornwall

*British Library Cataloguing in Publication Data*
A catalogue record for this book is available from the British Library

*Library of Congress Cataloging in Publication Data*
Heil, John.
Philosophy of mind: a contemporary introduction / John Heil.
p.     cm. – (Routledge contemporary introductions to philosophy; 3)
Includes bibliographical references and index.
1. Philosophy of mind.   I. Title.   II. Series.
BD418.3.H47   1998
128'.2–dc21          97–32598
CIP

ISBN 0–415–13059–X (hbk)
ISBN 0–415–13060–3 (pbk)

*For Mark, Gus, and Lilian*

# Contents

## Chapter 5: Interpretational theories of mind and eliminativism 129

## Chapter 6: Minds and their place in nature 173

## Bibliography   227

## Index   233

# Preface and acknowledgments

One aim of this book is to introduce readers with little or no background in philosophy to central issues in the philosophy of mind, and to do so in a way that highlights those issues' metaphysical dimensions. In this regard, my approach differs from those that emphasize connections between the philosophy of mind and various empirical domains: psychology, neuroscience, and artificial intelligence, for instance. It is not that I regard empirical work as irrelevant to the philosophy of mind. After years of skepticism, however, I have become convinced that the fundamental philosophical questions concerning the mind remain metaphysical questions – where metaphysics is understood as something more than the a priori pursuit of eternal verities: metaphysics, as I see it, takes the sciences at their word. More particularly, the fundamental questions are questions of ontology – our best accounting of what, in the most general terms, there is.

Like any other systematic pursuit, ontology is constrained formally: ontological theses must be internally coherent. Ontological theses ought, in addition, to be reconcilable with established scientific lore. When we consider every imaginable ontology that is consistent, both internally and with pronouncements of the sciences, however, we can see that the field remains wide open. Something more is required if our evaluation of competing approaches is to be anything more than a bare expression of preference. That something more lies in the relative power of alternative schemes. An ontology that not only strikes us as plausible (in the sense that it is both internally coherent and consistent with science and common experience) but at the same time offers solutions to a wide range of problems in a way that makes those solutions appear inevitable, is to be preferred to an ontology that provides only piecemeal solutions to a narrow range of problems.

At the present time, the field is dominated by David Lewis's ontology of possible worlds. Lewis postulates, in addition to the actual world, an infinity of real, but non-actual, possible worlds. Each world differs in some respect from the actual world and from every other possible world. By appealing to features of these worlds, Lewis lays claim to offering explanations of important truths holding in the actual world.

The Lewis ontology of possible worlds strikes many philosophers (and all non-philosophers) as implausible. Nevertheless, many of these same philosophers persist in resorting to possible worlds to explicate important concepts: the concept of causation, for instance, the concept of a causal power or disposition, the concept of necessity. If you reject the ontology of possible worlds, it is unclear what is supposed to ground such appeals. For Lewis, the truth-makers for claims about possible worlds are the possible worlds. If you disdain possible worlds, however, yet appeal to them in explicating, say, causation, what makes your assertions true or false? If non-actual possible worlds do not exist, then presumably your claims are grounded in features – intrinsic features – of the actual world. But then why not appeal directly to these features? What use is it to invoke non-actual possibilities?

I believe we have a right to be suspicious of anyone who embraces the formal apparatus of possible worlds while rejecting the ontology. Indeed, I think we might be more suspicious of formal techniques generally, when these are deployed to answer substantive questions in metaphysics and the philosophy of mind. So long as we remain at a formal level of discourse, it is easy to lose interest in what might ground our claims. And this, I think, has led to the kind of technical sterility characteristic of so much contemporary analytical philosophy.

I do not deny that formal techniques have their place. I want only to suggest that it is a mistake to imagine that these techniques can be relied upon to reveal hidden ontological details of our world. A good example of the detrimental effects of ungrounded formalism can be found in the tendency to conflate (if not officially, then in practice) predicates – linguistic entities – and properties. This can lead to specious puzzles. Are there disjunctive properties? Well of course, some reply: if $P$ is a property and $Q$ is a property, then $P \lor Q$ ($P$ or $Q$) is a property.

True enough, if $P$ and $Q$ are predicates denoting properties, then we can construct a disjunctive predicate, $P \lor Q$. What is less clear is whether this gives us any right whatever to suppose that $P \lor Q$ designates a property. The notion of a disjunctive property makes sense, I suspect, only so long as we imagine that a property is whatever answers to a predicate. But this is the linguistic tail wagging the ontological dog.

I mention all this by way of calling attention to the absence of formal devices, appeals to purely modal notions like supervenience, and invocations of possible worlds in the chapters that follow. If it accomplishes nothing else, my decision to omit such technical trappings will certainly make the book more accessible to the non-specialist reader. In any case, the philosophy of mind, indeed metaphysics generally, is not – or ought not to be – a technical exercise. Philosophical theses should be expressible without reliance on specialized terminology; and I have tried my best to say what I have to say without resorting to such terminology. This strikes me as an important exercise for every philosopher. Too much can be smuggled in, too much left unexplained when we allow ourselves to fall back on philosophical jargon.

Although this book is written with the non-specialist in view, it is intended to be more than a mere survey of going theories. I take up a number of issues that may be of interest to hardened philosophers of mind and to non-philosophers with a professional interest in minds and their nature. If nothing else, I am hopeful that my approach will encourage others to delve into the ontological basis of mentality.

Some readers will be surprised at my including certain views, and disappointed at my downplaying or ignoring others. In a book of this sort, however, one must be selective: it is impossible to do justice to every position. I have, then, chosen what seem to me to be central issues and points of view in the philosophy of mind, and concentrated on these. Ultimately I hope to lead open-minded readers to what amounts to a new perspective on the territory.

On a more practical note: I expect instructors who use this book as part of a course in the philosophy of mind to supplement it with readings of original materials. With that in mind, I have included, at the end of each chapter, a list of suggested readings. These readings can be used to fill perceived gaps and to compensate for infelicities in my exposition.

The inspiration for this book came to me as I was completing an earlier volume, *The Nature of True Minds* (Cambridge: Cambridge University Press, 1992). The centerpiece of that volume is an elaborate discussion of the problem of mental causation: if mental properties depend on, but are not identical with, material properties, how could mental properties affect behavior? As I struggled with details of my account of mental causation (an account that owed much to the work of my colleague, Alfred Mele), it gradually dawned on me that any solution to the problem would require a prolonged excursion into ontology. More generally, I began to see that attempts to answer questions in the philosophy of mind that ignored ontology, or depended (as mine did) on *ad hoc* ontological assumptions, were bound to prove unsatisfying. The upshot was something akin to a religious conversion.

My route to "ontological seriousness" was occasioned by conversations (pitched battles, really) with C. B. Martin. The first result was a book-length manuscript on metaphysics and the philosophy of mind completed during a sabbatical leave in Berkeley in 1993–4. The book before you is a distant relative of that manuscript. I am grateful to Davidson College and to the National Endowment for the Humanities for their generous support, and to the Department of Psychology, the University of California, Berkeley, for hosting me. I owe a particular debt to Lynne Davisson and Carolyn Scott for their administrative support and to the

Berkeley Presbyterian Missionary Homes for providing accommodation for my family.

Many people have contributed to my thinking on the topics covered here. Martin is foremost among these. My most fervent hope is that readers whose interest is stirred by the ideas discussed in chapter six will take the trouble to track down those ideas' sources in Martin's writings.

I have benefited immeasurably from discussions with John Carroll, Randolph Clarke, Güven Güzeldere, Michael Lockwood, E. J. Lowe, David Robb, Dan Ryder, Amie Thomasson, Peter Unger, and Peter Vallentyne, all of whom provided astute comments on portions of the manuscript. I am especially indebted to participants in my 1996 NEH Summer Seminar on Metaphysics of Mind at Cornell, including (in addition to Clarke and Thomasson) Leonard Clapp, Anthony Dardis, James Garson, Heather Gert, Muhammad Ali Khalidi, David Pitt, Eric Saidel, Stephen Schwartz, Nigel J. T. Thomas, and Michael Watkins. Many of the ideas found in the pages that follow emerged in seminar discussions. I cannot imagine a more congenial, philosophically discerning, and, yes, ontologically serious group anywhere.

A number of people have, in discussion or correspondence, influenced my thinking on particular issues addressed here. David Armstrong, Richard Boyd, Jaegwon Kim, Brian McLaughlin, Alfred Mele, Brendan O'Sullivan, and Sydney Shoemaker deserve special mention. Fred Dretsky and Kim Sterelny provided useful comments on a penultimate draft of the manuscript. I am especially indebted to E. J. Lowe for detailed and searching criticisms of every chapter. Lowe is, to my mind, one of a handful of contemporary philosophers whose views on minds and their place in nature reflect a deep appreciation of ontology. Finally, and most importantly, the book would not have been possible without the unwavering support – intellectual, moral, and otherwise – of Harrison Hagan Heil.

The manuscript was completed during a fellowship year at the National Humanities Center (1996–7) and was supported by the Center, by a Davidson College Faculty Grant, and by the National Endowment for the Humanities. I owe these institutions more than I can say.

John Heil
Spring, 1997

# CHAPTER 1
# Introduction

**Science and metaphysics**
**A look ahead**

# 1
# Introduction

Does a tree falling in the forest make a sound when no one is around to hear it? The question is familiar to every undergraduate. One response is that of course the tree makes a sound – why shouldn't it? The tree makes a sound whether anyone is on hand to hear it or not. And, in any case, even if there are no people about, there are squirrels, birds, or at least bugs that must hear it crashing down.

Consider a more measured response, versions of which have percolated down through successive generations of undergraduates. The tree's falling creates sound waves that radiate outwards in a spherical pattern. If these sound waves are intercepted by a human ear (or maybe – although this is more controversial – the ear of some non-human sentient creature) they are heard as a crashing noise. If the sound waves go undetected, they eventually peter out. Whether an unobserved falling tree makes a sound, then, depends on what you mean by sound. If you mean "heard noise," then (squirrels and birds aside) the tree falls silently. If, in contrast, you mean something like "distinctive spherical pattern of impact waves in the air," then, yes, the tree's falling does make a sound.

Most people who answer the question this way consider the issue settled. The puzzle is solved simply by getting clear on what we mean. Indeed, we can appreciate the initial question as posing a puzzle only if we are already prepared to distinguish two senses of "sound." But what precisely are these two senses? On the one hand, there is the physical sound, a spherical pattern of impact waves open to public inspection and measurement – at any rate, it is open to public inspection given the right instruments. On the other hand, there is the experienced sound. The experienced sound depends on the presence of an observer. It is not, or not obviously, a public occurrence: although a sound can be experienced by many people, each observer's experience is "private." And although we can observe and measure agents' responses to experienced sound, we cannot measure the experienced sound itself. This way of thinking about sounds applies quite generally. It applies, for instance, to the looks of objects, to their tastes, their smells, and to the way they feel.

The picture of the world and our place in it that lies behind such reflections has the effect of bifurcating reality. There is, on the one hand, the "outer" material world, the world of trees, forests, and sound waves. On the other hand, there is the "inner" mental world, the mind and its contents. The mental world includes conscious experiences: the looks of seen objects, ways they feel, heard sounds, tastes, smells. The "external" material world comprises the objects themselves, and their properties. These properties include such things as the mass and spatial characteristics of objects (their shapes, sizes, surface textures, and, if we consider objects over time, motions and changes in their spatial characteristics).

Following a long tradition, we might call those observed qualities properly belonging to material objects "primary qualities." The rest, "secondary qualities" are characteristics of objects (presumably nothing more than arrangements of objects' primary qualities) that elicit certain familiar kinds of experience in conscious observers. Experience reliably mirrors the primary qualities of objects. Secondary qualities, in contrast, call for a distinction between the way objects are experienced, and they way they are. This distinction shows itself in our reflections on the tree falling in a deserted forest. More generally, the distinction encourages us to view conscious experiences as occurring outside the material world.

You may doubt this, confident that conscious experiences occur in brains, and regarding brains as respectable material objects. But now apply our distinction between primary and secondary qualities to brains. Brains – yours included – have assorted primary qualities. Your brain has a particular size, shape, mass, and spatial location; it is made up of particles, each with a particular size, shape, mass, and spatial location, and each of which contributes in a small way to the brain's overall character. In virtue of this overall character, your brain looks (and presumably sounds, smells, feels, and tastes!) a particular way. This is just to say that your brain can be variously experienced. The qualities of these experiences, although undoubtedly related in some systematic way to the material reality that elicits them, differ from qualities possessed by any material object, including your brain. But if that is so, where do we situate the qualities of experience?

Your first instinct was to locate them in the brain. But inspection of the brain reveals only familiar material qualities. An examination of the brain – even with the kinds of sophisticated instrumentation found in the laboratory of the neurophysiologist and the neural anatomist – reveals no looks, feels, heard sounds. Imagine that you are attending a performance of *Die Walküre* at Bayreuth. Your senses are assaulted with sounds, colors, smells, feelings, even tastes. A neuroscientist observing your brain while all this is occurring would observe a panoply of neural activities. But you can rest assured that the neuroscientist will not observe anything resembling the qualities of your conscious experience.

The idea that these qualities reside in your brain, then, appears unpromising. But now, if the qualities of your experiences are not found in your brain, where are they? The traditional answer, and the answer that we seem driven to accept, is that they are located in your mind. And this implies, quite straightforwardly, that your mind is somehow distinct from your brain. Indeed, it implies that the mind is not a material object at all, not an entity on all fours with tables, trees, stones – and brains! Minds are non-material entities: entities with properties not possessed by any material object. Minds bear intimate relations to material objects, perhaps, and especially intimate relations to brains. Your conscious experiences of ordinary material objects (including your own body) appear to reach you "through" your brain; and the effects your conscious deliberations have on the world (as when you decide to turn a page and subsequently turn the page) require the brain as an intermediary. Nevertheless, the conclusion seems inescapable: the mind could not itself be a material object.

You may find this conclusion unacceptable. If you do, I invite you to go back over the reasoning that led up to it and find out where that reasoning went off the rails. In so doing you would be engaging in philosophy of mind. Your attention would be turned, not to the latest results in neuroscience, but to commonsense assumptions with which this chapter began and to a very natural line of argument leading from these assumptions to a particular conclusion. As you begin your reflections, you may suspect a trick. If you are right, your excursion into philosophy of mind will be brief. You need only locate the point at which the trick occurs.

I think it unlikely that you will discover any such trick. Instead you will be forced to do what philosophers since the time of Descartes have been obliged to do. You will be forced to choose from among a variety of possibilities, each with its own distinctive advantages and liabilities. You might, for instance, simply accept the conclusion as Descartes did: minds and material objects are distinct kinds of entity, distinct "substances." You might instead challenge one or more of the assumptions that led to that conclusion. If you elect this course, however, you should be warned that giving up or modifying an assumption can have unexpected and unwanted repercussions elsewhere. In any case, you will have your work cut out for you. The best minds in philosophy – and many of the best outside philosophy as well – have turned their attention to these issues, and there remains a notable lack of anything resembling a definitive, uncontested view of the mind.

Do not conclude from this that it would be a waste of time for you to delve into the philosophy of mind. On the contrary, we enjoy the advantage of hindsight. We can learn from the successes and failures of others. Even if we cannot resolve every puzzle, we may at least come to learn something important about our picture of the world and our place in it. If we are honest, we shall be obliged to admit that this picture is gappy and unsatisfying in many respects. This, I submit, represents an important stage in our coming to terms with ourselves and our standing in the order of things.

## Science and metaphysics

Some readers will be impatient with all this. Everyone knows that philosophers only pose problems and never solve them. Solutions to the important puzzles reside with the sciences. So it is to science that we should turn if we are ever to understand the mind and its place in the world. Residual problems, problems not susceptible to scientific answers, are at bottom phony pseudo-problems. Answers we give to them make no difference; any "solution" you care to offer is as good as any other.

Although perhaps understandable, this reaction is ill-considered. The success of science has depended on a well-defined division of labor coupled with a strategy of divide and conquer. There is no such thing as science; there are only sciences: physics, chemistry, meteorology, geology, biology, psychology, sociology. Each of these sciences (and of course there are others) carves off a strictly circumscribed domain. Staking out a domain requires delimiting permissible questions. In this way, every science passes the buck. The practice of buck-passing is benign because, in most cases, the buck is passed eventually to a science where it stops. Sometimes, however, the buck is passed out of the sciences altogether. Indeed, this is inevitable. The sciences do not speak with a single voice. Even if every science were fully successful within its domain of application, we should still be left with the question of how these domains are related, how pronouncements of the several sciences are to be measured against one another. And this question is, quite clearly, not a question answerable from within any particular science.

Enter metaphysics. One traditional function of metaphysics – or, more particularly, that branch of metaphysics called ontology – is to provide an overall conception of how things are. This includes, not the pursuit of particular scientific ends, but an accommodation of the pronouncements of the several sciences. It includes, as well, an attempt to reconcile the sciences with ordinary experience. In one respect, every science takes ordinary experience for granted. A science is empirical insofar as it appeals to observation in confirming experimental outcomes. But the intrinsic character of observation itself (and, by extension, the character of observers) is left untouched by the sciences. The nature of observation – outwardly directed conscious experience – stands at the limits of science. It is just at this point that the puzzle with which this chapter began rears its head.

Scientific practice presupposes observers and observations. In the end, however, the sciences are silent about the intrinsic nature of both. The buck is passed. Our best hope for a unified picture, a picture that includes the world as described by the sciences and includes, as well, observers and their observations, lies in pursuing serious ontology. The buck stops here. You can, of course, turn your back on the metaphysical issues. But, to the extent that you do so, you are diminished – intellectually, and perhaps in other ways as well.

This book concerns the ontology of mind. It revolves around reflections on questions about mind that fall partly or wholly outside the purview of the sciences. I should warn you that this is not a fashionable endeavor. Many philosophers are skeptical of metaphysics, and many more have arrived at the belief that our best bet for understanding the mind and its place in the world is to turn our backs on philosophy altogether. These philosophers promote the idea that the philosophy of mind is, or ought to be, one component of what has come to be called cognitive science. Cognitive science includes elements of psychology, neuroscience, computer science, linguistics, and anthropology. What has a philosopher to offer the scientists who work in these areas? That is a good question.

Perhaps philosophers can provide some kind of unifying influence, a general picture that accommodates finer-grained assessments issuing from the scientific contributors to cognitive science. This, it would seem, is simply to engage in a kind of attenuated metaphysics. The metaphysics is attenuated to the extent that it excludes traditional ontological concerns, and excludes as well consideration of the bearing of sciences like physics on the ontology of mind.

If I sound skeptical about attempts to assimilate the philosophy of mind to cognitive science, I am. This book is premised on the conviction that the philosophy of mind is continuous with metaphysics as traditionally conceived. The difficult questions that arise in the philosophy of mind – and some would say the difficult questions *tout court* – are at bottom metaphysical questions. Such questions are, to all appearances, both legitimate and unavoidable. More to the point, we can make (and in fact have made) progress in addressing them. This does not mean that we have in our possession a catalogue of fully satisfactory answers that could be succinctly reviewed in an introduction to the philosophy of mind. It does mean that you can reasonably hope to find, in subsequent chapters, some help in sorting through and eliminating options.

Am I just conceding the point: philosophers agree only on questions, not on answers? Not at all. Progress in philosophy, like progress in any domain, can be measured in two ways. We can focus on some definite goal, and ask ourselves whether we are approaching that goal. But we can also ask ourselves how far we have come. And, on this count, philosophy can be said to move forward. In any case, we have little choice. Philosophical questions about the mind will not go away. They occur, even in laboratory contexts, to working scientists. And as recent widely-publicized controversies over the nature of consciousness attest, ignoring such questions is not an option.

## A look ahead

The chapters that follow introduce a range of pre-eminent themes in the philosophy of mind. They do so in a way that presupposes no special background in the subject. The focus is on theories that have formed the basis of what might be regarded as the modern (or is it postmodern?) conception of mind. I have done my best to present each of these theories in a way that makes its attractions salient. Philosophers of mind have, in my judgment, been too quick to dismiss views they regard as quaint or outmoded. One result is that we may pass up opportunities to learn from predecessors who, as it turns out, had a good deal to teach. A second result of slighting unfashionable theories is that we risk repeating mistakes that we ought by now to have learned to avoid. I have tried to rectify this situation by providing sympathetic readings of positions that are sometimes caricatured or dismissed out of hand. At the same time, I have put less weight on criticism of positions covered than do many others. To my mind, my job is to illuminate the territory. I leave it to you, the reader, to decide for yourself what to accept and what to reject.

This is not to say that I take a neutral position on topics discussed. Where I offer my opinion, however, I have tried to make clear that it is my opinion, a consideration to be weighed alongside other considerations. In a concluding chapter I say what I think. There, I offer an account of minds and their place in the natural world grounded in what I consider to be a plausible ontology. A good deal of the chapter is devoted to spelling out that ontology. In so doing, I hope, not so much to convince you of the details of the view I prefer, but to convince you of the importance of serious ontology for the philosophy of mind.

But this is to get ahead of the story. My closing chapter follows on the heels of chapters devoted to the examination of a variety of conceptions of mind. Before venturing further, it might be worthwhile to provide a brief accounting of what you can expect in each of these intervening chapters.

Chapter two introduces Descartes's "dualist" conception of mind and assorted variants of that conception. Descartes divides the world into mental and non-mental – immaterial – substances. Having done so, he is obliged to confront the notorious mind–body problem: how could mental and non-mental substances interact? Dissatisfaction with Descartes's efforts to answer this question has led to amended versions of the Cartesian framework that include parallelism, occasionalism, and epiphenomenalism. Parallelism, conceding the impossibility of comprehending causal interaction between mental and material entities, supposes that mental and material substances do not interact, but undergo changes in parallel. Occasionalists introduce God as a connecting link between the mental and the material. God wills changes in both the material world and in minds in such a way that events in each world are aligned just as they would be were they causally related. Epiphenomenalists defend one-way, material-to-mental causation. Mental events are causally inert "by-products" of material events (most likely events in the brain).

Idealists reject the materialist component of the dualist picture. All that exists, they contend, are minds and their contents. Idealists do not simply deny that external, material objects exist; they contend that an external material world is literally unthinkable. The thesis that objects exist outside the mind is judged, not false, but unintelligible. Chapter two concludes with a discussion of non-Cartesian dualism: minds and bodies are distinct substances, but minds possess, in addition to mental properties, material properties as well. This version of dualism avoids obvious pitfalls of its Cartesian predecessor while accounting for a number of otherwise puzzling phenomena.

Idealists reject the materialist side of the dualist conception of mind: material substance is inconceivable. Materialists hold, in contrast, that every substance is a material substance. Chapter three investigates two materialist responses to Cartesianism: behaviorism and the identity theory. Behaviorism attempts to show that the Cartesian conception of minds as distinct from bodies is based on a fundamental misunderstanding of what we are up to in ascribing states of mind to ourselves and others. According to behaviorists, claims about minds can be analyzed into claims about behavior and dispositions to behavior. To say that you are in pain – suffering a headache, for instance – is just to say (if the behaviorist is right) that you are holding your head, moaning, saying "I have a headache," and the like, or at least that you are disposed to do these things. Your being in pain, then, is not a matter of your possessing a non-material mind that is undergoing pain; it is simply a matter of your behaving in a characteristic way or being so disposed.

Proponents of the identity theory side with behaviorists against the Cartesian notion that minds are non-material substances, but stand with Cartesians against the behaviorist contention that having a mind is nothing more than behaving, or being disposed to behave, in particular ways. Identity theorists argue that states of mind (like having a headache, or thinking of Vienna) are genuine inner states of agents possessing them. These states, as neuroscience will someday reveal, are states of our brains.

Mental states are identical with brain states: mental states are states of brains. The identity theory appeals to anyone attracted to the idea that minds are just brains. But, at the same time, the identity theory inherits problems associated with that doctrine mentioned earlier.

Chapter four turns to functionalism, the historical successor to behaviorism and the identity theory and certainly the present day's most widely accepted conception of mind. Functionalism identifies states of mind, not with states of brains, but with functional roles. To have a headache is to be in some state that has characteristic input–output conditions. (In this, functionalism resembles a dressed-up version of behaviorism.) Headaches are caused by alcohol, lack of sleep, eyestrain, and the like, and they produce characteristic responses that include, but are not exhausted by, overt behavior of the sort focused on by behaviorists: head-holding, moaning, utterances of "I have a headache." In addition to behavior, a headache gives rise to other states of mind. (And in this respect, functionalists depart from the behaviorist contention that claims about states of mind are fully analyzable in terms of behavior and behavioral dispositions.) Your headache likely leads you to believe that you have a headache, for instance, and to a desire for aspirin.

Central to functionalism is the idea that states of mind are "multiply realizable." To be in a particular mental state is to be in a state that has a certain characteristic role. But many different kinds of material state could realize the same role. You, an octopus, and an Alpha Centaurian could all be in pain despite your very different physiologies (pretend that Alpha Centaurians have a silicon-based "biology"). If being in pain were, as identity theorists suggest, solely being in a particular kind of neurological state, then octopods and Alpha Centaurians, lacking physiologies like ours, could not be in pain. But that seems absurd.

One prominent difficulty for functionalists, a difficulty that functionalists share with proponents of behaviorism and the identity theory, is that of finding a place for the qualities of conscious experience: the looks of objects, heard sounds, feelings, and the like. Some functionalists have suggested that these qualities might be analyzed away: claims about qualities could be shown to be nothing more than claims about beliefs or representations of qualities. Other functionalists have conceded the qualities, but argued that their connection with our mental lives is merely contingent. There could be creatures, indistinguishable from us both physically and psychologically, who nevertheless altogether lacked conscious experiences. Neither of these strategies is apt to appeal to anyone not antecedently committed to functionalism.

Chapter five takes up two "interpretationist" conceptions of mind. Interpretationists regard an agent's possession of a mind as a matter, not of that agent's possessing a particular material makeup (as identity theorists would have it) or a particular kind of internal organization (as functionalists claim), but a matter of the agent's being describable in a particular way. One version of interpretationism, a version defended by Donald Davidson, concentrates on one category of mental states, the "propositional attitudes." These include beliefs, desires, and intentions. Davidson argues that in ascribing propositional attitudes to one another, we employ a distinctive "theory of interpretation." This theory places significant constraints on propositional attitude ascriptions. Beliefs, for instance, are ascribable only to creatures possessing a language, only to creatures capable of describing their own beliefs in a language translatable into our own.

Daniel Dennett advocates a rather different brand of interpretationism. According to Dennett, the question whether a creature (or indeed anything at all) possesses, say, a belief, turns on the utility of the practice of ascribing beliefs to it. We find it useful to describe desktop computers (and even thermostats!) as believing particular things. Your desktop computer believes the printer is out of paper (and so alerts you to that fact); the thermostat believes that the room is too cool (and, in consequence, turns on the furnace). Insofar as such attributions of belief work, desktop computers and thermostats (and of course people, and many other creatures) have beliefs. There is no question of whether thermostats, for instance, really have beliefs or whether it is just that we can get away with treating them as though they do. All there is to having a belief is to be so treatable.

The practice of ascribing beliefs, desires, and intentions is, according to Dennett, a matter of taking up a particular stance: the "intentional stance." In pursuing science, however, we find surprising differences in creatures' responses to one another and to their environments. An understanding of these requires that we adopt the "design stance." In so doing, we discover that mechanisms responsible for behavior differ importantly across species. Actions indistinguishable from the intentional perspective look very different once we consider the "design" of creatures performing them. Eventually, the design stance gives way to the "physical stance." This is the move from considering a creature's software to looking at its hardware. Having a mind, then, is simply a matter of being describable from the intentional stance. The mystery of how minds are related to bodies vanishes, according to Dennett, once we recognize that truths expressible from the intentional stance can be explained by reverting to the design stance. For their part, design stance truths are grounded in facts uncovered from within the physical stance.

The book concludes with a chapter in which, as noted already, I lay out an account of the mind grounded in a particular ontology. The ontology, details of which occupy the first part of the chapter, regards objects as the basic entities. Objects possess properties, which I take to be ways objects are. A billiard ball is red and spherical. The ball's redness and sphericity are ways it – that ball, and nothing else – is. Every property contributes distinctively to an object's qualities and to its causal powers or dispositions. Indeed, every property is both qualitative and dispositional.

From this basis, I construct an account of the mind that occupies the remainder of the chapter. The construction is tentative and sketchy, but the fundamental ideas will be clear. The account differs from functionalism – which, I argue, has severe ontological liabilities – and from each of the other conceptions of mind treated in earlier chapters.

A final comment. This book will have achieved its purpose if it convinces you that any account of the nature of mind includes an important metaphysical component. I am less concerned with your agreeing with me on the details of this component. To my way of thinking, we shall have made considerable progress if only we recognize that the study of mind requires a measure of ontological seriousness.

# CHAPTER 2
# Descartes's legacy

# Descartes's legacy

What exactly is a mind? The question is one philosophers and non-philosophers have struggled with throughout recorded history. According to some, minds are spiritual entities that temporarily reside in bodies, entering at conception or birth and departing on death. Indeed, death is simply the departure of a body's spirit. Others imagine the relation between minds and bodies to be more intimate. Minds, they hold, are not entities. Minds resemble fists or laps: a mind is present when a body is organized in a particular way, and absent otherwise. Still others hold that minds are indeed entities, physical entities: minds are just brains.

The aim of this chapter is to make a start at sorting out some of these competing claims and thus to make clear what precisely is at stake when we ask what minds are. We shall see that the issues are rarely clear-cut. This is scarcely surprising. The puzzles posed by the investigation of minds are some of the deepest in philosophy. In the end we may find no proffered solution entirely satisfactory. Even if that is so, we shall at least have a better understanding of the attractions and liabilities inherent in different ways of regarding minds.

Having said this, I want to head off one natural line of response. A common attitude toward philosophy is that philosophers never answer questions, but merely pose them. Scientists, in contrast, are in the business of delivering answers. Questions the answers to which elude science, questions that seem scientifically unanswerable, are often dismissed as "merely philosophical." It is but a short step from this deflationary depiction of philosophy to the notion that, where philosophy is concerned, there are no settled truths: every opinion is as good as any other.

This conception of philosophy and its relation to science is inadequate and naïve. What eludes science need not be unsettled. The state of the universe immediately before and immediately after the Big Bang, for instance, may be forever unknowable. We are evidentially cut off from that state. It would be absurd to conclude, however, that there was no such state, or that every claim about its character is just as good as every other. Similarly, from the fact that there has been little agreement among philosophers as to the status of minds, it does not follow that minds have no definite status.

As we shall see in the chapters ahead, questions that arise in the philosophy of mind are rarely susceptible to straightforward empirical investigation. An empirical question is one decidable, at least in principle, by experiment. Although experimental results tell against some conceptions of mind, most competing traditional accounts of mind are consistent with whatever empirical evidence we now possess or might conceivably possess in the future. The philosophical question is what we are to make of this evidence. And here our guide cannot be science. Science provides a loose framework for representing empirical findings, but no strictly scientific principles tell us how to interpret or make sense of those findings. For that, we must turn to "common sense" and to philosophy. This does not mean that we must advance specifically philosophical theories in sorting through empirical evidence. Rather, the activity of sorting through scientific findings and reconciling these with ordinary experience, and with a constellation of beliefs we have adopted on the basis of other findings, is a kind of philosophizing: philosophers are not the only philosophers. Card-carrying philosophers are merely those who do their philosophizing self-consciously.

## Cartesian dualism

Let us take as a starting point the influential conception of mind advanced by René Descartes (1596–1650). Descartes held that minds and bodies are "substances" of distinct kinds that, in the case of living human beings, happen to be intimately related. This dualism of substances (subsequently labeled Cartesian dualism) nowadays strikes most philosophers and scientists interested in the mind as hopelessly misguided. Until quite recently, it was widely supposed that the source of the notorious mind–body problem stemmed from the acceptance of the Cartesian picture: a solution to the problem could be had by rejecting dualism. As we shall see, this diagnosis has not panned out. Nevertheless, we can begin to develop an appreciation of the mind–body problem by examining Descartes's approach to the mind.

As a preliminary, let us note some *prima facie* differences between mental and material objects and states. First, material objects are spatial; they occupy a location in space and exhibit spatial dimensions. Mental objects – thoughts and sensations, for instance – are apparently non-spatial. What is the size and shape of your desire for a Whopper? Is your thinking of Vienna triangular? These questions seem to make no sense.

You might think of sensations – some of them at least – as having spatial locations. A pain in your left big toe is, after all, in your left big toe.

(Does this mean it is big-toe-shaped?) But is this quite right? Consider the phenomenon of "phantom pain," a phenomenon well known to Descartes and his contemporaries. Amputees often seem to experience pains in their amputated limbs. Your big toe could be amputated, and you still might continue to experience the very same kind of throbbing pain you experienced prior to its amputation, and this pain might seem to you to be in the place at the end of your foot formerly occupied by your big toe. This suggests that, although we experience pains and other sensations as occurring in various bodily locations, it need not follow that experiences of pain occur at those locations. Following Descartes, we might say that an experience of pain-in-your-left-big-toe is a kind of experience, one differing in quality from an experience of pain-in-your-right-big-toe. There is no reason to think – and indeed good reason not to think – that such experiences must be located where they are felt to be located.

Mental states, then, unlike material states, appear to be distinctively non-spatial. This, at any rate, is Descartes's conclusion. A second important difference between the mental and the material is qualitative. Think of the qualities of your experience of a pain in your big toe. You may find these qualities difficult to talk about, but that need not affect your awareness of them. Now ask yourself whether you could ever expect to encounter these qualities in a material object. A neuroscientist observing your nervous system while you are experiencing pain will observe nothing qualitatively resembling your pain. Indeed, this possibility seems to make no sense.

The point can be summarized as follows. The qualities of our conscious experiences appear to be nothing at all like the qualities of material objects – indeed they seem unlike the qualities of any conceivable material object. The natural conclusion is that mental qualities are not qualities of material objects; mental qualities differ in kind from material qualities.

A third distinction between the mental and the material is partly epistemological – that is, it concerns the character of our knowledge of such things. The knowledge you have of your own states of mind is direct and unchallengeable in a way that your knowledge of material objects is not. Philosophers sometimes put this by saying that we have "privileged access" to our own states of mind. Descartes himself believed that this knowledge was incorrigible: your thoughts about your current states of mind could not be false. He believed, as well, that the contents of our own minds were transparent to us. In consequence, if you are in a particular state of mind, then you know you are in that state; and if you believe that you are in a particular state of mind, then you are in that state.

The Cartesian notion that the mind is in this way transparent strikes us nowadays as excessive. Freud long ago convinced us that much in the mind can be hidden. More recently, cognitive scientists have contended that most mental states and operations are inaccessible to consciousness. We can accept all this, however, without jettisoning Descartes's central insight. The access we have to our own states of mind is distinctive, even if not infallible. You entertain thoughts and experience pains self-consciously. I can only infer the occurrence in you of such goings-on. Your access to your own states of mind is direct and unmediated, my access to your states of mind is invariably indirect.

We might put this by saying that states of mind are "private." They are "directly observable" only by the person (or creature) having them; outsiders can only infer them from their material effects. You can tell me what you are thinking, or I can guess it from the expression on your face. Neuroscientists might eventually be able to infer what you are thinking by observing patterns of neurological activities. Our observations of your mental life, however, are never direct in the way yours appear to be.

The situation is very different for material objects and their states. If mental items are necessarily private, material things are necessarily public. When it comes to a material object, or the state of a material object, if you are in a position to observe it, then anyone else suitably situated could observe it as well by taking up your observational position. The asymmetry of access we find in the case of minds is entirely absent. Again, this suggests that minds and material bodies are very different kinds of object. And Descartes offers an explanation for this difference: minds and material bodies are distinct kinds of substance. A mental substance possesses properties not possessible by any material substance, and a material substance possesses properties no mental substance could possess. Indeed, according to Descartes, there is no overlap in the properties possessed by mental and material substances.

Before taking up Descartes's view in more detail, let us chart the three differences between the mental and the material we have just isolated (see figure 2.1). In later chapters, we shall reopen discussion of these distinctions. For the present, however, let us accept them as they stand and notice what follows.

| Material Bodies | Minds |
|:---:|:---:|
| Spatial | Non-spatial |
| Material qualities | Distinctively mental qualities |
| Public | Private |

Figure 2.1

## Substances, attributes, and modes

Descartes supposes that the world is made up of substances. A substance is not, as the term might suggest, a kind of stuff like water, or coal, or paint. Descartes, following tradition, regards substances as individual things or entities. The desk at which I am now writing is, in this traditional sense, a substance, as is the pen I hold in my hand, the tree outside my window, and the bird nesting in its branches. These substances are complex: they are composed of other substances, their parts. My desk is made up of pieces of wood, organized in a particular way. Each of these pieces of wood (and each of the screws holding them together) is a substance in its own right. Similarly, the pen, the tree, and the bird are all made up of parts that are themselves substances. And of course these substances are themselves made up of distinct substances. (A natural question to ask is whether every substance is made up of parts, each of which is a distinct substance. This seems unlikely. We shall return to this question in chapter six.) Substances, note, are individuals – "particulars" in the jargon of philosophers – as distinct from classes or kinds of thing. This bird and this tree are substances, but the class of birds is a class, not a substance; beech and oak are species of substance, not substances.

Substances are to be contrasted, on the one hand, with non-substantial individuals and, on the other hand, with properties. Non-substantial individuals include "concrete" items like events and "abstract" entities like sets and numbers. An event (a chicken's crossing the road, for instance) may be regarded as a dated, non-repeatable particular. In this respect, events resemble substances. Just as two exactly similar peas in a pod are nevertheless distinct peas, so your reading this sentence now is one event, and your reading the very same sentence tomorrow is a distinct event. Events are not substances, however, but changes substances undergo. Moreover, events are concrete particulars as distinct from abstract entities like the set of cows or the number two.

Properties are had by substances. Think of an ordinary substance, a particular red billiard ball. We distinguish the ball's redness from its sphericity and its mass. In so doing, we consider three of the ball's properties. But we can also distinguish the ball, as possessor of these properties, from its properties. On the view I am associating with Descartes, this ball is a substance that possesses a number of properties including redness, sphericity, and a particular mass. Properties and substances are inseparable. You cannot peel off an object's properties and leave the bare substance. Nor can properties float free of substances. Some philosophers have argued that substances are nothing more than collections or bundles of properties. This is not Descartes's view, however, and it is not a view that I should want to defend.

I have spoken of substances and properties. Descartes in fact speaks, not of properties but of "attributes" and "modes." An attribute is what makes a substance the kind of substance it is. A material (or physical: I shall use the terms interchangeably) substance is a substance possessing the attribute of extension. Extension is, roughly, spatiality. Thus, a material substance is one that occupies a position in space and possesses a particular shape and size. The particular shape and size possessed by material substances are modes, ways of being extended. What we would ordinarily think of as properties of everyday material objects are, for Descartes, modes of extension.

On this conception, the billiard ball's sphericity is a mode of extension; its sphericity is the way it is shaped. What of the ball's color? Here Descartes contends that the distinctive visual experience we have when we look at a red billiard ball does not resemble the feature of the ball that produces this experience in us. That feature might be the texture of the ball's surface, a texture that reflects light in a particular way. Texture – the arrangement of micro-particles making up an object's surface – is a mode of extension.

## The metaphysics of dualism

Descartes puts the attribute–mode distinction to work by supposing that each kind of substance possesses a distinctive attribute. A material substance is a substance possessing the attribute of extension. A mental substance, in contrast, is a substance possessing a very different attribute, the attribute of "thought." Descartes gives the term "thought" a broader sense than we do today. Anything we in everyday life would count as a state of mind – a sensation, an image, an emotion, a belief, a desire – Descartes regards as a mode of thought, a way of thinking.[1]

We can now begin to understand Cartesian dualism. Bodies are material substances possessing the attribute of extension. Minds, too, are substances, but not material substances. Minds possess the attribute of thought. One more step is required to yield dualism. Every substance possesses exactly one attribute. If a substance possesses the attribute of extension (and so is extended in particular ways), it cannot possess the attribute of thought. If a substance possesses the attribute of thought (and thus possesses various modes of thought: feelings, images, beliefs), it cannot possess the attribute of extension. Thought and extension mutually exclude one another. It follows that no extended substance thinks, and no

---

[1] In another respect, Descartes's conception of thought is narrower than ours. Descartes appears not to countenance the possibility of unconscious thoughts.

thinking substance is extended. Minds are thinking substances and bodies are extended substances, so minds are distinct from bodies.

Descartes embraces this conclusion, but he does not deny that minds and bodies are, as they clearly seem to be, intimately related. Think for a moment, as Descartes does, of the mind as the I or the self. You are related in an especially intimate way to a particular body, your body. When your finger comes too near the flame of a candle you feel pain. When my finger goes near the flame, in contrast, you feel no pain. When you decide to get up and walk across the room, it is your body that moves, not mine. To be sure you can control my body. You can ask me to get up and walk across the room, or order me to do so at gunpoint, or tie a rope around me and pull me across the room. In so doing, however, your decision affects my body only indirectly, only by way of some movement of your body. Movements of your own body (your tongue and vocal chords, or your limbs) seem, in contrast, largely under your direct voluntary control.

Let us pause briefly and take stock. Descartes holds that the world consists of two kinds of substance: material substances and mental substances. Material substances are extended and unthinking; mental substances think, but are unextended. Each mental substance bears an especially intimate relation to some particular material substance. (Or at any rate this is the arrangement with which we are most familiar. According to Descartes, it is possible for a mental substance to persist after the demise of the material substance to which it was intimately related: the self might survive the death of the body.) Mental and material substances, although utterly distinct, causally interact. Your body responds to your plans and decisions. Your mind receives signals from your body in the form of sensory experiences that provide you with information about the state of your body and, indirectly, the state of the world outside your body. The world causally impinges on your mind by way of your senses: your eyes, ears, nose, and your sense of touch.

The Cartesian picture is simple to spell out. Imagine that you sit on a tack planted in your chair by a malicious practical joker. Your sitting on the tack (a material event involving a pair of material objects, the tack and your body) gives rise to a distinctive sensation of pain (a mental event). This sensation or feeling in turn generates another mental event, a desire to leap upward, and this desire brings about an appropriate leaping bodily motion. (See figure 2.2.)

Cartesian dualism fits nicely with common sense. We see ourselves as having bodies, but as distinct from our bodies in at least the following sense. We can apparently conceive of our bodies changing dramatically, or ceasing to exist altogether, while we continue to exist. True, we speak of ourselves as having minds – and, for that matter, we speak of changing our minds. But, while you can perhaps imagine your body's being destroyed

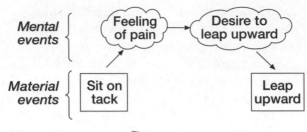

Figure 2.2

while you remain, it is less clear that you could coherently imagine your surviving the demise of your mind or self. You can imagine that you or your mind ceases to exist while your body continues to exist (in a vegetative state perhaps), but that is another matter. Moreover you might be able to imagine cases in which you swap bodies. This is a not uncommon occurrence in science fiction. But it seems to make no sense to suppose that you could swap minds or selves. Changing your mind is not a matter of replacing one mind with another, but a matter of changing your beliefs. When a chastened Scrooge becomes "a new person", he does not swap selves, but alters his attitudes.

In addition to fitting well with a commonsense conception of ourselves, Cartesian dualism also promises a reconciliation of our scientific picture of the world and ordinary experience. Science tells us – or at any rate physics tells us – that the world consists of colorless particles jumbled together to form middle-sized objects. Our experience of the world is quite different. Your visual experience of the red billiard ball is not an experience of a colorless spherical jumble. Sounds are vibrations in a medium (air or water, for instance). Yet your experience of a performance of an Offenbach overture differs qualitatively from anything science seems likely to turn up in its investigation of the physical world. Dualism makes sense of this apparent bifurcation. Material bodies are nothing more than colorless objects interacting in space. Such interactions, however, produce in the mind experiences with qualities that differ from the qualities of any material object.

The qualities of our experiences (at bottom, modes of thought) seem to differ dramatically from the qualities of material bodies (modes of extension). Despite these apparent differences, however, Descartes holds that experiential qualities are correlated with material qualities. The result is a correlation or isomorphism between our experiences of the world and the world. The presence of this isomorphism is what enables the qualities of experiences to serve as signs of the qualities of the material world.

## Mind–body interaction

We seem, then, following Descartes, to be in a position to account for apparent qualitative differences between our experiences and objects experienced, and for our capacity to "read off" qualities of the world from qualities of our experiences. Further, we can accommodate our own everyday view of ourselves as housed in, but in some way distinct from our bodies. All this is to the good. Unfortunately, Cartesian dualism comes at a price, a price few philosophers have been prepared to pay.

The difficulty is one that was immediately obvious to Descartes's contemporaries, one that Descartes himself understood keenly. Central to Descartes's view is the idea that minds and bodies causally interact. But if minds and bodies are distinct kinds of substance, it is hard to see how such causal interaction could occur. Minds or selves, you will recall, are immaterial substances possessing the attribute of thought, but lacking the attribute of extension. Material bodies, in contrast, are extended but lack thought. How could entities of such utterly different kinds affect one another causally? How could an event in an immaterial mind alter a material object? How could a physical event beget a change in an immaterial mind? The metaphysical distance Descartes places between minds and material bodies seems to preclude their causally interacting.

A Cartesian might bite the bullet here and contend that causal relations between a mental and a material substance are *sui generis* – that is, mental–material causation is not a species of causation as we encounter it in the material world, but something unique. This strategy leads us from the frying pan into the fire. Modern science is premised on the assumption that the material world is a causally closed system. This means, roughly, that every event in the material world is caused by some other material event (if it is caused by any event) and has as effects only material events. (The parenthetical rider allows us to leave room for the possibility of uncaused events.) We can reformulate this idea in terms of explanation: an explanation citing all of the material causes of a material event is a complete causal explanation of the event.

The notion that the material world is causally closed is related to our conception of natural laws. Natural laws govern causal relations among material events. Such laws differ from laws passed by legislative bodies. A natural law is exceptionless: it cannot be violated in the way a traffic law can be violated. An object that behaves in an odd or unexpected way nevertheless perfectly conforms to natural law. Evidence that an object's behavior violates a given natural law is evidence that what we had thought was a law is not.

Return now to Descartes's supposition that minds are non-material substances that can initiate events in the material world. This supposition obliges us to give up the idea that the material world is causally self-contained. To see why this is so, imagine how causal interaction between mental and material substances might work. Suppose your mind acts on your body by instigating changes in a certain region of your brain. Descartes himself believed that minds were linked to bodies by way of the pineal gland, a small structure near the center of the brain. Minute alterations in the motions of particles in the pineal gland radiated throughout the body via the nervous system producing muscular contractions and ultimately bodily motions. Let us pretend Descartes was right. Your pineal gland is made up of micro-particles that operate in accord with physical law. If your mind is to initiate a causal sequence in your pineal gland, then, it will have to affect in some way the behavior of these micro-constituents. Its interference with the behavior of micro-constituents, however, would appear to require violation of the laws governing them, an impossibility if we take the material world to be causally self-contained, laws of nature to be inviolable.

You might imagine that the mind could act on the body without violating laws governing its material constituents. Perhaps, as the quantum theory suggests, the laws governing those constituents are ultimately probabilistic or statistical in character. Imagine that a micro-system's being in a certain state, $S_1$, causes the system subsequently go into state $S_2$, but only with a certain probability: there is a 35 percent probability that a particular micro-system in state $S_1$ will go into state $S_2$. Now, imagine that you – a mental substance – decide to wave to a friend. You initiate a particular change in your body by making it the case that a particular $S_1$ micro-system in your pineal gland goes into state $S_2$. (We might imagine that when the constituents of such states "line up" in this way, the result is a signal sent to your right arm that causes a series of muscle contractions and ultimately a waving motion of your arm. Here you have decided to wave, and subsequently wave.) In this way, you, a mental substance, seem capable of making yourself felt in the material world without in any sense violating laws governing material bodies.

Consider a sequence of tosses of a fair coin, one that lands heads about half the time. When you toss the coin on a particular occasion, you snap your thumb in a characteristic way sending the coin tumbling through the air in a trajectory that leads it eventually to land on the ground, heads side up. We can suppose that there is a completely deterministic basis for the coin's landing as it does on this occasion: given features of the coin, the character of the movement of your thumb, the location and composition of the surface on which the coin lands, and so on, the coin is bound to land heads. Of course we are ignorant of all these factors. We can only guess how the coin will land on each toss. We express our ignorance by saying that, on any given occasion, the probability that the coin will land heads is 50 percent.

Imagine now an outsider who occasionally intervenes in the system by focusing a strong electromagnetic beam on the coin, insuring that it lands heads. The outsider might do this infrequently and in a way that is statistically undetectable: when we evaluate the relative frequency with which the coin landed heads over a long series of tosses, that frequency approaches 50 percent. The outsider, then, intervenes, but in a way that does not alter the statistical likelihood that the coin will land heads whenever it is tossed, and does not reveal itself when we examine the coin's behavior. Perhaps this is how the mind affects the body.

This example misses the mark. It misconstrues the nature of statistical or probabilistic causation as this might be thought to apply to the basic constituents of the material world. If probabilities are written into fundamental laws of nature, these probabilities are not the result of our ignorance in the face of the complexity of physical systems, nor do they simply express statistical frequencies. The probabilities are, as it were, built into the fundamental entities. In the imaginary case we are considering, it is an intrinsic, that is built-in, feature of an $S_1$ micro-system that it is 35 percent likely to go into state $S_2$. This does not imply that 35 percent of $S_1$ systems go into $S_2$. It is consistent with our imaginary law that the relative frequency of $S_1$ to $S_2$ transitions is much less or much greater than 35 percent. In fact it is possible, although of course highly unlikely, that no $S_1$ system ever goes into state $S_2$.

If we imagine a force from outside nature intervening in a physical transaction governed by a statistical law, then we must imagine the force as somehow altering the probabilities that hold for the physical system in question: if the probabilities are not affected, then it is hard to understand what the alleged intervention amounts to. But if these probabilities are built into the system, then their being altered would amount to a "violation" of physical law.

To grasp this point, it is important to see that the kinds of statistical law thought to govern the elementary constituents of the world exclude so-called "hidden variables." That is, the probabilistic character of these laws is not due to the "interference" of some factor the nature of which we might be ignorant of. It is, rather, irreducible, ineliminable, and grounded in the nature of the elementary entities themselves. If the mind intervenes in the operation of the material world in a way that is statistically undetectable, it does not follow that no "violation" of physical law has occurred. Genuine intervention would require minds to affect in some way the propensity of particular $S_1$ systems to go into state $S_2$. And that would necessitate alterations in the character of $S_1$ systems, alterations the occurrence of which would constitute "violations" of natural law.

Here is another possibility. Although mental events do not alter $S_1$, they can, on occasion, prevent $S_1$ from manifesting itself by going into $S_2$ – in the way you might prevent a fragile vase from shattering when it is struck with a hammer by swathing the vase in bubble wrap. Selective "blockings" of this sort, if suitably fine-grained and strategically placed, might account for the effects of thoughts on bodily goings-on. But it is hard to see how this could work without violating our conception of the material world as causally self-contained. (We shall consider propensities – or, as I prefer, dispositions – and the manifestations in more detail in subsequent chapters.)

Of course it is possible that immaterial minds do intervene in the material world. It is possible that the material world is not in fact causally closed and that natural law is subject to contravention. The argument against Cartesian dualism is not that minds do not intervene, and so dualism must be false. Such an argument would beg the question against Descartes. The argument, rather, is founded on considerations of plausibility. If we accept Cartesian dualism, then we must suppose that immaterial minds sometimes intervene in the operation of the material world. This conflicts with a fundamental presumption of modern science, a presumption we have every reason to accept. To the extent that we regard the intervention of non-material minds in the material world as implausible, we should regard Cartesian dualism as implausible.

An argument of this sort is scarcely conclusive. Metaphysical arguments rarely are. We might fairly ask, however, who bears the burden of proof here. The Cartesian dualist offers us an account of mind that fits nicely with much of what we believe about our world and with everyday experience. The account has the disadvantage of implying something we have little reason to believe, and many reasons to doubt. It is up to the Cartesian, then, to show that competing accounts of mind suffer equally serious defects. We shall be in a better position to evaluate the Cartesian's prospects when we have examined the alternatives.

## Modifying Cartesian dualism

Descartes's central difficulty revolves around mind–body interaction. Minds and bodies evidently interact causally. Your decisions lead you to act and so to move your body in particular ways. Goings-on in your body result in conscious sensory experiences. As we have discovered, however, it is hard to see how such interaction could occur if minds are non-material substances and bodies are material.

Perhaps we could modify Cartesian dualism in such a way that we

preserve what seems right about it. If the problem concerns causal interaction between material and non-material substances, what would happen
if we simply dropped the requirement of causal interaction? In so doing,
we move to a doctrine called "psycho-physical parallelism" or, for short,
"parallelism." Gottfried Wilhelm von Leibniz (1646–1716) is perhaps the
best-known proponent of parallelism, although my focus will not be on
Leibniz's considered view but on a simpler alternative.

## Parallelism

A proponent of parallelism accepts Descartes's bifurcation of the world
into extended material substances and unextended mental substances.
Parallelists deny, however, that mental and material substances interact
causally. This appears to fly in the face of ordinary experience. It surely
seems that goings-on in your mind affect your body, and through it,
affect the material world beyond your body. It seems no less clear that
events and objects in the world have an impact on your mind by way of
their effects on your body.

Consider again your sitting on a tack planted by a practical joker. You sit
on the tack, experience a sharp, painful sensation, recognize the source of
your discomfort, and leap from your chair. This sequence of events
includes both mental and material events that are, to all appearances, causally related. A defender of parallelism must say that all this is an illusion.
The picture is captured by figure 2.3 (compare figure 2.2).

Minds, parallelists contend, appear to interact with the material world,
but the appearance is just that: an appearance. Sequences of events involving minds, mental events, and sequences of material events run in parallel.
Your sitting on the tack (a material event) precedes your sensation of pain
(a mental event). You undoubtedly have the clear impression that the
former brought about the latter. In this you are mistaken, however. Similarly, when you decide to leap upward and subsequently leap, it feels to
you as though your decision caused your leaping, but it did not. Events in
the mind systematically covary with events in the material world, but
there are no causal connections between mental and material events.

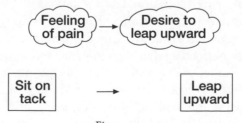

Figure 2.3

We know that $A$'s can covary with $B$'s without its being true that $A$'s cause $B$'s. If the covariation is extensive and systematic, however, we seek a causal explanation: perhaps $A$'s and $B$'s are themselves caused by $C$'s. A squeaking from under the hood of my Yugo is inevitably followed by the motor's quitting. The motor's quitting covaries with the squeaking, but is not caused by it. Rather some mechanical condition produces both the squeaking and the motor's quitting.

What explanation does a parallelist have to offer for the fact that sequences of mental events covary systematically and universally with sequences of material events? One possibility is that this is just a brute fact about our world, something not capable of further explanation. This response is scarcely satisfying, however. In the context, it appears suspiciously *ad hoc*. All explanation comes to an end somewhere, of course. But the notion that the delicate pattern of covariation of the mental and the material is incapable of further explanation appears in this case to be motivated solely by a wish to preserve the theory. This is particularly so in light of the fact that straightforward explanation seems to be available: mental events covary with material events because mental substances and material substances interact causally. To be sure, this explanation requires that we abandon parallelism, but that is the parallelist's problem, not ours.

Another defense of parallelism invokes God. God intervenes to insure that mental and material sequences run in parallel. You might think that an appeal to God to account for the covariation of mental and material events is obviously unpromising. God is not a material substance. Indeed, according to Descartes, God is not a mental substance either: God is a substance of a third sort. But if that is so, how is it any easier to understand how God could affect the course of material events than to understand how finite material substances could do so? All the difficulties associated with Cartesian interactionism appear to arise all over again.

You do not have to be a friend of parallelism to see that this complaint is misguided. The parallelist need not envisage God as continually adjusting the course of mental and material events. Rather God might create, once and for all, a world containing both material substances subject to unalterable natural law and mental substances, subject, perhaps, to psychological laws. The world is designed in such a way that events in the mental realm covary with events in the material realm. The model is a clock-maker who constructs a pair of perfectly synchronized clocks the movements of which covary, not because they are causally linked, but because the internal adjustments in one clock perfectly reflect the internal adjustments in the other.

Even so, the parallelist's appeal to God seems not to be much of an improvement over the brute fact account. Indeed, the appeal to God appears to be just a gussied-up way of saying that mental–material covariation is a brute fact. If we had independent grounds for believing that God acts in the way required by parallelism, then matters would be different. In the absence of such independent grounds, the appeal to God is an appeal to a *deus ex machina*, a contrived solution to an otherwise intractable problem.

## Occasionalism

A variant of parallelism, "occasionalism," accords God a more active role in the world. Occasionalism is most often associated with the writings of Nicholas Malebranche (1638–1715). My discussion will focus on occasionalism as a philosophical doctrine, and omit historical niceties. Parallelism suggests systems operating independently, but side by side, in the way an automobile on a highway might shadow a train. Occasionalism makes God actively responsible for the existence and character of event sequences. When you sit on a tack, God wills the occurrence of a sensation of pain in your mind (see figure 2.4). God's acting in this instance resembles, but is taken to be different from, causing.

It is hard to see occasionalism as an advance over parallelism, and hard to see either as an improvement on Descartes's original version of dualism. The sticking point for Descartes is the difficulty of understanding how unextended mental substances could interact causally with extended material substances. Parallelism and occasionalism concede the difficulty and attempt to cope with it by conceding that mental and material substances could not causally interact, and offering an explanation for the appearance of interaction. The strategy looks unpromising. It appears merely to push the original problem around without solving it.

## Causation

Perhaps this complaint is unfair. Occasionalism is motivated in part by a general thesis about causation. Let us suppose, as most philosophers do,

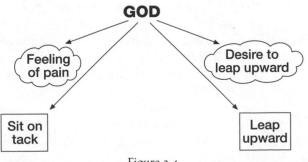

Figure 2.4

that causation is a relation holding between events: one event, the cause, brings about another event, the effect. Your striking a billiard ball with a billiard cue, one event, brings about the billiard ball's rolling in a particular direction, a second event. The difficulty is to understand what exactly this "bringing about" amounts to. We ordinarily distinguish cases in which one event merely follows or accompanies another, from those in which one event causally necessitates another. But what is the basis of this distinction? This is the problem of the causal nexus: when events are linked causally, what is the character of the linkage?

One possibility is that there are no genuine links between events, only bare event sequences. We regard two events as standing in a causal relation, not because we observe the first bringing about or necessitating the second, but because the event sequence resembles sequences we have previously observed. A view of this sort is often associated with David Hume (1711–76).

Note that, although tempting, it would be misleading to describe this view as one that denies that events are causally related. The idea rather is that this is just what particular causal relations come to: a causal sequence is simply an instance of some regularity. Your striking the billiard ball now (a particular, dated event) causes it to roll across the table (another particular event), just in case it is true that, whenever an event of a kind similar to the first occurs, an event of a kind similar to the second occurs as well.

Hume was hardly an occasionalist, but his influential observations on causality bear on the occasionalist hypothesis. (Indeed, Malebranche, the best-known occasionalist, advanced "Humean" arguments long before Hume did.) If causal relations boil down to nothing more than regularities, the covariation of events of particular sorts, then it is a mistake to regard the absence of a mechanism or causal link between mental events and material events as a special problem. On the contrary, there are no such links, not even among events in the material world. To be sure, we are often under the impression that we have observed connections among events. But according to Hume this is merely a "projection" of our conviction that, when an event of a given sort occurs (the striking of a billiard ball by a billiard cue), an event of another sort (the ball's moving in a particular way) will follow. And this conviction arises in us after we have been conditioned by prior observations of similar event sequences.

If causal relations amount to no more than regularities among types of event, then there is nothing especially problematic or mysterious about mental events causing material events. The appearance of a problem stems from the tacit assumption that causal relations require an intervening mechanism or link. If no such links are discoverable, that is scarcely surprising. They are absent as well from ordinary sequences of material events. The Cartesian and parallelist pictures of mental causation are, on such a view, indistinguishable.

Where does this leave occasionalism? Occasionalists might argue that, in the absence of a causal nexus, a connecting mechanism or linkage between causes and effects, we require some explanation for the pattern of regularities among kinds of event we find in the world. These regularities encompass purely material event sequences as well as sequences involving both mental and material components. When an event of one kind is invariably followed by an event of another kind, this is not because events of the first kind somehow necessitate or bring about events of the second kind. Events are discrete occurrences; no event has the power to induce another event. How then are we to explain the obvious fact that event sequences are tightly structured, regular, and orderly? Their orderliness is captured by scientific theories, which postulate natural laws, and it is enshrined in everyday causal generalizations.

Here, the occasionalist invokes God. If events are discrete, wholly self-contained episodes, the occurrence of one event cannot by itself account for the occurrence of any subsequent event. The occurrence of every event is, in an important sense, miraculous. God, as it were, creates every event *ex nihilo* – from nothing. One way to think about a view of this sort is to imagine that the world is divided into momentary temporal stages or segments (see figure 2.5).

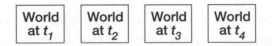

Figure 2.5

Alternatively, we could think of the world over time as comprising a sequence of worlds, each world differing slightly from its predecessor in something like the way each image on a movie film differs from the image preceding it. In our billiard ball example, the cue's striking the ball belongs to one temporal segment (one world), and the ball's subsequent rolling belongs to a subsequent temporal segment (a distinct world). Every segment in the sequence that makes up what we commonly regard as our world must be created *ex nihilo*.

It is widely held that no event in the world could account for the existence of the world (a world that includes that event as a part). And if what we call the world is more accurately thought of as a sequence of metaphysically independent worlds, then it follows that no event in any world in the sequence can account for any event in a subsequent world. We have a choice, it seems. We could accept the existence of each world in the sequence as a brute, inexplicable fact; or we could explain the existence of the sequence by postulating a benevolent God. God wills anew each world

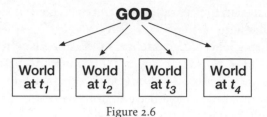

Figure 2.6

in the sequence of worlds in accord with a divine plan. We can rest content that the sequence will preserve the kind of complex order we find when we engage in scientific inquiry because we can be confident that it belongs to God's nature to do so (figure 2.6).

An occasionalist can point out that it is one thing for a scientist to allow that the existence of a single world is simply a brute fact, a fact for which there is no explanation. It is quite another matter, however, to hold that each member of a patterned sequence of metaphysically independent worlds or world stages is a brute fact. If no event in any stage explains the occurrence of that stage or the occurrence of any event in any other stage, then, it would seem, every fact is merely a brute fact.

Suppose you find this conclusion unappealing, and suppose you accept the occasionalist's conception of the world as a sequence of momentary stages. You then seem faced with a choice. Either every fact is a brute, unexplained and unexplainable fact (figure 2.5), or God exists and provides an explanation for things being as they are (figure 2.6). In this case, unlike the case of parallelism, God is offered as a plausible explanation of an otherwise baffling situation. Of course, you might question the occasionalist's take on causation, and question as well the notion that the world is a sequence of metaphysically independent momentary segments. But then it is up to you to provide a plausible alternative.

If nothing else, these reflections make it clear that we cannot hope to evaluate claims about minds and the material world without first coming to grips with a host of fundamental metaphysical issues. Whatever plausibility occasionalism possesses rests on a particular metaphysical conception of causation. If the occasionalists are right about causation (and right, as well, about mental and material substances), then they are in a relatively strong position. Before we can evaluate the occasionalist's brand of dualism, however, we shall need to build up our grasp of the metaphysical options.

Idealism

Parallelism and occasionalism hold that our impression that minds and bodies are causally linked is an illusion. You make up your mind to wave and subsequently wave. It seems to you that your decision brings about your waving. But that is not so – or, if it is so, it is only because God insures that, in the world segment subsequent to the world segment in which you decide to wave, you wave.

Suppose we go further, however, suppose we allow that, not only is the impression of mind–body causal interaction an illusion, but that the material world is itself an illusion! We have experiences that we should describe as experiences of material objects and events existing outside our minds, but these are at bottom nothing more than elaborate and prolonged dreams or hallucinations. Of course, everyday activities lack the peculiar dreamlike character of dreams, but that is just because everyday experiences are more orderly, regular, and unforgiving.

On a view of this sort, "idealism," the world consists exclusively of minds and their contents. (On a variant of idealism, "solipsism," the world is just a single mind – your mind – and its contents.) There are no non-mental material objects or events, hence no worrisome causal interactions between minds and mind-independent material objects, no mysterious parallelism between independent mental and material realms. We explain the regularity and order we find in our experiences, not by reference to a regular and orderly material world, but by reference to the intrinsic nature of minds (figure 2.7) or by supposing that the order is secured by a benevolent God who insures that our ideas occur in orderly, hence predictable, patterns( figure 2.8). (The Irish philosopher and Anglican bishop, George Berkeley (1685–1753) is the most famous proponent of the latter view.)

Idealism has the advantage of saving the appearances. If idealism is true, then our experiences of the world would be no different in any way from what they would be were the world populated by material objects. Idealism does not imply that what appear to us to be solid, extended material objects would take on a ghostly air. On the contrary, we would have experiences

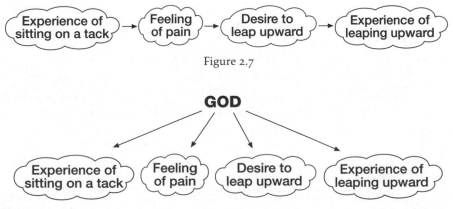

Figure 2.7

Figure 2.8

"as of" solid extended objects and spatial expanses, just as we sometimes do in dreams.

Suppose you set out to disprove idealism by conducting experiments designed to establish the existence of mind-independent material bodies. These experiments might be crude – as in Dr Johnson's kicking a stone and announcing "thus I refute Berkeley" – or sophisticated – including, for instance, the deployment of expensive detectors to identify the material particles that science tells us are the building blocks of a mind-independent reality.

An idealist will point out that experimentation is a matter of arranging matters so as to yield certain observations. Your kicking the stone provides observational evidence of an especially vivid sort that the stone exists. A scientist's observation of a particular kind of streak in a cloud chamber provides rather more indirect evidence that an $\alpha$-particle has passed through the chamber. Observations are conscious experiences, however, and so do not carry us outside the mind. Further, our experimental equipment – stones, cloud chambers, and the like – are, if the idealist is right, no less mental. What is a stone or a cloud chamber other than something that looks a particular way, feels a particular way, sounds a particular way, and so on? But looks, feels, and sounds, are nothing more than sensory states. Experiment, the idealist concludes, cannot provide us with grounds for inferring the existence of anything non-mental.

Idealism certainly covers the bases. It banishes problems associated with causal interaction between minds and the material world, and it does so in a way that bypasses worries associated with parallelism and occasionalism. Rightly understood, idealism is consistent with all the evidence we could possibly have. Moreover, idealism has a kind of elegant simplicity of the sort valued in the sciences. Idealism postulates nothing more than minds and their contents and explains all the phenomena by appeals to these without needing to resort to messy questions about extra-mental material objects and events.

Even so, most of us find idealism hard to swallow. This may be in part because idealism appears to take the easy way out. Idealism explains the appearances by identifying the appearances with reality. Most of us, however, hold out hope that there might be some way to keep the distinction and to reconcile our minds and their contents with a non-mental material world. In the end, we may be forced to accept idealism. But until we are forced to accept it, we can continue to seek less dramatic alternatives.

## Mind and meaning

Having said this, I should note that traditionally idealists have not offered idealism simply as a replacement for Cartesian dualism. At the heart of most species of idealism is a view about meaning and the contents of our thoughts. Idealists argue that opposing views, views that sharply distinguish minds and their contents from a mind-independent world, are literally incoherent. They do not immediately strike us as incoherent, of course, but once we understand what is involved in the having of a particular thought we can see that such views are nonsense; they are at bottom unthinkable. The upshot is that there really are no options, no alternatives to idealism.

This is a strong thesis. If true, idealism would be unassailable. However, this is not the place to examine the idealist's arguments in detail. Let us look, rather, at a streamlined version of the kind of argument to which idealists might appeal.

The line of argument I have in mind is advanced by Berkeley. Berkeley is not interested in showing that there is, as a matter of fact, no material world but only minds and their contents, or that idealism enjoys certain metaphysical advantages over its dualistic competitors. His aim is to show that, in the final analysis, there are no serious competitors. Berkeley holds that when philosophers pretend to talk about the material world, they are endeavoring to talk about something literally inconceivable. More starkly: philosophical talk about a mind-independent material world is not talk about anything at all. Dualistic hypotheses, then, are not merely false or implausible. They altogether lack meaning.

Consider, says Berkeley, what we are talking (or thinking) about when we talk (or think) about familiar objects: tables, stones, cats. We are talking (or thinking) about things that look, sound, taste, smell, and feel a certain way. But the looks of things, the sounds we hear, their tastes and feels are not external to us, not outside our minds. They are simply experiences of certain characteristic sorts. We commonly distinguish our experiences of things from the things, of course, but Berkeley is out to show us that this is an empty distinction.

Suppose you are now perceiving a ripe tomato in bright sunlight. You have a particular visual experience of a reddish roundish sort. If you grasp the tomato and bite it, you will have additional tactile, olfactory, gustatory, and auditory experiences: the tomato feels, smells, and, when you bite it, tastes and sounds a particular way. Berkeley argues that your thoughts about the tomato are exhausted by these sensory features. When you think about the tomato, your thought concerns something that looks, feels, smells, tastes and sounds a particular way. But looks, feels, and the like are, properly understood, nothing more than qualities of conscious experiences, and conscious experiences are mental phenomena.

So our thoughts about the tomato are, in the end, nothing more than thoughts about certain characteristic mental episodes. It makes no sense to suppose that mental episodes – Berkeley calls them "ideas" – could exist outside the mind, however. Our thoughts about tomatoes, then, are really thoughts about mental goings-on: conscious experiences of a particular sort we have had, or would have under the right conditions. Philosophers tell us that these experiences correspond to and are caused by a mind-independent tomato "out there." But, when we examine our idea of tomatoes, we find only experiences. We find nothing answering to the expression "mind-independent tomato." The expression "mind-independent tomato," then, is empty of significance. In that regard, it resembles "colorless green ideas." You can say these words, but they sig-nify nothing. You can, as well, entertain a thought that you might describe as a thought of colorless green ideas. But in so doing you entertain an empty thought, a thought with no content.

You might think that there is an obvious response to this line of reason-ing. Of course, you say, we can think of a mind-independent tomato. Nothing could be easier. Mind-independent tomatoes resemble our tomato experiences: they are red, spherical, and acidic. We can think of a mind-independent tomato by entertaining thoughts of the kinds of conscious experience we normally have in the presence of tomatoes, and adding to these thoughts the thought that they are of something outside the mind, something outside our experiences.

Berkeley rejects this move. Experiences, he contends, can only resemble experiences. In setting out to imagine a mind-independent tomato, I first call to mind certain experiences, then subtract from these that they are experi-ences. This, Berkeley argues, is nonsense. It resembles calling to mind the idea of a triangle and then subtracting from this idea that it is three-sided. We are left with nothing but an empty thought. Of course, we still have words: "unexperienced tomato"; "triangle without three sides." The words lack significance. But, at least in the former case, philosophers have not noticed this. They have prattled on about a mind-independent world in the way a child might prattle on about a triangle that is not three-sided.

The conclusion – a world of material objects residing outside the mind, is literally unthinkable – seems outrageous. Berkeley, however, insists on a point mentioned earlier, one that softens the blow. Suppose idealism were true: all that exists are minds and their contents. How would our everyday experiences be different than they would be were idealism false? The answer, according to Berkeley and other idealists, is that nothing would be detectably different. If that is so, however, it is hard to accuse idealists of confuting ordinary expectations. What idealists deny is simply a certain philosophical interpretation of these expectations. In rejecting material objects, idealists insist that they are not rejecting tables, trees, galaxies, and the like. Rather, they are rejecting the notion that "table," "tree," and "galaxy" designate mind-independent material objects. The terms in fact designate collections of actual and possible experiences.

Idealism, despite its apparent implausibility, is notoriously difficult to confront head-on. Rather than rehearsing detailed arguments against idealism here, I propose to move forward and discuss alternative views. It may turn out that there are grounds for preferring one or more of these to idealism, even though there are no obvious chinks in the idealist's armor. My own view is that idealism represents a kind of failure of nerve: unable to reconcile minds and the material world, the idealist gives up the game and places the material world inside the mind.

## Epiphenomenalism

Descartes depicts minds as causally interacting with the material world: events in the material world produce experiences in minds, and mental events yield bodily motions. We have seen that this kind of two-way causal interaction is difficult to reconcile with the conviction that the material world is causally self-contained: the causes of every material event are exclusively material. Suppose, however, we grant that the material world is "causally closed," but allow that material events can have mental products. Mental events exist. They are the effects of certain material causes. But no mental event has a material effect; no mental event disrupts causal sequences in the material world. Mental events are "epiphenomena," offshoots or "side-effects" of material phenomena, that themselves yield no effects of any kind (see figure 2.9).

Epiphenomenalists, then, hold that mental phenomena (conscious experiences, for instance) are by-products or side-effects of complex physical systems. In this regard, they resemble smoke produced by a locomotive, or the shadow cast by a billiard ball rolling across a billiard table, or the squeaking noise produced by a pair of new shoes. The smoke, the shadow, and the squeaking noise play no causal role in the operation of the systems that produce them. Of course, the smoke, the shadow, and the squeaking noise are material phenomena, and so have some physical effects: the smoke makes your eyes burn, the shadow alters the distribution of light radiation in the region on which it falls, and the

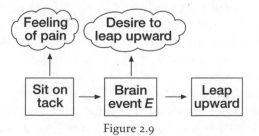

Figure 2.9

squeaking produces minute vibrations in the eardrums of passers-by. Mental phenomena, in contrast, have no effects whatever – material or mental.

Epiphenomenalism appears to fly in the face of common experience. Surely your experience of pain as you move your hand closer to the fire is what brings about your withdrawing it. And surely your deliberation and subsequent decision to obtain a Whopper are what lead you to pull into the Burger King. According to the epiphenomenalist, however, all the causal work in these cases is done by events in your nervous system. Those events have, as a by-product, the production of certain conscious experiences, perhaps. The conscious experiences, however, are causally inert. They appear to have causal clout because they are caused by, hence invariably accompany, material events that themselves bring about various effects. Suppose a loose fan belt causes both the overheating of my Yugo and a distinctive squeaking noise. The squeaking accompanies, but does not cause, the overheating. According to the epiphenomenalist, this is how it is with mental phenomena generally.

The fact, then, if it is a fact, that it feels to you as though your states of mind make a causal difference is entirely consistent with the truth of epiphenomenalism. In deciding to reach for a Whopper and subsequently reaching, you have the distinct impression that your decision caused your reaching (or, at any rate, that it contributed to the occurrence of that material event). Certainly, you can reliably count on your body's moving in a way that reflects your decisions. And it will be true that had you not decided to reach for the Whopper, you would not have done so. It does not follow, however, that decisions – kinds of mental event – move anything. If epiphenomenalism is right, then the cause of your body's moving is some neurological event. This neurological event has, as an inevitable auxiliary effect, a decision – just as, in figure 2.9, a neurological event, $E$, yields both a desire to leap and a subsequent leaping.

Neuroscientists have sometimes found epiphenomenalism attractive. In studying brain function, if we accept epiphenomenalism, we can ignore the qualities of mental phenomena altogether, and focus exclusively on physical mechanisms and processes in the brain. If mental phenomena are epiphenomenal then they are undetectable (except, presumably, by those undergoing them), and they could make no difference to anything that transpires in the material realm. This would leave neuroscientists free to explore mysteries of the brain without having to concern themselves with the messy details of conscious experience.

Epiphenomenalism faces a number of difficulties, however. First, the nature of material-to-mental causal relations is none too clear. Most philosophers accept the idea that causal relations hold among events. The epiphenomenalist contends that some material events cause mental events, but mental events cause nothing. One might think that there would be no harm in allowing that mental events could cause other mental events. After all, mental events (according to the epiphenomenalist) have no material effects, so causal relations among mental events would pose no threat to the causal integrity of the material world. But this possibility is out of step with the epiphenomenalist's broader picture. If mental events could themselves cause mental events, then some mental events would have a life of their own. It is of the essence of epiphenomenalism, however, that mental events are by-products of material events.

We must suppose then that mental events, although themselves causally inert, are caused by material events. "Dead-end" causal relations of this sort differ from ordinary causal relations, however. In the case of ordinary material causation, events are both effects (of prior events) and causes (of subsequent events). So causal transactions that include mental events appear to be very different from those encountered elsewhere in the universe. This, by itself, is no objection to epiphenomenalism. It is merely a consequence of the epiphenomenalist's conception of mental events. Nevertheless, it is clear that, if an alternative view were available, one that accounted for all that epiphenomenalism accounted for, but that did so without recourse to a special kind of causal relation, that view would be preferable.

This way of thinking invokes the principle of parsimony or Ockham's Razor (named for William of Ockham, 1285–1347). Ockham's Razor bids us not to "multiply entities beyond necessity." The idea is that simpler, more parsimonious, accounts of phenomena, accounts that refrain from introducing new kinds of entity or process, are preferred to less simple competitors. The notion of simplicity in play here is notoriously difficult to spell out. And, of course, there is no guarantee that the world is a simple place. Such matters, however, needn't detain us. We are bound to judge competing theories on their merits. We can think of Ockham's Razor, not as a principle that tells us how the world is organized, but as one that encourages us to place the burden of proof on proponents of "less simple" theories. If an alternative to epiphenomenalism avoids "dead-end" causal relations, then the burden is on the proponent of epiphenomenalism to convince us that epiphenomenalism nevertheless affords a better account of the phenomena.

## Non-Cartesian dualism

Cartesian dualism, as I have characterized it, includes a number of components. First, minds and material bodies are taken to be distinct substances. Second, minds and material bodies are assumed to interact causally. This interaction goes in both directions: mental events cause and are caused by material events. We have seen that it is possible to start with Cartesian dualism and modify particular elements to produce new conceptions of minds and their relation to the material world. Parallelists and occasionalists deny that minds interact with material bodies. Idealists reject material substance and with it the notion of mind–body interaction. Epiphenomenalists disavow mental substances, but allow mental events as causally inert by-products of events involving material substances.

There is, however, a third component of the Cartesian view. Mental and material substances are distinguished by unique attributes. Minds are thinking substances, bodies are extended substances. No material body thinks, no mind is spatially extended. Suppose we retained the first two components of Cartesian dualism, and rejected this third component. On such a view, minds and bodies would be regarded as distinct substances capable of causal interaction, but minds might nevertheless possess properties Descartes would have restricted to material bodies.

Why should anyone be attracted to such a view? One reason is that by allowing that minds can be spatially extended, the notion that they interact causally with material bodies becomes less mysterious. We can make a start on understanding what is at stake here by first considering a little more carefully the principles we deploy in distinguishing substances.

Think of a boat made of wooden planks. How is the boat related to the collection of planks? It is tempting to think that boat just is the collection of planks (and nothing more). After all the boat goes where the collection of planks goes; the boat weighs what the collection of planks weighs; if you purchase the boat, you thereby acquire the collection of planks. A long tradition in philosophy, stemming from Aristotle (384–322 BC), rejects this picture. Ordinary substances are distinguished from one another by conditions of individuation and persistence. These conditions tell us, in effect, what counts as a particular thing or substance and what sorts of change it could undergo without ceasing to exist. Consider the collection of planks that makes up the boat. Suppose you remove a plank from the collection, burn it, and replace it with a new plank (as you might do in refitting the boat). The collection no longer exists; in its place is one that differs from the original collection by a single plank: a new collection. The boat, however, survives this transformation. You have changed the boat, you have not destroyed it. Imagine now that you dismantle the boat and use the planks to build a belvedere. The collection survives, but the boat does not.

This line of reasoning requires an especially strict understanding of what constitutes a collection. Collections, in this strict sense, cannot gain or lose parts without ceasing to exist: a collection just is the sum of its members (or perhaps the sum of its members in a particular relationship). Our everyday understanding of collections is less rigid. You can add to your collection of baseball cards or stamps, or replace some with others, and the collection remains. (We shall return to these matters in chapter six.)

We might explain these facts about the boat and the collection of planks that makes it up by allowing that the conditions of individuation and persistence for a boat differ from those for a collection of planks. Now the tricky bit. If a boat could continue to exist when the collection of planks that now makes it up does not, and if a collection of planks that now constitutes a boat could exist when the boat does not, then a boat cannot be identified with the collection of planks that makes it up at a given time. More generally, if $A$ can exist when $B$ does not, then $A$ and $B$ cannot be the selfsame thing. A boat and a collection of planks can spatially coincide during a period of time. The boat, during that period, is made up of the collection of planks. Indeed, at a particular time, the boat's existence depends on the existence of the collection of planks. This merely shows, however, that material composition and dependence do not add up to identity.

I have been tossing around a number of unfamiliar technical notions: substance, composition, identity, dependence. The best way, indeed the only way, to get a grip on these notions is to see how they function in metaphysical theories. It is possible, however, to say a word about each at the outset and thereby to avoid potential confusion.

We have encountered the traditional notion of substance already, the notion of a particular thing: this particular billiard ball, the tree in the quad, your left ear. Substances can be made up of substances. The billiard ball, the tree, and your ear, are made up of bits arranged in particular ways, and these bits are themselves substances. Simple substances can be distinguished from complex substances. Complex substances have simple substances as parts. Simple substances, in contrast, lack parts.

This last claim needs qualification. A simple substance cannot have parts that are themselves substances – substantial parts. A simple substance might, however, have non-substantial spatial or temporal parts. Suppose a simple substance is square, for instance. Then it has a top half and a bottom half. If the square is four inches on a side, then its surface comprises sixteen distinct regions, each of which is one inch square. However, the square, if it is simple, is not composed or made up of these regions in the way a watch is composed of gears, springs, and a case. Gears, springs, and cases can exist when no watch exists, but its spatial regions cannot exist independently of the square.

What of composition? The composition relation holds among substances. Several substances compose or make up a complex substance when they are grouped together appropriately. What constitutes an appropriate grouping will depend on the character of the collection. The cells making up your left ear are densely packed together and have a more or less definite boundary. In contrast, the atoms making up my desk are, at the microscopic level, widely scattered. Not every collection of substances makes up a substance. Consider the collection of substances consisting of your left ear, this billiard ball, and the tree outside my window. Such a collection does not add up to a substance. Complex substances are collections of substances appropriately organized, where the organizing principle stems from the nature of the substance in question. The organizing principle of the planks making up a wooden boat differs from the organizing principle of the cells that at a given time make up your left ear.

When we asked whether the boat was nothing more than the collection of planks, we were asking whether the boat and the collection were identical. The notion of identity thus appealed to is that of selfsameness. A is identical with B, in this sense, just in case A and B are the selfsame individual. This notion of identity, strict identity, is to be distinguished from a weaker colloquial notion. We may say that two dresses are identical, meaning, not that the dresses are one and the same dress, but that they are exactly similar. Henceforth, in speaking of identity, I shall mean strict identity, selfsameness. In cases where the weaker sense is intended, I shall speak of similarity or exact similarity.

The notion of dependence, or metaphysical dependence, is the notion of the existence of one thing's absolutely requiring the existence of some other thing. An A metaphysically depends on some B when A could not exist unless B exists. Metaphysical dependence is to be distinguished from causal dependence. You could not exist in the absence of oxygen, and so your existence depends on the existence of oxygen. The dependence here is causal, however, not metaphysical. You might have existed (if only for a brief period) in the absence of oxygen. Compare dependence of this sort with the metaphysical dependence of a whole (the wooden boat, for instance) on its parts at a given time. Although we can imagine the boat surviving the replacement of individual parts over time, we cannot imagine the boat's continuing to exist at a time when none of its parts exist.

Armed with this vocabulary, we can begin to see how a dualism of substances need not imply Cartesian-style dualism. The boat, let us suppose, is a substance distinct from the collection of planks that make it up at a given time. The boat metaphysically depends, at that time, on the collection of planks. Moreover, the boat, although distinguishable from the collection of planks, is not an immaterial substance. Indeed, at any given time it shares a number of properties with the collection of planks that make it up. The boat and the collection of planks have the same mass, the same spatial dimensions, and occupy the same region of space-time.

Now suppose we extend this point to the relation minds bear to bodies. Imagine that minds – or, following Descartes, selves – were regarded as substances distinguishable from, but dependent on, the material substances in which they were embodied. Selves, thus considered, could possess ordinary material properties: mass, size, and spatial location, for instance. In this regard, they would differ from Cartesian selves.

A view of this kind has been eloquently defended by E. J. Lowe. Lowe distinguishes selves from their bodies in the way we have distinguished a boat from the collection of planks making it up. A self has a body, a complex material substance, on which it depends for its existence. When you identify yourself, you are identifying a substance that has, and depends on, a body, but which is not identical with that body. Nor are you to be identified with any part of your body (your brain, for instance). At this point the boat analogy breaks down. Although the self shares some properties with the body, it is not made up of the body or the body's parts as a boat is, at a particular time, made up of a collection of planks.

Bodies and selves have very different persistence conditions, so you are not identical with your body. Similar considerations lead to the conclusion that you are not identical with any part of your body, your brain, for instance. Your body is a complex biological substance that includes complex substances as parts. Your brain is one of these substantial parts. Your brain could exist when you do not. Further, you have a particular height and mass. These you share with your body, not with your brain and not with any other part of your body.

Even if we accept all this, even if we grant that the self is a substance, distinct from the body but nevertheless sharing some of the body's properties, why should we imagine that the self is a simple substance, one without substantial parts? Lowe turns the question around: what could parts of the self be? If we grant that the self is not the body or a part of the body, then parts of the body could not be parts of the self, unless the self has, in addition, other, non-bodily parts. But what might these parts be? There are no obvious candidates.

One possibility is that the self has psychological parts. It is common nowadays (as it was in Descartes's day) to suppose that minds include distinct "faculties" or "modules." You have various perceptual faculties, for instance, as well as a faculty for memory, and a faculty of imagination. Might these faculties be regarded as parts of the self? Again, Lowe holds that this is unlikely. In the sense in which faculties might be regarded as parts of selves, they are not substantial parts, they are not substances in their own right capable of existence independently of the self in the way a brain or a heart is capable of existing independently of the body of which it is a part.

Let us suppose that Lowe is right about this: the self is a simple substance distinct from the body and from any substantial part of the body. What characteristics do selves possess? You – that is, your self – possess some characteristics only derivatively. Your having a left ear, for instance, amounts only to your having a body that has a left ear. But you also have a particular height and mass. These characteristics are, in addition to being characteristics of your body, characteristics of you, your self. This is where Lowe and Descartes part company. According to Descartes, selves, but not bodies, possess mental characteristics; bodies, but not selves, possess material characteristics.

What accounts for the distinction between material characteristics you have and those you have only in having a body that possesses them? If the self is simple, then it can possess only characteristics capable of possession by a simple substance. Because ears have substantial parts, ears can be possessed only by complex substances. In contrast, being a particular height or having a particular mass does not imply substantial complexity.

In addition to possessing a range of material characteristics, selves possess mental characteristics. Your thoughts and feelings belong, not to your body, or to a part of your body (your brain), but to you. More generally, selves, but not their bodies, possess mental characteristics.

Because selves, on a view of this sort, are not regarded as immaterial substances, the Cartesian problem of causal interaction between selves and material substances does not arise. Still, we are bound to wonder how a self, which is not identical with a body or with any part of a body, could act on the world. You decide to take a stroll and subsequently move your body in a characteristic way. How is this possible? The causal precursors of your strolling include only bodily events and external causes of bodily events.

Lowe contends that the model of mental causation inherited from Descartes is inappropriate. Descartes imagines selves initiating causal sequences in the brain. One worry about such a view is that it apparently violates our deep conviction that the material world is causally self-contained. Perhaps such a conviction is, in the end, merely a prejudice or, more charitably, a presumption that we could find good reason to abandon. Until we are presented with such a reason, however, we should do well to remain suspicious of those who would deny it solely in order to preserve a favored thesis.

Lowe argues that there is, in any case, a more telling difficulty for the Cartesian model. Consider your decision to take a stroll, and your right leg's subsequently moving as a consequence of that decision. A Cartesian supposes that your decision, a mental event, initiates a causal chain that eventually issues in your right leg's moving, a bodily event. This picture is captured in figure 2.10 ($M_1$ is your deciding to stroll; $B_1$ is your right leg's moving; $E_1$ and $E_2$, intervening events in your nervous system; $t_0$ is the time of the decision; and $t_1$, the time at which your right leg moves).

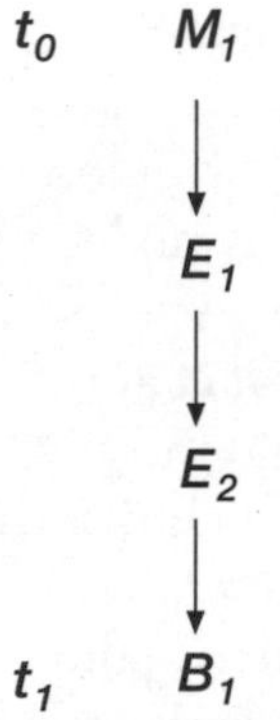

$$t_0 \quad M_1$$
$$\downarrow$$
$$E_1$$
$$\downarrow$$
$$E_2$$
$$\downarrow$$
$$t_1 \quad B_1$$

Figure 2.10

The Cartesian picture, Lowe thinks, includes a distortion. Imagine tracing the causal chain leading back from the muscle contractions involved in the motion of your right leg. That chain presumably goes back to events in your brain, but it goes back beyond these to earlier events, and eventually to events occurring prior to your birth. Further, and more significantly, when the causal chain culminating in $B_1$ is traced back, we discover that it quickly becomes entangled in endless other causal chains issuing in a variety of quite distinct bodily movements. (See figure 2.11.)

Here, $B_1$ is your right leg's moving, and $B_2$, and $B_3$, are distinct bodily motions. $B_2$ might be your left arm's moving as you greet a passing

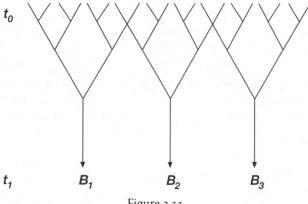

Figure 2.11

acquaintance, and $B_3$ might be the non-voluntary movement of an eyelid. The branching causal chains should be taken to extend up the page indefinitely into the past.

Now, although your decision to take a stroll is presumed to be responsible for $B_1$, and not for $B_2$ and $B_3$, the causal histories of these bodily events are inextricably entangled. Prior to $t_0$, there is no identifiable event sequence causally responsible for $B_1$, but not for $B_2$ or $B_3$. It is hard to see where in the complex web of causal relations occurring in your nervous system a mental event might initiate $B_1$.

Lowe contends that we can abandon the Cartesian model of mental causation, and replace it with a model reminiscent of one proposed by Immanuel Kant (1724–1804). The self affects the material world, although not by initiating causal chains. Indeed, in one important respect (and excluding uncaused events), nothing in the world initiates a causal chain. Rather, to put it somewhat (and perhaps unavoidably) mysteriously, the self makes it the case that the world contains a pattern of causal sequences issuing in a particular bodily motion. A mental event (your deciding to stroll, for instance) brings about a material event (your right leg's moving), not by instigating a sequence of events that culminates in your right leg's moving, but by bringing it about that a particular kind of causal pattern exists.

Consider a spider moving about on its web. Although the web is causally dependent on the spider, it is a distinct substance in its own right, not identifiable with the spider's body or with a part of the spider. Moreover, the web affects the spider's movements, not by initiating them, but by "enabling" or "facilitating" them. The web, we might say, makes it the case that the world contains motions of one sort rather than another. In an analogous way, the self might be regarded as a product of complex physical (and, Lowe thinks, social) processes, a product not identifiable with its body or a part of its body. The self accounts for the character of bodily motions, not by initiating causal chains, but by making it the case that those causal chains have the particular shape they have.

I do not pretend that any of this is entirely clear or persuasive. My aim, however, has not been to offer a brief on behalf of non-Cartesian dualism, but merely to propose it as an option worthy of serious consideration. (An alternative view of the same territory is put forward in chapter six.) Given the tentative nature of our understanding of minds and their relations to bodies, it would be unwise to dismiss such options prematurely.

## Taking stock

In the chapters that follow, we shall return to many of the metaphysical themes introduced here, refining our understanding of those themes and their bearing on questions about minds and their relation to the material world. In the end, we may be in a better position to assess the options open to us.

Thus far we have seen that dualism of the sort promoted by Descartes, a dualism of substances, can be spelled out, transformed, and fine-tuned in a number of ways. Descartes himself holds that minds – or selves – and bodies are utterly distinct kinds of substance. Even so, mental and material substances can bear especially intimate relations to one another. At the very least, mental and material substances interact causally.

Descartes never fully explains how an unextended, non-spatial, thinking substance could affect or be affected by an unthinking, extended substance. In one respect, of course, there is only so much anyone can do to "explain" causal relations. And in this respect, Descartes is no worse off than his latter-day materialist critics. In another respect, however, Descartes's picture apparently conflicts with our deeply-held belief that the material world is "causally closed." We are a long way from knowing whether this belief is true, or even whether it is warranted. Even so, there is something decidedly unsettling about accepting the Cartesian picture, if options are available that do not oblige us to regard the world as bifurcated along mental–physical lines.

Parallelists and occasionalists accept Descartes's dualism and resolve the problem of causal interaction by denying that it occurs. The appearance of causal interaction between mind and body is explained away by supposing, as proponents of parallelism do, that sequences of events in the mental realm are perfectly correlated with material event sequences, or that God wills into existence both mental events and their material correlates.

Idealists agree with parallelists and occasionalists that observed causal interactions between minds and bodies are illusory. But idealists abandon the dualist premise that the world contains both mental and material substances: all is mental. Indeed the notion of objects existing independently of minds is deemed unintelligible.

We might try to preserve causal interaction between minds and bodies and still maintain that minds and bodies are distinct substances, by rejecting the Cartesian doctrine that mental substances lack material characteristics. Minds or selves possess characteristics not possessed by bodies (they undergo experiences, for instance). But minds can possess characteristics Descartes reserves for unthinking substances. This common ground apparently leaves open the possibility of causal interaction between minds and bodies.

A dualism of this stripe is left with a residual difficulty. As we noted above, modern science has encouraged a commitment to the causal autonomy of the material world. If mental substances causally intervene in material affairs, this would seem to require us to abandon the idea that the material world is causally self-contained. This would be so even if those mental substances possessed, in addition to mental characteristics, physical characteristics.

Suppose, however, we reject the conception of mental causation implicit in the Cartesian picture. Minds causally influence bodies, perhaps, but not by initiating sequences of material events. Every event in such a sequence is caused by some other material event. This is just the thesis of the causal autonomy of the material world. It is consistent with causal autonomy, however, that minds "shape" causal sequences – not by altering the directions of motion of elementary particles, as Descartes supposed, but by constraining sequences in the way a spider's web constrains the motions of a spider.

Before embracing any of these views, however, we should do well to consider the alternatives. This we shall do in the chapters that follow. The goal is not to promote a single account of mind and matter, but rather to provide you the reader with the tools to make an informed choice.

## Suggested reading

Substance dualism is given scant consideration in contemporary philosophy of mind. The focus has been, instead, on "property dualism," a view according to which the mental and the physical are not distinguishable kinds of substance, but distinct families of properties. Dualisms of this sort have troubles of their own, and have been much discussed in recent years. I have elected to dwell on substance dualism partly in the hopes of encouraging a fresh look at a range of well-worn issues. Thus, I have tried to present versions of traditional dualism in a favorable light. I have not said all that I might have said, and I have ignored many details; my goal has been only to introduce a range of issues. Readers interested in pursuing these should consider the readings discussed below. (A complete bibliography appears at the end of this volume.)

Descartes's views on the mind are developed in his *Meditations on First Philosophy* (1641/1986). This edition of the *Meditations* includes selections from the "Objections and Replies" that illuminate certain of Descartes's positions.

Hume's discussion of causation occurs in his *A Treatise of Human Nature* (1739/1978), i, 3, §§ 1–6, 11, 12, 14, 15; and in *Enquiry Concerning Human Understanding* (1748/1975), §§ 4, 7.

Malebranche's account of occasionalism can be found in *Dialogues on Metaphysics and Religion* (1688/1997). Leibniz advances a version of parallelism in his *Monodology* (1787/1973). Berkeley's idealism is discussed at length and defended in his *Treatise Concerning* the *Principles of Human Knowledge* (1713/1983); and in *Three Dialogues between Hylas and Philonous* (1710/1979). John Foster brings idealism up to date in *The Immaterial Self* (1991).

Epiphenomenalism is described and defended by T. H. Huxley in his *Methods and Results: Essays* (1901). See also C. D. Broad's *The Mind and Its Place in Nature* (1925), chap. 3. Nowadays, epiphenomenalism is most often taken to concern, not mental events, but mental properties: an object's possession of mental properties makes no non-mental difference. Frank Jackson's defense of property epiphenomenalism in "Epiphenomenal Qualia" (1982) has been widely influential.

E. J. Lowe's defense of non-Cartesian dualism is developed in his *Subjects of Experience* (1996). Lowe's depiction of the self has much in common with that advanced by P. F. Strawson in his *Individuals: An Essay in Descriptive Metaphysics* (1959), chap. 3. Lowe's "Substance" (1988) provides an especially readable account of the traditional conception of substance introduced in this chapter. Lowe's view of the nature of mind-to-body causation is reminiscent of Kant's in his discussion of the "third antinomy"; see *The Critique of Pure Reason* (1787/1964).

Peter van Inwagen's *Metaphysics* (1993) includes a discussion of composites (which van Inwagen calls "collections"), although his conclusions differ from those defended here.

# CHAPTER 3
# Varieties of materialism:
## Behaviorism and psycho-physical identity

# Varieties of materialism–
## Behaviorism and psycho-physical identity

In chapter two, we began with an examination of Descartes's contention that minds and material bodies are distinct kinds of substance. We then examined a number of related views, views that could be spun out from our Cartesian starting point by rejecting or modifying one or another of its components. In this chapter, we shall explore two materialist accounts of the mind.

Materialists deny that the world includes both mental and material substances. Every substance is a material substance. Minds are fashioned somehow from the same materials from which rocks, trees, and stars are made. If we take the fundamental particles that make up inanimate objects and arrange them in the right way, the result is a creature with a mind. The mind is not a separate, non-material entity, but only matter, suitably organized.

Materialism has a long history. Democritus (c. 460–370 BC) described the world as a fleeting arrangement of atoms swirling in the void. Hobbes (1588–1679) and La Mettrie (1707–51) regarded mental phenomena as nothing more than mechanical interactions of material components. Nowadays, materialism of one stripe or another is more often than not taken for granted. The belief that minds are just brains is evidently widespread. Francis Crick's recent description of this as "the astonishing hypothesis" flies in the face of my own experience with undergraduate philosophy students who seem to use "mind" and "brain" interchangeably.

Although many philosophers would, if pressed, describe themselves as materialists, materialism comes in different flavors. Disagreements among materialists tend to overshadow their common rejection of dualism. In recent years, dissatisfaction with materialist assumptions has led to a revival of interest in forms of dualism. Surprisingly, much of this interest has been spawned by work in the neurosciences where difficulties in reconciling characteristics of complex material systems with characteristics of conscious experiences are especially acute.

In this chapter, we shall examine a pair of precursors to the contemporary debate: behaviorism and the mind–brain identity theory. Behaviorism as a philosophical doctrine about the nature of mind differs from behaviorism as a movement in psychology. Philosophical behaviorism is associated with a thesis about the nature of mind and the meanings of mental terms. Psychological behaviorism emerged from a particular conception of scientific method as applied to psychology. This brand of behaviorism dominated experimental work in psychology until the 1960s when it was eclipsed by the information-processing model, a model inspired by the advent of the computing machine.

The relation between philosophy and the empirical sciences, including psychology, is scarcely straightforward. On the one hand, philosophers of mind have had an important part in shaping conceptions of mentality that guide empirical investigators. On the other hand, philosophers have periodically re-evaluated their theories in light of advances in the sciences. One result is that philosophical influences on the sciences find their way back into philosophy. When this happens, a philosophical thesis can gain an undeserved air of empirical respectability in the minds of philosophers eager to embrace the pronouncements of science.

Philosophers, impressed by behaviorism in psychology, sometimes failed to appreciate the extent to which the behaviorist conception of mind was the product of a definite philosophical conception of scientific method. Ironically, the roots of that conception lay in a positivist tradition that many of these same philosophers would have found unappealing. One lesson is that it is a mistake for philosophers of mind to accept uncritically or at face value claims issuing from psychology or the neurosciences.

## Behaviorism

Until the twentieth century, the study of mind the was assumed to revolve around the study of conscious states and processes. Subjects in psychological experiments (very often the experimenters themselves or their students) were trained to "introspect," and report on features of their conscious experiences. In this milieu, mental imagery and subtle qualities of sensory episodes had a central place.

At the same time, psychologists were concerned to integrate the study of the mind with the study of the brain. It had long been evident that occurrences in the brain and nervous system were intimately related to mental goings-on. The difficulty was to understand precisely the nature of the relation between minds and brains. It is tempting to think that minds (or selves: I shall continue to use the terms interchangeably, without intending to suggest that they are synonymous) are nothing more than brains. Properties of brains, however, seem to differ importantly from properties of minds. When you undergo a conscious experience, you are vividly aware of characteristics of that experience. When we examine a living brain, the characteristics we observe appear to be utterly different. Think of what it is like to have a headache. Now imagine that you are able to peer at the brain of someone suffering a headache. What you observe, even aided by instruments that reveal the fine structure of the brain, is altogether different from what the headache victim feels. Imagine a neuro-scientist, intimately familiar with the physiology of headache, but who has never experienced a headache. There is, it would seem, something the scientist lacks knowledge of, some characteristic the scientist has not encountered and could not encounter simply by inspecting the brain. But then this characteristic would appear not to be a neurological character-istic. When we look at the matter this way, it is hard to avoid concluding that mental characteristics are not brain characteristics, and thus that minds are not brains.

If this were not enough, we would do well to remind ourselves that we evidently enjoy a kind of "access" to our conscious experiences that others could never have. Your experiences are "private." Your awareness of them is direct and authoritative; my awareness of those same experiences is, in contrast, indirect, inferential, and easily overridden. When you have a headache, form an image of your grandmother, or decide to comb your hair, you are in a position to recognize immediately, without the benefit of evidence or observation, that you have a headache, that you are imagining your grandmother, or that you have decided to comb your hair. I can only infer your state of mind by observing your behavior (including your lin-guistic behavior: I can interrogate you). If mental goings-on are correlated with neurological processes, then I may be able to infer your state of mind by observing your brain. But my access to that state is still indirect. I infer your state of mind by observing a neurological correlate. I do not observe your state of mind.

All this is exactly what we should expect were dualism true. But dual-ism, or at any rate Cartesian dualism, apparently leads to a bifurcation of the study of intelligent agents. We can study the biology and physiology of such agents, but in so doing we ignore their minds; or we can study their minds, ignoring their material composition.

Now, however, we are faced with a difficulty. Science is limited to the pursuit of objective, "public" states of affairs. An objective state of affairs can be apprehended from more than one perspective, by more than one observer. The contents of your mind, however, are observable (if that is the word) only by you. My route to those contents is through observations of what you say and do. This appears to place minds outside the realm of scientific inquiry. We can study brains, and we may conclude that par-ticular kinds of neurological goings-on are correlated with kinds of mental goings-on. This would enable us reliably to infer states of mind by observing brain activity. But we should not be observing or measuring those states of mind themselves, except in our own case.

## Privacy and its consequences

Once we start down this road, we may come to doubt that states of mind – as distinct from their physiological correlates – are a fit subject for scientific examination. Eventually, the very idea that we are in a position even to establish correlations between mental occurrences and goings-on in the nervous system can come to be doubted. Imagine that, every time you have a particular kind of experience – every time you see a certain shade of red, for instance, the red of a ripe tomato – your brain goes into a particular state, $S$. Further, whenever your brain goes into state $S$, you experience that very shade of red. It looks as though there must be a correlation between experiences of this kind and neurological states of kind $S$.

Suppose, now, you observe my brain in state $S$. I announce that I am experiencing a certain shade of red, a shade I describe as the red of a ripe tomato. It might seem that this provides further evidence of the correlation already observed in your own case. But does it? In your own case, you have access both to the mental state and to its neurological correlate. When you observe me, however, you have access only to my neurological condition. What gives you the right to assume that my mental state resembles yours?

True, I describe my experience just as you describe yours. We agree that we are experiencing the color of ripe tomatoes. But of course this is how we have each been taught to characterize our respective experiences. I have a particular kind of visual experience when I view a ripe tomato in bright sunlight. I describe this experience as the kind of experience I have when I view a ripe tomato in bright sunlight. You have a particular kind of experience when you view a ripe tomato under similar observational conditions. And you have learned to describe this experience as the kind of experience you have when you view a ripe tomato in bright sunlight. But what entitles either of us to say that the experiences so described are exactly similar? Perhaps the experience you have is like the experience I would have were I to view a lime in bright sunlight. Our descriptions perfectly coincide, but the state of mind I am describing is qualitatively very different from yours.

It would seem, then, that attempts to correlate kinds of neurological goings-on and kinds of mental occurrences boil down to correlations of neurological goings-on and descriptions of mental occurrences. We learn to describe the qualities of our states of mind by reference to publicly observable objects that typically evoke them. And this leaves open the possibility that, while our descriptions match, the states to which they apply are wildly different.

This may seem an idle worry, a purely philosophical possibility. But ask yourself: what earthly reason do you have for thinking that your states of mind qualitatively resemble the states of mind of others? It is not as though you have observed others' states of mind and discovered they match yours. You lack a single example of such a match. Might you infer inductively from characteristics of your own case to the characteristics of others? (Inductive inference is probabilistic: we reason from the characteristics of a sample of a population to characteristics of the population as a whole.) But canons of inductive reasoning proscribe inferences from a single individual to a whole population unless it is clear that the individual is representative of the population. If you assume that characteristics of your states of mind are representative, however, you are assuming precisely what you set out to establish.

The problem we have been scouting is the old problem of other minds. Granted you can know your own mind, how can you know the minds of others? Indeed, once we put it this way, we can see that the problem is deeper than we might have expected. How can you know that others have minds at all? They behave in ways similar to the ways you behave, and they insist they have pains, images, feelings, and thoughts. But what reason do you have for supposing that they do? You cannot observe others' states of mind. Nor do you have adequate inductive grounds for inferring that they enjoy a mental life from what you can observe about them.

A recent twist on this ancient puzzle introduces the possibility of "zombies," creatures identical to us in every material respect, but altogether lacking conscious experiences. The apparent conceivability of zombies has convinced some philosophers that there is an unbridgeable "explanatory gap" between material qualities and the qualities of conscious experience.

You may be growing impatient with this line of reasoning. Of course we know that others have mental lives similar to ours in many ways – and different as well: it is also possible to know that. Well and good. But it is hard to see how this confidence could be justified so long as we accept the notion that minds and their contents are private affairs, incapable of public scrutiny.

## The beetle in the box

Perhaps our starting point is what is responsible for our predicament. We have been led down the garden path by a certain conception of mind inherited from Descartes. If we begin to question that conception, we may see our way clear to a solution to our problem, one that better fits our commonsense idea that we can know that others have minds and that their minds resemble ours.

Wittgenstein (1889–1951), in his *Philosophical Investigations* (1953/ 1968), § 293, offers a compelling analogy:

> Suppose everyone had a box with something in it: we call it a "beetle". No one can look into anyone else's box, and everyone says he knows what a beetle is only by looking at his beetle. – Here it would be quite possible for everyone to have something different in his box. One might even imagine such a thing constantly changing.

The picture here resembles the picture of the relation we bear to our own and others' states of mind that we have been taking for granted.

Wittgenstein argues against this picture, not by presenting considerations that imply its falsity, but by showing that our accepting it leads to a paradoxical result: if this is the relation we bear to our own and others' states of mind, then we should have no way of referring to them.

> Suppose the word "beetle" had a use in these people's language? – If so it would not be used as the name of a thing. The thing in the box has no place in the language-game at all; not even as a something: for the box might even be empty. – No, one can "divide through" by the thing in the box; it cancels out, whatever it is. That is to say: if we construe the grammar of the expression of sensation on the model of "object and designation" the object drops out of consideration as irrelevant.

What is Wittgenstein's point? You report that your box contains a beetle. Your report is perfectly apt. You have been taught to use the word "beetle" in just this way. Imagine, now, that the object in my box is very different from the object in your box. If we could compare the objects, this would be obvious, although we could never be in a position to compare them. Suppose now that I report that my box contains a beetle. In so doing, I am using the word "beetle" exactly as I have been taught to use it. My utterance, like yours, is perfectly correct.

Suppose, now, we each report, say, that our respective boxes contain a beetle. Is either of us mistaken? No. In the imagined situation, Wittgenstein argues, the word "beetle" is used in such a way that it makes no difference what is inside anyone's box. "Beetle," in our imagined dialect, means, roughly, "whatever is in the box." To wonder whether your beetle resembles my beetle is to misunderstand this use of "beetle." It is to treat "beetle" as though it named or designated a kind of object or entity. But "beetle" is used in such a way that "the object drops out of consideration as irrelevant."

Wittgenstein's point is not merely a linguistic one. Any thoughts we might harbor that we would express using the word "beetle," are similarly constrained. Those thoughts turn out not to concern some particular kind of entity. Differently put: if the word "beetle" does not refer to entities of a particular sort, then neither do thoughts naturally expressible using "beetle."

## Philosophical behaviorism

How might the analogy be extended to states of mind? As a child, you react in various ways to your surroundings. On some occasions, you moan and rub your head. Adults tell you that what you have is called a headache. Others are taught to use "headache" similarly. Does "headache" designate a kind of entity or state?

Perhaps not. Perhaps when you tell me that you have a headache, you are not picking out any definite thing or private condition at all (think of the beetle), but merely evincing your headache. You have been trained in a particular way. When you are moved to moan and rub your head, you are, as a result of this training, moved as well to utter the words "I have a headache." When you ascribe a headache to me, you are saying no more than that I am in a kind of state that leads me to moan, rub my head, or utter "I have a headache." The private character of that state could differ across individuals. It might continually change, or even, in some cases (zombies?), be altogether absent. The function of the word "headache" is not to designate that private character, however. It "drops out of consideration as irrelevant."

Suppose that this account of our use of "headache" applied to our mental vocabulary generally. Then mental terms would not in fact be used to designate kinds of entity or qualitatively similar private episodes as Descartes would have it. Their role is quite different. And in that case, the question whether the state you designate by "experience I have when I view a ripe tomato in bright sunlight" qualitatively matches the state I designate when I use the same expression could not so much as arise. To raise the question is to mischaracterize the use of mental terminology, and thus to utter nonsense.

This line of reasoning supports what is often dubbed philosophical behaviorism. (It is dubbed thus by its opponents. Few philosophers routinely so characterized have applied the label to themselves.) The philosophical behaviorist holds that the Cartesian conception of mind errs in a fundamental way. Minds are not entities (whether Cartesian substances or brains); and mental episodes are not private goings-on inside such entities. We are attracted to the Cartesian picture only because we are misled by what Wittgenstein calls the grammar of our language.

So long as we deploy our language in everyday life we steer clear of philosophical puzzles. Words owe their significance to the "language games" we play with them. An appropriate understanding of any word (hence the concept it expresses) requires a grasp of the part or parts it plays in these language games. When we engage in philosophy, however, we are apt to be misled by the fact that "mind," like "brain," or "baseball," is a substantive noun. We reason that "mind" must designate a kind of entity, and that what we call thoughts, sensations, and feelings refer to qualitatively similar states or modes of this entity. We can avoid confusion only by looking carefully at the way our words are actually deployed in ordinary circumstances.

This prescription is intended by Wittgenstein to apply to philosophy generally. Philosophical problems arise "when language goes on holiday," when we lose touch with the way our words are actually used. In our everyday interactions with one another, we are not puzzled by our capacity to know how others feel or what they are thinking. The philosophical problem of other minds arises when we wrench "mind," "thought," "feeling," and their cognates from the contexts in which they are naturally deployed, put a special interpretation on them, and then boggle at the puzzles that result.

Gilbert Ryle (1900–76) extends Wittgenstein's point. According to Ryle, the supposition that minds are kinds of entity amounts to a "category mistake": "it represents the facts of mental life as if they belonged to one logical type or category ... when actually they belong to another" (1949, p. 16). Suppose I show you around my university. We stroll through the grounds; I show you various academic and administrative buildings; I take you to the library; I introduce you to students and members of the faculty. When I am done, I ask whether there is anything else you would like to see. You reply: "Yes. You've shown me the grounds, the academic and administrative buildings, the library, students, and faculty; but you haven't shown me the university. I'd like to see that." You have made a category mistake. You have taken the term "university" to designate an entity similar to, but distinct from, those you have seen already.

If you persisted in the belief that "university" designates such an entity despite failing ever to encounter it, you might come to imagine that the entity in question is "non-material." An analogous mistake, says Ryle, encourages Cartesian dualism. We begin with the idea that minds are entities, distinct from, but similar to brains or bodies. When we have trouble locating such entities in the material world, we assume that they

must be non-material. We see the mind, to use Ryle's colorful phrase, as
the ghost in the machine. But minds are not entities at all, ghostly or
otherwise, a fact we should immediately appreciate if only we kept firmly
before us the way "mind" functions in ordinary English.

> The theoretically interesting category mistakes are those made
> by people who are perfectly competent to apply concepts, at
> least in the situations with which they are familiar, but are still
> liable in their abstract thinking to allocate those concepts to
> logical types to which they do not belong.
>
> (1949, p. 17)

At the risk of confusing matters by piling analogies on top of analogies,
an example of Wittgenstein's may help here. Suppose you look into the
cab of a locomotive (or the cockpit of a jetliner). You see levers, knobs,
buttons, and switches. Each of these operates in a particular way (some are
turned, some slide back and forth, some are pushed or pulled), and each has
a particular function in the locomotive's (or jetliner's) operation. We
should be misled if we assumed that levers or knobs with similar shapes
had similar functions. In the same way, the fact that "mind" is a substantive noun, or that we speak of "states of mind" should not lead us to
assume that "mind" functions to designate a particular entity, and that
states of mind are states of this entity.

If "mind," like "university," does not function to name a particular
kind of material or immaterial ("ghostly") entity, how does it function?
Perhaps we ascribe minds to creatures with a capacity to comport themselves, as we should say, "intelligently." A creature possesses a mind, not
in virtue of being equipped with a peculiar kind of private ingredient, its
mind, but in virtue of being the sort of creature capable of engaging in
behavior that exhibits a measure of spontaneity and a relatively complex
organization. For their part, states of mind – headaches, intentions, beliefs
– are possessed by intelligent creatures in virtue of what they do or would
do. Your believing that there is a bear in your path, for instance, is a matter
of your taking appropriate evasive measures, your assenting to "There is a
bear on the path," and the like. Your intending to attend the World Series
is a matter of your being moved to purchase tickets, arranging for trans-
portation, announcing "I'm going to the World Series," and so on. (In
chapter five, we shall encounter Daniel Dennett's updated version of this
view.)

On a view of this sort, an agent is correctly describable as having states
of mind, not only in virtue of what that agent does, but also in virtue of
what he would do, what he is "disposed" to do. Thus, if you have a headache, you may be disposed to moan, rub your head, seek out aspirin, and

announce "I have a headache." You may do none of these things, however. Imagine, for instance, that you do not want anyone to know that you have a headache. In that case, although you are disposed to behave in particular ways, you do not behave in those ways.

But now we are confronted with a new question. What is it to "be disposed" to behave in a particular way? What are dispositions? A fragile vase possesses a disposition to shatter. In shattering, when struck by a tire iron, for instance, it manifests this disposition. A salt crystal possess a disposition to dissolve in water. In dissolving upon being placed in water, it manifests its solubility. An object can possess a disposition, however, without manifesting that disposition. A fragile glass need never shatter; a salt crystal need never dissolve.

I shall have more to say about dispositions in later chapters (see especially chapter six). For now, it is important only to appreciate that any plausible version of philosophical behaviorism requires their introduction. Among other things, dispositions take up the slack between what I do and what I would do. I do, presumably, what I am disposed to do; but I may be disposed to do many things that I never do because the opportunity to do them does not arise or because they are overridden by competing dispositions. You might be disposed to act bravely when faced with danger, but pass your life in tranquil surroundings. This need not detract from your bravery. Of course if you never manifest your bravery, we should have no reason to think you brave – nor, for that matter, need you have any inkling of it. Similarly, we should have no reason to think that a particular unfamiliar substance was water-soluble if its solubility is never manifested. You may be disposed to remain steadfast in a dangerous encounter but nevertheless flee because you are disposed, as well, to spirit away a threatened companion. Similarly, a salt crystal disposed to dissolve in water may fail to dissolve if it is subjected to a powerful electromagnetic field.

In what sense, exactly, does philosophical behaviorism "tie states of mind to behavior"? Behaviorists hold that assertions concerning states of mind can be translated into statements about behavior or dispositions to behave. We have had a taste of this already. If you believe there is a bear in your path, you are disposed to take evasive action, to assent to "There is a bear on the path," to warn your companions, and the like.

The guiding idea is that, if talk about states of mind can be analyzed or paraphrased into talk about behavior (or dispositions to behave), then states of mind will have been "reduced to" (shown to be nothing more than) behavior (or dispositions to behave). Analysis of this sort amounts to the reduction of something to something else. To see the point, think of a parallel case. We sometimes speak of the average family. The income of the average family in rural areas has declined from what it was a decade ago. Is there an average family? Is there an entity (or, for that matter, a collection of entities) designated by the phrase "the average family"? That seems unlikely. In this case, we can see how talk about the average family's income might be reductively analyzed into talk about the income of individual families summed and divided by the number of families. There is nothing more to the average family than this. If we could analyze away claims about minds and mental goings-on, replacing it with claims about behavior and dispositions to behave, then (so the argument goes) we would have succeeded in showing that there is nothing more to an agent's possessing a mind than the agent's behaving or being disposed to behave in appropriately mindful ways.[1]

What are the prospects for reductive analyses of states of mind? One worry is that behavioral analyses are open-ended. There is no limit on the list of things you might do or be disposed to do if you harbor the belief that there is a bear on the trail, for instance. What you do will depend on the circumstances, and the circumstances can vary in indefinitely many ways. Moreover, it seems clear that among the things you will be disposed to do is to form new beliefs and acquire new desires. Each of these beliefs and desires will need its own behavioral analysis.

This complicates the picture, certainly, but it need not pose an insuperable problem for the philosophical behaviorist. The envisaged analyses need not be finite. We can accept a reductive analysis, provided we can see how it could be extended, even when we are in no position to do so ourselves.

Another difficulty is less easily dismissed. You see a bear on the path and form the belief that there is a bear on the path. But what you do and what you are disposed to do evidently depends on your overall state of mind: what else you believe and want, for instance. And this is so for any state of mind. Suppose you believe that there is a bear on the path, but want to have a closer look, or believe that bears are not dangerous, or suppose you have a yen to live dangerously.

It would seem that your belief is compatible with your behaving or being disposed to behave in any way at all depending on what else you believe and what you want. In that case, however, it looks as though no reductive analysis of states of mind is in the cards. The problem is not just that each of these additional states of mind requires a further behavioral analysis, thus complicating and extending the analytical task. The problem, rather, is that there is apparently no way to avoid mention of further

---

[1] Berkeley, whom we encountered in chapter two promoting idealism, defends a reductive analysis of talk about material objects to talk about "ideas" (Berkeley's catch-all term for states of mind). If successful, such an analysis would show that we do not need to suppose that material objects are anything "over and above" ideas. Behaviorists' analyses run in the opposite direction.

states of mind in any statement of what behavior a given state of mind is likely to produce. It is as though we set out to analyze away talk about the average family only to discover that our analysis reintroduced mention of average families at every turning.

To appreciate the magnitude of the problem, think of your belief that there is a bear on the path. This belief, in concert with the belief that bears are dangerous, and a desire to avoid dangerous animals, may lead you to hurry away. But now imagine that you believe that there is a bear in your path, believe that bears are dangerous, and desire to avoid dangerous animals (your beliefs and desires are as before) but that you believe, in addition, that hurrying away will only attract the attention of bears. In this case, you will be disposed to behave, and behave, very differently.

The example illustrates a general point. Any attempt to say what behavior follows from a given state of mind can be shown false by producing an example in which the state of mind is present but, owing to the addition of new beliefs or desires, the behavior does not follow. Nor will it help to try to rule out such cases by means of a general excluder: if you believe that there is a bear on the path, believe that bears are dangerous, and desire to avoid dangerous animals, then, providing you have no further conflicting beliefs or desires, you will be disposed to turn tail. The problem here is that we have reintroduced mention of states of mind in the exclusion clause. And these are precisely what we were trying to analyze away. The analytical project looks hopeless. (In chapter four, we shall encounter a technique – associated with Frank Ramsey and David Lewis – for dealing with cases of this sort that a behaviorist could adopt. The question then arises whether this is sufficient to render behaviorism an attractive option.)

## The legacy of philosophical behaviorism

If the attempt to analyze talk of states of mind into talk of behavior is unworkable, what is left of philosophical behaviorism? It is true, certainly, that our grounds for ascribing states of mind to one another are largely behavioral. This is an epistemological point, however, a point about what constitutes evidence for our beliefs about one another's mental lives, and a point a Cartesian could happily accept.

What of Ryle's contention that it is a mistake to regard your possessing a mind as a matter of your body's standing in a particular relation to a distinct entity, your mind? And what of Wittgenstein's suggestion that terms used to ascribe states of mind are not used to designate objects of some definite sort? Both of these ideas are independent of the behaviorist's analytical project, and both survive in accounts of the mind that are self-consciously anti-behaviorist. Thus, one might suppose that to have a mind is just to possess a particular sort of organization, one that issues in what we should call intelligent behavior. And one might imagine that to possess a given state of mind is just to be in some state or other that contributes in a characteristic way to the operation of this organized system.

These themes are central to functionalism, a conception of mind that we shall examine in more detail in chapter four. For the moment, let us simply register behaviorism's lack of concern for the qualitative dimension of states of mind. If your having a headache is solely a matter of your behaving, or being disposed to behave, in a particular way, then the intrinsic qualitative nature of whatever is responsible for your so behaving, or being disposed to behave, is irrelevant. This is explicit in Wittgenstein's beetle in the box analogy. And, as we shall see, this feature of behaviorism is inherited by functionalism.

What could be meant by "intrinsic qualitative nature"? The notion of an intrinsic quality is best understood in contrast to the complementary notion of an extrinsic characteristic. An intrinsic quality is a quality an object has in its own right. Being spherical is an intrinsic quality of a billiard ball. Being near the center of the billiard table is, in contrast, a non-intrinsic, extrinsic feature of the ball.[1] Think of intrinsic qualities as being built into objects, extrinsic characteristics as being possessed by objects only in virtue of relations those objects bear to other objects. In the beetle in the box case, imagine that one person's box contains a marble, and another's contains a sugar cube. Then the intrinsic nature of what is in each box differs. And it is precisely this that "drops out of consideration as irrelevant."

We can distinguish an object's intrinsic qualitative nature from its dispositionalities or causal powers. The billiard ball has the power to roll across the table, the power to shatter a pane of glass, and the power to reflect light in a particular way. But the ball has, as well, a particular qualitative nature: a particular shape, a particular size, a particular temperature. The relation between an object's powers or dispositionalities and its qualitative characteristics is a subtle business, as we shall see later. For the present, we need only recognize that it seems possible to distinguish an object's qualitative aspects from its causal propensities or powers. And, again, behaviorism regards the intrinsic qualitative nature of states of mind as irrelevant.

One way to put this is to say that, according to the behaviorist, states of mind, "*qua* states of mind," lack an intrinsic qualitative nature. Think

---

[1] I prefer to contrast intrinsic with extrinsic rather than relational. That two cells bear a certain relation to one another is a relational feature of the cells, but an intrinsic feature of the organism to which they belong.

again of the beetle in the box analogy. Whatever is in the box has some intrinsic qualitative nature. But this nature is irrelevant to its being true that the box contains a beetle: *qua* beetle – considered solely as a beetle – what the box contains lacks intrinsic qualities.

A view of this sort might seem wildly implausible. Surely your headache has an intrinsic qualitative nature, and this is an important part of what makes a headache a headache. These days it is fashionable to put this point by saying that "there is something it is like" to have a headache. What it is like to have a headache differs from what it is like to have other kinds of conscious experience. Part of what makes a given conscious experience a headache is just this "what-it's-likeness."

I have said that the denial of all this might seem implausible. Yet behaviorists do deny it. And, as we shall see, many other philosophers, philosophers dismissive of behaviorism, deny it as well. These philosophers argue that states of mind owe their identity, not to their intrinsic qualitative nature (if indeed they have any such nature at all), but exclusively to their causal powers or, as I prefer, their dispositionalities. We can evaluate such claims only after we have built up an understanding of the underlying metaphysical issues. Before embarking on that project, however, let us look briefly at psychological behaviorism.

## Psychological behaviorism

Philosophical behaviorism is a thesis about the meaning of mental terms and, ultimately, about the nature of mental concepts. Its proponents consider philosophical questions about the nature of mind to be reducible to questions about the character of such concepts. They reason that, if we want to know what minds are, we must make explicit what "mind" and its cognates mean. This, they contend, is a matter of spelling out how "mind" and its cognates are used in everyday discourse. Minds are whatever answers to "mind."

A conception of this sort neatly divides philosophy from psychology. Philosophers are in the business of making clear the subtleties of the conception of mind enshrined in ordinary language. Psychologists, and other empirical scientists, investigate the character of the world. Our language carves up the world in a particular way. We can interpret scientific claims only after comparing the concepts deployed in those claims with the concepts encoded in ordinary language. When psychologists speak of a belief, or an emotion, or a mental image, do they mean what is ordinarily meant by "belief," "emotion," "mental image"? To find out, we must see how these expressions function in psychological theories and compare this with their use in everyday language.

When we do this, according to philosophers like Wittgenstein and Ryle, we discover that psychology has more often than not made use of familiar terminology in unfamiliar ways. This can lead to a systematic misunderstanding of psychological theses. Wittgenstein put it this way: "in psychology there are experimental methods and *conceptual confusion*" (1953/ 1968, p. 232). This "conceptual confusion" applies as much to the psychologists' interpretation of their own work as it does to the layperson's interpretation. We introduce a technical notion using a familiar term. The technical notion may be importantly different from the sense of the term in its everyday use. We then establish truths that pertain to the technical notion. Confusion results when we interpret these as applying to whatever the original term applies to. It is as though we decided to give "pigeon" a rigorous sense: a four-legged artifact with a flat surface used for supporting objects. We then go on to establish that the common belief that pigeons can fly, lay eggs, and reproduce is a myth.

Behaviorism in psychology was spawned, not by worries about the meanings of mental terms, but by a concern for the scientific status of psychology. On a traditional view of the mind, a view accepted without question by psychologists in the nineteenth century, states of mind are private states not amenable to public scrutiny. While "access" to your own states of mind is direct, others can only observe their effects on your behavior. If we suppose, as early behaviorists like J. B. Watson (1878–1958) and B. F. Skinner (1904–90) supposed, that only what is publicly observable is a fit subject for science, we shall exclude states of mind, as traditionally conceived, from scientific consideration. If we suppose, as well, that talk about items not susceptible to public verification is unsavory, or perhaps meaningless, we shall have in effect ruled the traditional conception of mind out of bounds for serious consideration.[1]

We could put this by saying that, on the behaviorist conception, minds, conscious experiences, and the like do not exist. Talk of such things reflects only a superstitious past in which the observable characteristics of objects were explained by reference to ghosts and spirits taken to inhabit them. To deny ghosts and spirits – and mental states – is not to deny that objects and intelligent creatures have complex observable traits, nor that these are susceptible to rigorous scientific explanation. Just as we have put behind us explanations of demented behavior that appeal to possession by evil spirits, so we must put behind us explanations that appeal to private inner occurrences. This is what behaviorists set out to do.

The data for psychological behaviorism are instances of behavior, "behaviors," what organisms do. We explain an instance of behavior, not

---

[1] In fairness, I should note that early behaviorists were reacting to what was widely perceived as the uniform failure of introspective psychology to deliver on the goods.

Figure 3.1

by postulating unobservable interior states of mind, but by reference to environmental stimuli that elicit the behavior. The governing model is the simple reflex. I tap your knee, and your leg bobs in a characteristic way. Here, a bit of behavior, a response – your leg's bobbing – is explained by the occurrence of a stimulus – my tapping your knee. What connects stimulus and response is an unadorned reflex mechanism. We describe that mechanism exclusively by reference to its role in stimulus–response (S–R) relations.

Behaviorists held that all behavior, even complex behavior, could be fully explained in S–R terms. Complex responses were simply the result of complex stimuli. The job of the psychologist was to provide a systematic accounting of these S–R relations. As far as psychology is concerned, the organism is a "black box," something the psychological nature of which is exhaustively describable by reference to its response to stimuli (figure 3.1). Black boxes and organisms have an internal structure, something capable of being investigated in its own right. But this is the province of the biologist or the physiologist, not the psychologist.

Behaviorists proscribe mention of inner mechanisms except insofar as these are capable of exhaustive characterization in terms of relations between stimuli (observable inputs) and output responses (observable behavior). Complex organisms are capable of learning, capable, that is, of modifying their S–R relations. Again, the mechanism is straightforward. A particular kind of response can be "reinforced" if its occurrence is "rewarded." A rat may not be inclined at the onset of a particular sound to respond by pressing a bar in its cage. But if, perhaps by accident, the rat discovers that it will receive a food pellet if it presses the bar when the sound is heard, then a bar-pressing response to the aural stimulus will be reinforced.

Of course, talk here of the rat's "discovering" a connection between the sound, the bar in its cage, and the receipt of a food pellet is purely metaphorical. It suggests an inner process of the sort behaviorists disdain. If we stick to the purely behavioral facts, we find that the rat presses the bar at the onset of a particular sound and receives a food pellet. Subsequently, the rat's bar-pressing comes to be associated with the onset of instances of the sound. More precisely: the probability that the rat will press the bar at the onset of the sound increases dramatically. Eventually, the rat presses the bar during, and only during, a period immediately following the onset of the sound. This is, at bottom, what the rat's "discovering" the connection amounts to.

Behaviorists assume that all learning can be explained in terms of simple associative mechanisms. This assumes that complex tasks – your learning to play Parcheesi, for instance, or your coming to master English – can be broken down into simpler tasks, each of which can be explained in something like the way the rat's bar-pressing is explained. In 1959, Noam Chomsky published a review of Skinner's *Verbal Behavior* in which he argued that Skinner's attempts to extend the behaviorist model of learning to the linguistic performances of human beings were hopelessly inadequate. Chomsky claimed that linguistic abilities could not, even in principle, be explained without assuming that human beings possessed a sizable repertoire of complex cognitive structures that governed their use of language.

This attack on central behaviorist themes had a devastating effect on the behaviorist program. Many psychologists had grown dissatisfied with rigid behaviorist doctrines, and were already moving in new directions. Chomsky's review, combined with a growing interest in "rule-governed" activities generally, sealed behaviorism's fate. Behaviorism was never again to possess the kind of authority it once did. It became increasingly clear that behaviorism was founded on a view about scientific legitimacy, a view rooted in unappealing philosophical doctrines going back at least to Berkeley. By requiring that every scientifically respectable expression be characterizable in terms of observations that would confirm its application, behaviorists foreclosed modes of explanation that had proved fruitful in other sciences. These modes of explanation distinguished, as behaviorists often did not, between entities postulated to explain observable features of the world and observations that constituted evidence for these entities.

One further difficulty inherent in the behaviorist program is worth mention. Consider the central notion of behavior. What constitutes an instance of behavior? When do two "behaviors" count as instances of the same behavior, and when are they different? Answers to these questions are important. The behaviorist requires a rigorous pairing of stimuli and response behavior. The model we began with was the patella reflex: your knee is tapped, and your leg bobs. This same response – your leg's bobbing – happens whenever your knee is tapped. If your leg's bobbing is an example of behavior, then it would seem that behavior is to be understood as bodily motion. Two instances of behavior are the same just in cases they are instances of the same bodily motion.

Unfortunately, matters are not so simple. Consider the rat's bar-pressing. Suppose that on one occasion the rat presses the bar with its right paw, then later with its left paw. We count these as instances of the same behavior – "bar-pressing behavior" – even though the bodily motions are not the same. But now we have moved away from the basic reflex model. It is relatively easy to envisage a simple mechanism that accounts for your leg's bobbing when your knee is tapped. But the mechanism responsible for a rat's pressing a bar at the onset of a particular sound is not like this. That mechanism connects the onset of a particular sound with a variety of different kinds of bodily motion. What these bodily motions have in common is just that they each result in the bar's being pressed. And now it looks as though any mechanism behind the rat's bar-pressing behavior must be specified by reference to what we non-behaviorists might blushingly describe as the rat's desires or purposes. Unfortunately, such things are unobservable states of mind, and so officially out of bounds for the behaviorist.

When it comes to complex human behavior, the situation is worse still. Think of your answering the door when the doorbell rings. We might call this door-answering behavior. But there need be no bodily motions in common among instances of this behavior. Sometimes you walk calmly to the door and open it. On other occasions you may trot to the door, or go on tiptoe, or, if you are otherwise occupied, merely shout "Come in!" Again, it is difficult to imagine that the mechanism connecting the doorbell's ring with your door-answering behavior is a simple reflex mechanism. It looks, for all the world, like a relatively complex state of mind.

Similar considerations hold of the behaviorist notion of stimulus. When we look at what behaviorists count as instances of the same stimulus, we discover that these lack the sorts of common feature that the approach would seem to demand. Your "door-opening behavior" might be elicited by a loud banging on the door, or a soft knock; by the ringing of a doorbell; or by a glimpse through the window of a neighbor striding up the walk. These stimuli have little in common beyond being in some respect responsible for your opening the door.

Suppose we cannot come up with a non-circular, independent characterization of "door-opening stimulus," one that does not invoke the very thing for which it is the postulated stimulus – "door-opening behavior." Then it looks as though appeals to such stimuli in explanations of behavior will be trivial. A response is elicited by a stimulus. Which one? The response-eliciting stimulus. This does not mean that the behaviorist contention that all behavior is explicable by reference to stimulus–response relations and that learning is explicable purely by reference to contingencies of reinforcement of such relations is thereby condemned. It does strongly suggest, however, that the central notions of stimulus and response gain credence only by taking in one another's washing. And if this is so, the theory is uninformative.

Perhaps these worries about the emptiness of behaviorist explanation can be overcome. Even so, there is some reason to suspect that the behaviorist model is fundamentally misguided. Think for a moment of your response to a given stimulus, the appearance of a bear in your path, for instance. Strictly speaking, it would seem not to be the bear that elicits your response (whatever it might be), but your perceiving or in some way taking note of the bear. If a bear appears in your path, but you remain oblivious to it, you will be unmoved by the bear. Just so, you may be moved to a bear-avoiding response, even if a bear is absent. You may be so moved if, for whatever reason, you take there to be a bear in your path.

The example suggests that behavioral responses are determined, not by behaviorist-style stimuli, but by our perceptions of those stimuli, their effects on us, or by apparent perceptions of stimuli. The bear's presence explains your behavior only if it leads you to the perception of a bear. This perception mediates your subsequent behavior. Perceiving (or apparently perceiving) a bear, however, includes a mental component. And it was just such mental intermediaries that behaviorism was supposed to eliminate.

None of these reflections yields a knock-down argument against behaviorism. Behaviorists have attempted to respond to worries of the sort we have addressed. I shall not pursue those responses here. Instead, let us push ahead to what may be more promising realms.

## The identity theory

Let us, for the nonce, banish thoughts of behaviorism – philosophical and psychological – and revert to our Cartesian starting point. Let us pretend that states of mind are states of an individual substance, the mind, and that the mind is distinct from the body. If states of mind are not states of the body, they are not states of some part of the body – the brain, for instance – either.

The more we learn about the nervous system, however, the more we discover apparent correlations between mental occurrences and neurological goings-on in the brain. (I follow custom and speak of goings-on in the brain. This should, however, be understood as shorthand for goings-on in the central nervous system. Alternatively, we could think of the brain as distributed throughout the body.) Suppose these correlations were perfect: every mental state or process could be matched to some neurological state or process. What should we make of this? One possibility is that endorsed by the Cartesians: the correlations are based on causal interaction between minds and brains. In this regard, they would resemble correlations between falling barometers and rain. Another possibility is epiphenomenalism: the correlations are the result of mental goings-on being produced as epiphenomenal by-products of neurological activity. A third possibility: each mental and material event is willed by God in such a way that they occur in orderly patterns.

These possibilities are all founded on the assumption that mental states or events are distinct from physical states or events. The identity theory rejects this assumption. Despite appearances, mental occurrences are taken to be nothing more than goings-on in the brain. If this is so, then it is misleading to say that mental occurrences are correlated with brain processes. Mental goings-on are brain processes, and a thing is not correlated with itself. The correlations we discover are merely apparent. They are like correlations in the whereabouts of the butler and the murderer, when the butler is the murderer.

Its proponents argue that, other things equal, the identity theory is preferable to its dualist rivals for two reasons. First, and most obviously, the identity theory provides a straightforward solution to the mind–body problem. If mental events are nothing but neurological events, then there is no special difficulty in understanding causal relations holding between mental events and material events: a mental event's causing a material event (or vice versa) is simply a matter of one neurological event's causing another.

A second consideration favoring the identity theory is parsimony. Both the identity theory and dualism grant the existence of brains and neurological goings-on. But dualism must suppose that, in addition to – "over and above" – brains and neurological goings-on, there are minds and mental goings-on. But why posit these additional items unless we are forced to? If we can account for mental phenomena solely by reference to brains and their properties, why follow the dualist in envisaging an independent realm of minds and mental properties?

We have encountered appeals to parsimony earlier within the dualist camp. Epiphenomenalists hold that epiphenomenalism provides a simpler, hence preferable account of the mind and its relation to material bodies than do competing dualist theories. In assessing this line, we noted that appeals to simplicity ought not to be understood as based on the assumption that the world must be simple – whatever that could mean. Rather, if two theories both account for the phenomena, but one theory is simpler – in the sense of positing fewer kinds of entity or process – then the burden of proof lies with proponents of the less simple theory. Simple theories are preferred by default.

It would seem then that, provided the identity theory and dualism both account for the phenomena, the identity theory wins by default. Ah, but does the identity theory account for the phenomena?

## The attraction of the Cartesian picture

Let us begin by asking whether states of mind could be states of the body, more specifically, states of the brain or central nervous system. The chief reason for supposing that states of mind could not be brain states is that mental and material states appear to be radically different in kind. These differences are both epistemological and ontological.

On the epistemological front, as we have had occasion to note already, the "access" we enjoy to states of mind is notably asymmetrical. Your mental life is "private" in a way that no material object or state ever is. You are aware of your own states of mind and the qualities of your conscious experiences directly and without evidence or observation. I, in contrast, have access to your mental life only indirectly. I infer your thoughts and feelings by observing your behavior, verbal or otherwise. Suppose I observe goings-on in your brain, and suppose these goings-on are reliable indicators of your mental condition. Then I am in an epistemologically strong position to know what you are thinking and feeling. Still, my access to your thoughts and feelings differs from yours. I must infer what you experience "directly."

A Cartesian explains this epistemological asymmetry by noting that others' knowledge of one's states of mind depends on observations, not of the states themselves, but only of their effects on material bodies. Knowledge of one's own mental life is unmediated, however. Indeed it is misleading to imagine that you literally observe your own thoughts and feelings. Take thoughts. Every thought carries with it the potential for self-awareness (a point emphasized long ago by Kant). Thinking is not something that occurs to you, like the beating of your heart, something concerning which you are a mere spectator. Thinking is something you do. And like anything you consciously do, you need not observe yourself in the act to recognize what it is you are up to. (Let us leave aside for the moment consideration of non-conscious states of mind.) When you entertain the thought that it is raining and consciously recognize that this is what you are thinking, your conscious recognition is not based on some further act of inward observation of the original thought. That thought, rather, is thought self-consciously. If every thought is potentially self-conscious, then this self-conscious thought could itself be entertained self-consciously: you can be aware that you are thinking that you are thinking that it is raining. Try it. And note that this thought is perfectly self-contained; it is a single thought, not a sequence of distinct thoughts.

Any account of the mind must, it would seem, accommodate this kind of self-consciousness. The Cartesian view does so by building it into the nature of the mental: that their states have this capacity is just one way minds differ from material bodies. Anyone who hopes to assimilate minds to bodies – or, more particularly, to brains – must be prepared to answer the Cartesian on this score.

A second hurdle facing anyone aiming to replace the Cartesian picture is ontological. Mental events, states, and properties appear to be utterly different in kind from material events, states, and properties. The difference is striking when we consider the qualities of our own conscious states of mind and compare these with the qualities of material bodies, including the qualities of brains. Your visual experience of a ripe tomato in bright sunlight seems qualitatively very different from goings-on in your nervous system. Neurological occurrences can be observed and described in great detail. But observe as we will, we seem never to observe anything at all like a conscious experience.

You might try to sidestep this problem by appealing to the apparent fact that science often tells us that things are not as they seem. Take the ripe tomato. We experience the tomato as possessing a particular color. But physicists tell us that the experienced color is in a certain sense an illusion. The tomato's surface exhibits a particular molecular texture. Surfaces with this texture reflect light in a particular way. And reflected light of this sort, when analyzed by the human visual system, gives rise to an experience of red. It would be a mistake to locate a feature of our experience in the tomato. Considered in its own right, the material world is colorless.[1] If this is so, then it is hardly surprising that we never observe anything with the features of our experiences when we observe the workings of brains. Brains, after all, are material entities.

This line of reasoning does little to advance the case of the anti-Cartesian. If the characteristics of conscious experiences of colors are not characteristics of material bodies, then what are they characteristics of? A physicist can banish them to the mind. But this implies that minds are not themselves locatable in the material world. More generally, if we distinguish appearance from material reality by assigning appearances to the mind, then we seem to place minds outside the material realm. Assuming that science is devoted to the investigation of the material world, we seem to be back with a Cartesian conception: minds are distinct from material bodies.

Notwithstanding these difficulties, many philosophers (and many non-philosophers) have been attracted to the view that, at bottom, minds are nothing more than material bodies. When a material body is organized in a particular way, organized in the way a human brain is organized, for instance, the result is a mind: a conscious, feeling, intelligent entity. In the end, mental characteristics are, despite appearances, material characteristics.

The impetus for a theory of this sort is two-fold. First, the more we investigate the brain, the more we uncover an intimate relation between

---

[1] Similar arguments can be concocted to show that sounds, tastes, smells, and the way things feel are, in the sense described, absent from the material world. A long tradition, going back at least to Galileo, Descartes, and Locke, dubs colors, sounds, and the like, "secondary qualities." Secondary qualities are thought to be powers possessed by material bodies to produce experiences of certain kinds in conscious observers.

neurological goings-on, and our mental lives. Second, a view according to which there is at most one kind of substance, material substance, is preferable to a dualistic view, on grounds of simplicity. If we could somehow account for central features of our mental lives without having to introduce non-material substances, then there would no longer be any reason to suppose that there are non-material substances.

## Properties and predicates

What has come to be called the identity theory of mind emerged independently in the United States and Australia in the 1950s in papers published by Herbert Feigl, U. T. Place, and J. J. C. Smart. According to the identity theory, minds are material entities – brains – and mental properties are, as a matter of empirical fact, material properties of brains and nervous systems. In claiming that mental properties are material properties, Feigl, Place, and Smart were not claiming merely that mental properties were properties of material bodies. One might think this, and yet imagine that mental properties were quite different from non-mental material properties. The result would be a substance monism coupled with a dualism of properties. The identity theorists, however, argued that every mental property is in reality a physical property, that is, a property of the sort independently countenanced by the physical sciences.

Earlier, I spoke of mental (and material) characteristics, states, and the like. Identity theorists talk of identifying mental processes with brain processes. Now I am formulating the identity theory as a theory about properties. These terminological vacillations deserve comment.

In chapter two, we distinguished attributes and modes from substances. Descartes's modes are what are more familiarly called properties; Cartesian attributes are kinds of property. To put it somewhat unhelpfully, a substance is an individual thing that possesses properties; and properties are what substances possess. Substances themselves differ from one another with respect to their properties. A material substance, according to Descartes, possesses the attribute of extension; a mental substance possesses the attribute of thought. Properties possessed by material bodies are modes of extension – ways of being extended; and particular thoughts, feelings, or sensory experiences possessed by non-material substances are modes of thought – ways of thinking. No substance that possesses properties of the one sort possesses properties of the other sort; indeed the possession of one kind of property precludes possession of the other.

A non-Cartesian dualist would reject this latter claim. Although minds are distinct from material bodies, mental substances – substances possessing mental properties – can possess material properties as well. You yourself are a mental substance. You have thoughts, feelings, and conscious experiences. But you are also extended: you are a certain height and you have a particular mass. These properties (Descartes would call them modes) belong to the same substance that thinks and feels. A view of this sort maintains the Cartesian distinction between mental and material properties, but rejects Descartes's contention that such properties could not be shared by a single substance. Such a substance, having both mental and material properties, is simultaneously mental and material. Minds or selves are distinct from the biological substances in which they are embodied. But selves share properties with those bodies.

You might balk at a substance dualism of this sort, yet join the dualist in insisting on a distinction between mental and material properties. On such a view, there is a single substance, the body, and this substance possesses both mental and material properties. This is not what identity theorists have in mind, however. Their contention is that every mental property is identical with some material property. (We shall examine the notion of identity more closely in a moment.)

We have looked briefly at properties, but what of states, events, processes, and the like? Think of a state as the possessing of a property by an individual substance. Suppose that being angry is a property we should classify as a mental property. Then your possessing this property is for you to be in a state of anger. If the state of anger turns out to be some neurological state, then this is so because the property of being angry is identical with (just is) a certain neurological property. We can think of events and processes as state transitions. When an object comes to be in a particular state (comes to possess a certain property), its coming to be in this state is an event. A process is a sequence of events. A state, event, or process, $\alpha$, is identical with state, event, or process $\beta$, only if the properties involved are identical.

Suppose that your feeling giddy is a matter of your being in a particular state of mind. Your being in this state is your possessing a certain, possibly complex, mental property. Now suppose the question arises whether your feeling giddy – your being in this mental state – is just your being in a particular brain state (and nothing more). If you agree with the identity theorist that this is what your feeling giddy is – your brain's being in a particular state – then you will accept the identification of the mental property of being giddy with a particular neurological property.

The moral: so long as we bear in mind that state, event, and process identity requires property identity, we can speak indifferently of the identity theory as identifying mental and material states, processes, events, or properties.

Before discussing property identity, it will be useful to pause and distinguish properties from predicates. Predicates are linguistic devices used to designate properties. The English expression "is round" is a predicate that designates a particular property, the property possessed by many coins, for instance. This predicate holds of a given coin, in virtue of that coin's being round. The predicate "is copper" holds of the same coin in virtue of its possession of a different property: its being copper.

One reason to call attention to the distinction between predicates and properties is that, as we shall see below, we must do so in order to understand what claims about property identity amount to. Another reason is that many philosophers assume without argument that every predicate capable of meaningful application designates a property. Such a view is ill-advised. What the properties are is largely a question for science. Predicates can be constructed *ad lib*. Consider the predicate "is a left ear or made of copper." This predicate holds of many objects. It holds of anything that is a left ear (so it holds of your left ear) and anything that is made of copper (so it holds of the penny on your dresser top). Moreover, the predicate holds of objects in virtue of properties they possess. It does not follow, however, that the predicate designates a property.

These are deep waters, and we shall return to them in later chapters. In the meantime, we need only bear in mind that properties and predicates, even those predicates that designate properties, belong to different orders: predicates are linguistic, properties are non-linguistic features of objects.

## The concept of identity

Identity theorists contend that mental properties are identical with material or physical properties. It is time to say what exactly this means. Let us first consider how identity applies to objects.

Our concept of identity, or selfsameness, is useful because it is common to speak or think of a single object in different ways. Suppose you discover that John Le Carré is David Cornwell. The "is" here, the "is" of identity, must be distinguished from the "is" of predication, as in: Le Carré is English. To say that Le Carré is Cornwell, that Le Carré and Cornwell are identical, is to say that the man called "Le Carré" and the man named "Cornwell" are the selfsame individual.

Any object can be given multiple names, any object can be described in different ways. You may know an object under one name or description, but not under another. Imagine that you are traveling in Australia, intending to visit Ayres Rock. *En route*, you hear talk of an impressive rock edifice called Uluru, and regret not having enough time to visit it as well. Much later you discover that Uluru is Ayres Rock. In hiking around Ayres Rock, you visited Uluru without knowing it.

The identity theory extends the notion of identity to properties. Like objects, properties can be the subject of identity claims. Red is the color of ripe tomatoes. A single property, a color, is designated by distinct predicates, "is red" and "is the color of ripe tomatoes." And just as one might be familiar with Ayres Rock and with Uluru without knowing that Ayres Rock and Uluru are identical, so one might fail to realize that two predicates in fact designate the selfsame property. You might know that a particular color is red without knowing that it is the color of ripe tomatoes – if, for instance, you were ignorant of tomatoes.

Identity theorists focus on what Smart calls theoretical identities. Such identities are uncovered by scientists exploring the way the world is put together. Lightning, we came to discover, is an electrical discharge; water is $H_2O$; temperature is mean kinetic energy of molecules; liquidity is a particular kind of molecular arrangement. An identity theorist holds that it is a good bet that research on the brain will lead to the discovery that certain properties we now designate using mental terms are properties of brains. Pain, for instance, might turn out to be the firing of C-fibers in the brain. (This, the standard example, has been empirically discredited, but it will do to illustrate the point.) If this is so, then the property of being in pain would be identified with the neurological property of being a C-fiber firing.

The identity theory does not pretend to offer particular identity claims. The establishment of these is the job of brain researchers who discover correlations between goings-on in the brain and subjects' reports of experiences. Rather, the identity theory offers an interpretation of these results: in reporting conscious experiences, we are reporting goings-on in our brain. The details will be revealed as the neurosciences move forward.

## The $64 question

The question we must now face, the question we can postpone no longer, is whether it is even remotely plausible to suppose that mental properties, the kinds of property the having of which might constitute your undergoing a conscious experience, for instance, could be nothing more than properties of the brain. There appear to be powerful reasons to doubt this. As noted earlier, the qualities we encounter when we undergo a conscious experience seem to be nothing at all like the qualities we find when we inspect brains. (For a convenient listing, see figure 2.1.)

Imagine that it is a sunny day and you are standing in Trafalgar Square watching a red double-decker bus rumble past. You have a visual experience of the red bus, you hear it, and very probably smell it, and, through the soles of your feet, feel its passing. The qualities of your conscious experience are vivid and memorable. But now, could anyone seriously think that, were we to open your skull and observe the operation of your brain while you were undergoing this experience, we would encounter those qualities? And if this is implausible, how could we suppose that your experience is just a process in your brain?

One preliminary point deserves mention. Suppose for a moment that the identity theory is correct: states of mind are brain states. Your undergoing an experience – seeing, hearing, feeling, smelling the passing bus – is presumably a matter of your brain undergoing a complex sequence of processes. Now imagine that a scientist is observing your brain undergoing this sequence of processes. Presumably the scientist's conscious experiences of your brain are themselves nothing more than a complex sequence of processes in the scientist's brain. (Remember, we are assuming for the sake of argument that the identity theory is correct.) But is it really so obvious that the qualities of your experience differ from qualities scientists observe when they investigate brains? (Do not confuse qualities of the scientist's experience of your brain with qualities of your experience of the passing bus or, what comes to the same thing if the identity theory is true, qualities of your brain.)

The qualities to compare in this case are qualities of processes in the scientist's brain that coincide with his observation of your brain. What we are comparing, after all, is, to put it crudely, how a conscious experience looks to an observer and how it is to someone undergoing it. This means that we must compare qualities of the observing scientist's conscious experiences of your brain (which, by hypothesis, are themselves neurological goings-on) with qualities of your conscious experiences (also, we are assuming, neurological events). And, although these will be different – observing a brain differs qualitatively from observing a passing bus – there is no reason to think that these must be dramatically different in kind.

The moral is that, if we aim to compare the qualities of conscious experiences with the qualities of brains, we must be careful to compare the right things. If the identity theory is correct, then, your enjoying a conscious experience is a matter of your brain's undergoing a complex process. If we want to compare the qualities of your conscious experience with observations of your brain, then the appropriate target of comparison is the brain of the observer. Goings-on in the observer's brain are what constitute, for the observer, the "look and feel" of your brain.

All this is just to insist on a simple point: undergoing an experience is one thing, observing the undergoing of an experience (a distinct experience) is something else again. The qualities of these will certainly be different. Looking at a brain, after all, is nothing at all like watching a passing bus. But the qualities need not be radically different in kind – radically different in the way harped on by dualists.

This may seem to miss the point of our original worry. That point was that, when we consider what it is like to observe the passing bus, when we reflect on the qualities of this experience, those qualities seem not to be candidates for possible qualities of brains. We know what our conscious experiences are like, and we know what brains are like, and it is obvious that conscious experiences are not like neurological goings-on. If that is so, however, the identity theory cannot get off the ground.

We must move cautiously here. It is tempting to reason as follows. When you observe the passing bus, you observe something red, loud, and smelling of diesel fumes. But redness, loudness, and that distinctive diesel odor are not found in your brain. If I scrutinize your brain when you are undergoing this experience, I will not find anything that possesses these qualities. The philosopher Leibniz provides an analogy.

> We are moreover obliged to confess that perception and that which depends on it cannot be explained mechanically, that is to say by figures and motions. Suppose there were a machine so constructed as to produce thought, feeling, and perception, we could imagine it as increased in size and while retaining the same proportions, so that one could enter it as one might a mill. On going inside we should only see only the parts impinging on one another; we should not see anything which would explain a perception.
>
> (1787/1973, p. 181)

(Leibniz goes on to argue that "the explanation of perception must be sought in a simple substance, and not in a compound or in a machine.")

This line of reasoning is flawed. When you undergo a conscious experience – when you observe the passing bus, for instance – your experience is qualitatively saturated. But what exactly are its qualities? Whatever they are, they are not to be confused with the qualities of the object observed, in this case the bus. Your experiencing a passing bus is one thing, the bus is another. Similarly, what it is like to experience the bus, the qualities of your experience of the bus, are not to be confused with qualities of the bus.

The identity theory identifies your experience of the bus with some occurrence in your brain. For the most part, we describe our experiences by reference to objects that typically cause them. You can convey to me an experience you had at Trafalgar Square by telling me that it was an experience of a passing red double-decker bus. I have a decent idea what it is like to observe passing red double-decker buses, and so I acquire a sense of what you experienced. But, again, the qualities of the experience are not to be confused with the qualities of objects that give rise to them. An experience of something red, massive, and smelly is not itself red, massive, and smelly.

This point was one insisted on by Smart in his original defense of the identity theory, but it has not always been fully appreciated. The rhetorical punch of the claim that it is just obvious that qualities of experiences differ from brain qualities relies heavily on our tacitly identifying, as Leibniz apparently does, qualities of experiences with qualities of objects experienced. Once we distinguish these (and we must distinguish them on any view), it is much less obvious that qualities of experiences could not turn out to be neurological qualities. Anyone who persists in claiming that experiential qualities differ in kind from neurological qualities owes us an argument. What exactly are the qualities of experience? And what reason do we have for thinking that they could not be qualities of brains?

I have suggested that the distinction between qualities of experiences and qualities of objects experienced is theory-neutral. The distinction must be made by dualists as well as materialists. It is worth pointing out that, so long as we keep the distinction firmly in mind, we can begin to make sense of a range of mental phenomena that might appear puzzling otherwise. This is so, whatever we ultimately conclude about the status of mental properties.

Consider dreams, mental images, hallucinations, and the like. Some theorists have wanted to downplay such phenomena, or to reduce them to purely cognitive processes. The worry is that there is no room in the brain for images, hallucinations, or dreams, the qualities of which appear to differ dramatically from qualities discoverable in brains. Suppose you hallucinate a pink penguin (or dream, or form an image of a pink penguin). Nothing in your brain is pink or penguin-shaped. Indeed, it is entirely possible that nothing anywhere in your vicinity (or, for that matter, anywhere at all) is pink and penguin-shaped.

But if this is supposed to cast doubt on hallucination, dreaming, or imagery, it relies on our confusing qualities of objects hallucinated (or dreamed, or imagined) with qualities of the hallucinating (dreaming, imagining). Visually hallucinating a pink penguin resembles having a visual experience of a pink penguin, it does not resemble a pink penguin. Just as the experience is not pink and penguin-shaped, neither is the hallucinating pink or penguin-shaped. Nor need we suppose that hallucinating, or imagining, or dreaming of a pink penguin is a matter of inwardly observing a picture-like image of a pink penguin. Appreciating these points enables us to relax a bit and think more clearly about the character of hallucination, mental imagery, and dreaming. (I shall have more to say about the importance of imagery and the qualities of conscious experiences in chapter six.)

## Epistemological loose ends

What can an identity theorist say about the asymmetry of "access" to states of mind? You have "privileged access" to your thoughts and sensory experiences. The rest of us have, at best, indirect access to your mental life. But if the mind is the brain, if mental properties are neurological properties, it is hard to see how this could be so. Mental properties are private; neurological properties are public.

These are difficult issues. If we are to have a prayer of explicating them within the materialist framework afforded by the identity theory, we must somehow explicate the asymmetry without resorting to the notion that mental items and goings-on are hidden in an inner chamber and visible only to the agent to whom they belong. This is the model nicely captured by Wittgenstein's beetle in the box example. But how else might the asymmetry be captured?

Consider, first, an observation made earlier concerning conscious thought. Thinking is something we do. Like anything we do, in doing it, we are in a position to appreciate that we are doing it. To be sure, we rarely bother to reflect on the fact that we are doing what we are doing. But, when we do reflect, we are not acting as observers – epistemologically well-placed observers – of what we are doing. Your recognition of what you are about stems from the fact that it is you who are about it.

Imagine that you draw a diagram on the blackboard to illustrate a lecture on the economy of pre-Roman Britain. I am in the audience. Compare your understanding of the diagram with mine. I observe what you have drawn and endeavor to interpret it in light of your lecture. You, in contrast, grasp its significance immediately. You are able to do this, not because you have a better, more intimate view of the diagram, but because it is your diagram: you drew it with this significance. You bear a similar relation to your own thoughts. You grasp the significance of those thoughts, not because of your view of them is especially good or unimpeded, but because you think them. The point holds, not simply for thought, but for any sort of deliberate action. Your capacity to skip rope includes a capacity to recognize that this is what you are doing.

Because we do not always do what we set out to do, our capacity to recognize what we are doing is not infallible. I take myself to be walking west, when I am, in reality, walking east. In the same way, I may take myself to be thinking of my grandmother, when in reality I am not: the person I have always assumed was my grandmother is an impostor.

What of our apparently privileged "access" to sensory episodes? Your recognition that you are suffering a headache is apparently direct and unmediated in a way my access to your headache never is. Must we assume that headaches are objects or episodes visible only to those undergoing them?

Two points bear mention. First, in undergoing a conscious sensory experience, you do not (1) have the experience and (2) observe – perhaps in an especially intimate way with an inward-directed perceptual organ or scanner – the experience. Your awareness of the experience is constituted, at least in part, by your having it. This is why talk of "access" to one's sensory experiences is misleading. Your recognition that you have a headache is constituted, in part, by your having or undergoing the headache. Differently put: your conscious experience of the headache is a matter of your having it. It is not that the headache occurs and, in inwardly observing it, you experience its occurring.

Second, and to echo a point made earlier, we must distinguish a system's undergoing some process or being in some state, from observations of a system's undergoing a process or being in a state. My refrigerator defrosts automatically. The system's defrosting on an occasion is, in an obvious way, very different from my observing its defrosting. Similarly, your undergoing a pain is very different from my observing your undergoing it. Now, if "directly observing a sensation" just amounts to having that sensation, then there is no puzzle at all in the idea that only you can "directly observe" your sensations. This is just to say that only you can have your sensations. And this is no more mysterious than the thought that only my refrigerator can undergo its defrosting.

Considerations of this sort tell against the Cartesian picture, not by providing a refutation of that picture, but by offering an alternative depiction of what might be included in self-awareness. On the Cartesian model, self-awareness resembles the awareness of "external" objects and events turned inward. As the foregoing discussion makes clear, however, we need not embrace this way of looking at the matter. And, the Cartesian conception aside, it would seem that we ought not to accept it.

This does not mean that we must abandon dualism and accept the identity theory or some other form of materialism. It does mean that one consideration apparently favoring dualism needs to be re-evaluated. It may be possible to accommodate the epistemological asymmetry we discover when we consider states of mind without recourse to dualism. We shall, in chapter six, have occasion to return to this topic.

## Taking stock

The identity theory offers itself as a replacement for dualism, one that accounts for the phenomena accounted for by dualism, but more elegantly. I have touched on one respect in which the identity theory is vindicated. Dualists sometimes argue as though it is just obvious that the properties of states of mind could not be properties of brains – or indeed properties of any material entity. I have suggested that the force of this argument depends in large measure on a tacit conflation of the qualities of experiences and the qualities of objects experienced. The latter are indeed very different from the qualities we experience in the course of observing brains. This, however, is not something that ought to trouble an identity theorist. If the dualist continues to insist that qualities of conscious experiences could not be possessed by brains, then the ball is back in the dualist's court.

I do not mean to leave the impression that this is the end of the matter. I noted that it is not obvious that the qualities of experiences could not be identified with qualities of ordinary material bodies, but neither is it obvious that they can be. I counsel suspicion of anyone who claims that either answer to this question is obvious.

Another worry that I have left untouched concerns the unity of experience. On the one hand, the brain is a complex system that we are only gradually coming to understand. On the other hand, our experience of the world is peculiarly unified. Although we all possess many different mental faculties, at any given time each of us seems to be a single ego with a single point of view or perspective. (Arguably, this is so even for persons said to possess multiple personalities.) How is this unity of experience to be reconciled with the widely dispersed and fragmented character of neural processing? Hopes for finding a neurological "Central Processing Unit," a neurological analog of a computing machine's CPU, have faded. Even if we were to locate a neurological CPU, however, it is by no means clear that its operation would account for the unity of experience. A point of view is just that: a point from which the world is apprehended. The relation of this point to the experienced world resembles the relation of the eye to the visual field. The eye is not within the visual field, but stands at its limit.

Science traditionally sought to reconcile appearance with reality by banishing appearances to the mind. Many apparent features of the world – colors, for instance – were taken to belong not to the world, but to us, to our point of view on the world. If we hope to make minds parts of a single reality, however, we are faced with the task of finding a place for appearance within that reality. And this requires locating points of view on the world wholly within the world. The trick, as we have seen in considering the qualities of experience, is to be clear on the nature of appearance, the character of points of view

Although these strike me as central points, they have not played an appreciable role in philosophical attacks on the identity theory. Those attacks have centered on the claim that states of mind are functional states of creatures possessing them, not material states. Functionalism will take center stage in chapter four.

# Suggested reading

Although Democritus' own writings have not survived, his defense of atomism – the view that everything that exists is nothing more than a fleeting arrangement of "atoms in the void" – is discussed by Aristotle, Plutarch, Galen, and other Greek philosophers. See Barnes, *Early Greek Philosophy* (1987), pp. 247–53; and McKirahan, *Philosophy Before Socrates* (1994), especially pp. 322–4 on "Compounds." A standard collection of texts can be found in Kirk, Raven, and Schofield, *The Presocratic Philosophers* (1983), pp. 406–27.

Francis Crick's brand of materialism is developed in *The Astonishing Hypothesis: The Scientific Search for the Soul* (1994). Whether Crick's hypothesis is "astonishing" is a matter of dispute. Thomas Hobbes defends materialism in part i of *Leviathan* (1651/1994). Julien Offraye de la Mettrie offers another early materialist model in *Man a Machine* (1747 and 1748/1994). For the biologically inclined, this edition includes, as well, La Mettrie's *Man a Plant*.

The possibility of a neuroscientist who has mastered the neurophysiology of headaches but has never suffered from a headache touches on an argument that has come to be associated with Frank Jackson: the "knowledge argument." The argument moves from the claim that, unless you have undergone an experience, you do not know what it is like to undergo that experience, to the conclusion that qualities of conscious experiences (so-called "qualia") do not fit the materialist picture. You can know all the material facts (facts about brain goings-on, and the like) and yet fail to know facts about conscious experiences (what they are like), so facts about conscious experiences are not material facts. See Jackson's "Epiphenomenal Qualia" (1982).

David Chalmers's account of zombies appears in his *The Conscious Mind: In Search of a Fundamental Theory* (1996), chap. 3. The presence of an "explanatory gap" between material properties and the qualities of conscious experiences – what philosophers call "qualia" – is discussed by Joseph Levine, "Materialism and Qualia: The Explanatory Gap" (1983).

Wittgenstein's best-known discussion of states of mind occurs in *Philosophical Investigations* (1953/1968). The extent to which Wittgenstein's views are compatible with behaviorism is controversial. The philosopher most closely associated with behaviorism as a philosophical doctrine is Gilbert Ryle. Ryle's position is developed in *The Concept of Mind* (1949). Readers of *The Concept of Mind*, however, may doubt that Ryle's position is adequately captured by what is commonly called philosophical behaviorism.

On the psychological front, there is less ambiguity. J. B. Watson's "Psychology as the Behaviorist Views It" (1913) sets out the position clearly. More up-to-date discussion and defense of psychological behaviorism can be found in B. F. Skinner's *Science and Human Behavior* (1953). See also Skinner's "Behaviorism at Fifty" (1963). Skinner's *Verbal*

*Behavior* (1957) is attacked in a famous review by Noam Chomsky (1959). See also Chomsky's *Cartesian Linguistics: A Chapter in the History of Rationalist Thought* (1966).

Herbert Feigl defends the identity theory in "The 'Mental' and the 'Physical' " (1958). Perhaps the best introduction to the identity theory is J. J. C. Smart's "Sensations and Brain Processes" (1959). See also U. T. Place's pioneering "Is Consciousness A Brain Process?" (1956).

Finally, Leibniz's defense of substance dualism, and his insistence that mental substances (selves) must be metaphysically simple, can be found in his *Monadology* (1787/ 1973).

# CHAPTER 4
# Functionalism and the Representational Theory of Mind

# Functionalism and the Representational Theory of Mind

The identity theory enjoyed only a brief period of popularity among philosophers. Its decline was not the result of dualist counterattacks, however, but a consequence of the rise of a new conception of mind: functionalism. Functionalists were not put off by identity theorists' commitment to materialism. Although, as we shall see, functionalism is not a materialist theory *per se*, functionalism can be seen as compatible with the spirit of materialism, and most functionalists regard themselves as materialists of one sort or another. Thus functionalists allow that, although immaterial substances – spirits, for instance – are conceivable, in all probability every substance is a material substance. If this is so, then every property possessed by a substance is possessed by a material substance. Does this imply that every property is a material property? Are mental properties a species of material property? The issues here are murky. We shall explore them in the sections that follow.

These days functionalism dominates the field in the philosophy of mind, in cognitive science, and in psychology. Functionalism offers a perspective on the mind that suits the needs of many empirical scientists, one that offers solutions to a host of long-standing philosophical puzzles about minds and their relation to material bodies. Clearly functionalism – the doctrine, if not the label – has etched its way into the popular imagination by way of television and the press. When the basic tenets of functionalism are put to non-philosophers, the response is, often enough, "Well, that's obvious, isn't it?"

This is not to say that functionalism lacks critics. On the contrary, plenty of philosophers and empirical scientists have found functionalism wanting. There is scant agreement among its opponents, however, concerning where exactly functionalism falls down. Indeed, opponents are typically willing to concede that functionalism is right about some things – though, again, what these things are is something concerning which there is little consensus. In the absence of clear competitors, many theorists have opted to stick with functionalism despite what they admit are gaps and deficiencies, at least until something better emerges. In this way, functionalism wins by default.

# The functionalist picture

The emergence of functionalism coincided with the meteoric rise of interest in computation and computing machines in the 1950s and 1960s. When we consider the computational operations a computing machine performs, we abstract from its hardware. Two very differently constructed mechanisms can perform identical operations. Charles Babbage (1792–1871) is usually credited with the design of the first programmable computing machine. Babbage's design called for a device made of brass gears, cylinders, rods, levers, and assorted mechanical gizmos. Fully assembled, this mechanical marvel – Babbage christened it the Analytical Engine – would have been the size of a railway locomotive. Although the machine was never completed, had it been, there is no reason to doubt that it could have performed (although much more slowly) the very sorts of computation that electronic computing machines of today perform. Where Babbage used gears and cylinders, early computing machines, those constructed in the 1950s and early 1960s, made use of vacuum tubes. Today we use arrays of millions of minuscule transistors embedded in slivers of silicon.

Economies of scale result when we move from brass gears and cylinders to vacuum tubes, and again when we move from vacuum tubes to transistors. These economies make a practical difference in the range of computations we could expect a given device to perform. When we consider only the computations themselves, however, all such devices are on a par. One might be faster, or more reliable, or less expensive than another, but all carry out the same kinds of computation. For this reason, when we discuss computations – the manipulation of symbols in accord with formal rules – we abstract from the material nature of the device performing them. And in so doing, we characterize the behavior of computing devices at a "higher level."

Are computational processes material processes? Those of a functionalist bent prefer to say that computational processes are "realized" in material systems. The material process that realizes a given computational sequence in a Babbage machine differs from the material processes that realize it in a modern computing machine or in an antique device equipped with vacuum tubes instead of transistors. (And if there are immaterial substances, perhaps the very same process could have an immaterial realization.) Functionalists sum up these points by describing computational processes as "multiply realizable."

We can think of a computing machine as a device that operates in a way that allows us to describe it as performing computations over symbols. Such a device could be made of any number of materials – or even, perhaps, of immaterial spirit-stuff – and organized in any number of ways. In considering a device as a computing machine, then, we consider it without concern for its material composition. Just as we abstract from the size, color, and spatial location of a geometrical figure when it is the subject of a geometrical proof, so we abstract from a computing machine's material composition when we consider it as a computational device.

## Minds as computing machines

Now suppose we thought of minds in roughly the same way. A mind is a device capable of performing particular sorts of operation. States of mind resemble computational states, at least to the extent that they are shareable, in principle, by any number of material (and perhaps immaterial) systems. To talk of minds and mental operations is to abstract from whatever realizes them; it is to talk at a higher level.

This preliminary characterization is intended only to impart the flavor of functionalism. You should not be put off by the idea that creatures like us, creatures possessing minds, are "nothing more than machines." The point of the computing machine analogy is not to suggest that we are mechanical robots, rigidly programmed to behave as we do. The point, rather, is that minds bear a relation to their material embodiments analogous to the relation computer programs bear to devices on which they run. Every program is "embodied," perhaps, in some material device or other. But the very same program can run on very different sorts of material device. In the same vein, we might suppose that every mind has some material embodiment, although minds may have very different kinds of material embodiment. In the case of human beings, our brains constitute the hardware on which our mental software runs. Alpha Centaurians, in contrast, might share our psychology, our mental software, yet have very different, perhaps non-carbon-based, hardware.

If this is right, then there would seem to be no deep mystery as to how minds and bodies are related. Minds are not distinct immaterial substances causally related to bodies. Talk of minds is merely talk of material systems at a "higher level." Feeling a pain or thinking of Vienna are not brain processes, any more than a computational operation, summing two integers, for instance, is a transistor process. Brain processes and hardware processes realize thoughts and computations. But such things – thoughts, feelings, and computations – are multiply realizable. They are capable of being embodied in a potentially endless array of organisms or devices.

## Functional explanation

Sticking for the moment with the computing machine analogy, we can identify two strands in the functionalist approach to the mind. One strand is explanatory; another is ontological. Let us look first at functional explanation.

Imagine that you are a scientist confronted with a computing machine deposited on Earth by an alien starship. You might want to know how the device was programmed. Doing so would involve a measure of "reverse engineering." You would "work backwards" by observing inputs and outputs, hypothesizing computational operations linking inputs to outputs, testing these hypotheses against new inputs and outputs, and gradually refining your understanding of the alien device's program. Functionalists think of the scientific investigation of the mind as an analogous enterprise. Psychologists are faced with "black boxes," the mechanisms controlling human behavior. Their task is to provide an account of the software governing the operation of these mechanisms. (Recall figure 3.1.)

Compare the task of understanding a device's program with that of understanding its mechanical nature. An alien computing machine would attract considerable interest among electrical engineers. They would want to know how it is put together, how it operates. Their interest is in its physical nature, not in its software. A programmer's explanation of the operation of a computing machine and an engineer's explanation of its operation are quite distinct kinds of explanation: one explains at the "hardware level," one at a higher level, the "software level." These explanations need not be seen to be in competition: they are explanations of the same thing – the operation of a particular device – at different levels.

In the same way, we can imagine neuroscientists examining the nervous systems of intelligent creatures, and offering hardware-level explanations of their operations and behavior. These explanations need not be seen as in competition with the software-level explanations advanced by psychologists.

Although it is convenient to think of hardware and software levels as distinct, in practice we could expect a good deal of cross-level communication among scientists. If you are engaged in an attempt to decipher the program of a particular computing machine, you may be helped by understanding certain things about the machine's mechanical organization. And an engineer trying to comprehend the device's hardware might benefit considerably from an understanding of how it is programmed. Suppose we introduce a third party into the picture, a trouble-shooter, whose job is to fix the device when it misbehaves. A trouble-shooter will need to understand both the device's software and its hardware. A computing machine can "crash" because of a software "bug," or because of a hardware defect or failure. (Indeed, the expression "bug" stems from the days when computing machines took up whole rooms filled with wires and vacuum tubes and could be brought to their knees by real live bugs. Legend has it that the term "bug" originated when Lieutenant Grace Hopper discovered a moth trapped inside ENIAC, the first modern-day digital computer.)

Similarly, we should expect psychologists and neuroscientists to benefit from looking over one another's shoulders in pursuing their respective enterprises. And trouble-shooters – physicians, clinical psychologists, psychiatrists – must be equipped to diagnose assorted malfunctions as psychological (software bugs) or physiological (glitches in neural hardware).

## Functionalist ontology

Functionalists appeal to levels of explanation analogous to hardware and software levels we encounter in explanations of the operation of computing machines. But functionalism is also committed to a distinction of ontological levels. It is not merely that talk of minds and their operation is a higher-level way of talking about what is, at bottom, a purely material system. Rather, higher-level mental terms designate properties taken to be distinct from properties designated by lower-level terms deployed by scientists concerned with the material composition of the world. Although mental states and properties are realized by material states and properties, mental states and properties are not identifiable with those material states and properties. Pains, for instance, are, according to the functionalist, realized in the nervous system. But the property of being in pain is not a material property. How could this be so?

Reflect, again, on the computing machine analogy. A given computational operation can be realized in a variety of distinct material devices: in Babbage's Analytical Engine, in a room full of vacuum tubes and wires, in a device consisting of silicon and transistors, even in a hydraulic device consisting of water-filled tubes and valves. Brains, and indeed many biological systems, seem capable of performing computations; and if there are immaterial spirits, there is every reason to think that these too could realize computational operations. In fact there is no end to the kinds of device that might be capable of engaging in a given computation. But if this is so, then performing a computation cannot be a kind of material process.

Think of the process that realized a particular computational operation – the summing of 7 and 5 to yield 12 – in an early computing machine. This process consisted of electrical goings-on in an array of wires and vacuum tubes. But the summing of 7 and 5 to yield 12 is not a vacuum-tube-and-wire process. If it were, it could not be performed on an abacus (a calculating device consisting of beads strung on rods in a rigid frame) or occur in the brain of a 6-year-old learning to do sums. Abacuses and brains contain neither wires nor vacuum tubes.

Now, the functionalist goes on, the same point applies to states of mind. Consider being in pain. Although it is perfectly possible that your C-fibers firing is in fact responsible for your being in pain – your being in pain is realized by your C-fibers firing – being in pain is not, as identity theorists would have it, a kind of C-fiber firing. If it were, then creatures lacking C-fibers could not experience pain. Yet there is every reason to think that creatures with vastly different material compositions (and perhaps immaterial spirits, if there are any) could be in pain.

In claiming that mental properties (or, for that matter, computational properties) are not material properties, a functionalist is not suggesting that mental properties are immaterial properties, properties of non-material substances. Fantasies aside, the possession of a mental property (or engaging in a computation) might well require a material "base," the possession of some material property or other that realizes the mental (or computational) property. The functionalist's point is just that higher-level properties like being in pain or computing the sum of 7 and 5 are not to be identified with, "reduced to," or mistaken for their realizers.

We shall eventually need to look more closely at the notion of realization appealed to here. Before doing so, however, let us endeavor to fill out this sketchy preliminary account of functionalism.

## Functionalism and materialism

Earlier I described functionalism as compatible with the spirit of materialism, the view that every object, state, and process is a material object, state, or process. In light of what has been said about the ontology of functionalism, we can now see why functionalists resist what they regard as the reductive tendencies inherent in materialist conceptions of mind. Think again of the computing machine analogy. As we have just seen, a computational process can be multiply realized: although a process of a particular sort in a material system might realize a given computational process, computational processes are not to be identified with material processes of this sort. Suppose, for instance, that Babbage's Analytical Engine sums 7 and 5 by lining up a row of brass gears. We should be off base were we to imagine that the summing operation is a matter of the aligning of rows of brass gears. The hand-held calculator you use to balance your checkbook can perform the very same computation, but it contains no gears at all.

As we have seen already, functionalists contend that in such cases there are two things: the computation and the processes that realize or embody the computation. The identity theory of chapter three errs in running these together. This, the functionalist holds, is to confuse higher-level features of systems with their lower level realizing features. True enough, in undergoing certain changes of state, your pocket calculator or Babbage's Analytical Engine perform particular computations. But compare: in moving your arm in a particular way you signal a left turn. We should not conclude, however, that signaling a left turn is a kind of arm motion. (Think of the ways in which you might signal without moving your arm in that way.) And performing a particular computation is not a kind of silicon state change or a kind of gear motion.

Perhaps computational processes, like signaling one's intention to turn, although multiply realizable, must be realized in some material system or other. Were this so, then materialism might be vindicated. But is it so? It seems at least imaginable that there are disembodied spirits, non-material entities capable of undergoing various non-material changes of state. In that case, it might turn out that a particular multiply realizable computational process could be realized in a non-material ectoplasmic system. If such systems are possible, then it would seem that functionalism, as thus far characterized, is not consistent with materialism: computations need not be materially embodied.

The issues here are tricky. And, in any case, we shall need a much clearer view of the metaphysical territory before we will be in any position to evaluate them. We shall return to them in due course. Meanwhile, let us conclude tentatively that functionalism, as we have spelled it out thus far, could be true, even if it turned out that there are no immaterial objects, properties, or events, even that immaterial objects, properties, and events are for some reason impossible. To embrace functionalism, then, is not thereby to turn one's back on materialism.

## Elements of functionalism

Functionalism, like most *isms* in philosophy, is not a single, univocal view. Functionalists begin with a shared set of insights and convictions, then spin these out in different ways. Earlier, we saw that functionalism blossomed with the advent of computing machines. We distinguish programs and computations from the hardware said to realize these. And, functionalists contend, we can deploy the same distinction in explicating the mind. Think of minds as devices running software on complex chunks of hardware – in the case of human beings, the human brain. Just as computational operations are realized by processes in the hardware of a computing machine without being identical with those processes, so states of mind are realized by states of the brain without being identical with those states.

## Functional properties

This computer analogy is just a special case of a more general idea. Consider Wayne. Wayne is a male human being, 5' 10" tall, and a vice-president of Gargantuan Industries, Inc. Wayne, it would seem, possesses a number of properties: the property of being a human being; the property of being male; the property of being 5' 10" tall; and the property of being a vice-president.

Let us look more closely at the the last of these: the property of being a vice-president. Wayne's possessing this property is a matter of his satisfying a particular job description. Wayne is a vice-president in virtue of his role in the operations of Gargantuan Industries, Inc. Anyone at all who filled the same role, regardless of gender, height, and even biological makeup (we might imagine Wayne's being replaced by a brainy chimpanzee or a more cost-effective android) would thereby possess the property of being a vice-president.

The property of being a vice-president is a functional property. The possession of a functional property by an object is a matter of that object's satisfying a certain job description. To see the point, think of another functional property, the property of being a clock. An object possesses this property (in plain English, an object is a clock), not because it has a definite kind of composition or internal organization, but because of what it does – its job description. Clocks can be made of candles, gears and pendulums or springs, vibrating crystals, and systems of water-filled tubes and valves. An object is a clock, not because it is put together in a particular way or made of materials of a particular sort, but because of what it does: it keeps time. So the property of being a clock is, if it is a property, a functional property. (One might insist that a clock must be an artifact: a natural object that kept time would not count as a clock. I leave aside this complication; it makes no difference to the point at issue. I also leave aside, for the time being, whether being a clock or being a vice-president are genuine properties.)

The example of the property of being a clock, and my describing functional properties as those possessed by things in virtue of their job descriptions might engender the impression that functional properties are in some way artificial or "made up." But consider the biological property of being an eye. To a first approximation, an eye is an organ that extracts information about objects from structured light radiation reflected by those objects. Eyes can be and are made of many different materials, and take many different forms. The compound eye of a honeybee differs from the eye of a horse, and the eye of a horse is unlike the eye of a human being. We might imagine eyes more different still in robots or in creatures elsewhere in the universe. Something is an eye, something possesses the property of being an eye, just in case it fills a particular role in the system to which it belongs: it (let us suppose) extracts information from light radiation and makes that information available to the system it subserves.

An object possesses a functional property, we might say, in virtue of filling a particular role. But what is it to "fill a role"? Functionalists like to think of roles causally. Something occupies a particular role if it responds in particular ways to causal inputs with particular kinds of output. A heart is an organ that circulates blood. An object possesses the property of being a heart provided it occupies this causal role. Hearts, like eyes, may differ dramatically across species. And, as the advent of artificial hearts has brought home, a heart need not be a biological entity at all.

Although your heart is a material object, the property of being a heart is, if we accept the functionalist picture, not a material property. It is a property your heart possesses in virtue of its particular material constitution, a constitution that suits it for a particular role in the operation of your circulatory system. Its material constitution, an instance of a straightforward material property, realizes the functional property of being a heart. It realizes this functional property because it endows the object possessing it with the right sort of causal role. Figure 4.1 represents the relationship between the property of being a heart and the lower-level property of being a particular kind of biological configuration. The latter property realizes the former. The properties are not identical; being a heart is not reducible to being a particular kind of biological configuration. Something that has the property of being a heart in virtue of possessing the property of being a biological configuration of kind $K$, has both properties. (As we shall see in chapter six, this is a particularly significant consequence of functionalism.)

Returning to computing machines, we can see that computational operations are representable by means of boxes or nodes in flow charts. Each box or node represents a function that takes particular kinds of input and yields particular kinds of output. A device that realizes these functions does so because it possesses the right sort of causal structure; it possesses

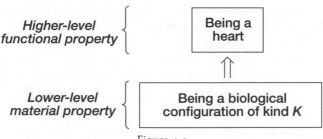

Figure 4.1

this structure in virtue of the constitution and arrangement of its material parts.

## Mental properties as functional properties

Functionalism takes states of mind and mental properties to be functional states and properties. A state is a functional state of a particular sort just in case it answers to a particular job description, that is, just in case it plays a particular sort of causal role in the system to which it belongs. A property is a functional property when its possession by an object turns on that object's satisfying a particular sort of causal role.

In introducing functionalism I have spoken both of properties and states. I shall reserve detailed discussion of properties for a later chapter. For the present, we can continue to distinguish states from properties as we did in chapter three. A state is the possessing of a property by an object at a time. Events or processes involve changes of state. When an object goes into a particular state, it comes to possess a particular property; when an object changes state, it ceases to possess some property and comes to possess some distinct property. We can think of processes as patterned sequences of events.

I mention all this simply in order to assuage potential worries about moving back and forth from talk about properties to talk about states (or processes or events). A state is not a property, nor a property a state. Nevertheless, in discussing functionalism, it is convenient sometimes to speak of properties, and sometimes to speak of states.

The picture of functionalism on the table incorporates the central idea of multiple realizability. Mental properties are realizable by, but not identical with, material properties. The same mental property, the property of being in pain, for instance, might be realized by one property in a human being, and quite another property in an invertebrate. Imagine that you are now suffering a particular pain, a headache, say. And pretend that a particular neural state realizes this pain. That neural state has an identifiable material constitution. This might be studied by a lower-level "hardware" science; neurobiology, perhaps. What makes the state a realization of pain, however, is not its material constitution, but its occupying a particular kind of causal role within your nervous system. Following Ned Block, we might put this by saying that what makes a pain a pain is not its having a particular material nature, but its occupying the right sort of causal role.

A caveat. In characterizing functionalism as I have, I exclude a kind of functionalism advanced by D. M. Armstrong and David Lewis. Armstrong and Lewis take mental properties to be functional properties, but identify these with what other functionalists would regard as their realizers. A mental state, on the Armstrong–Lewis view, is the occupant of a particular causal role. The functionalism discussed in this chapter identifies states of mind with the roles, not their occupants.

## Functionalism and behaviorism

Functionalists, then, reject the identity theory. Functionalists regard identity theorists as narrow-minded reductionists, philosophers who aim to reduce the mental (and perhaps everything else) to the physical. Functionalism is staunchly anti-reductionist, firmly committed to a conception of the world as containing distinct and irreducible levels of properties. Although higher levels are thought to be "autonomous" with respect to lower levels – higher levels are not reducible to, identifiable with, or collapsible into lower levels – higher levels are typically said to "supervene" on (to "depend on" and/or to be "determined by") lower levels. (I shall have more to say about supervenience and inter-level determination and dependence in chapter six.)

Functionalists are no less adamant in rejecting behaviorism. According to behaviorists, to be in a particular state of mind is to respond to stimuli in a particular way. To be in pain is to respond to certain sorts of stimuli in familiar ways, or at least to be disposed so to respond. The notion of a disposition to which behaviorists appeal is notably thin. Behaviorists do not regard dispositions as genuine states of objects. If a vase is fragile, this is not a matter of its being in a particular state. Rather, the vase's being fragile is simply a matter of its being true of the vase that, other things equal, if it is struck, it will shatter. All there is to the vase's possession of this disposition is its answering to this (qualified) conditional. The qualification, the "other things equal" clause, is designed to accommodate "exceptions." The vase will not shatter, for instance, if it is surrounded by bubble-wrap, or if it is struck by a styrofoam club.

If you find it difficult to understand how an object's having a particular disposition could fail to be a matter of that object's being in a particular state, you are not alone. This issue aside, however, behaviorist accounts of states of mind apparently fail on their own terms. When we try to say what an agent who possesses a given state of mind is disposed to do, we are invariably compelled to mention other states of mind. You will be disposed to eat the Whopper in front of you if you are hungry, for instance, only if you recognize it as food, believe it is edible, and you do not accept assorted vegetarian precepts. The lesson here is perfectly general. Your possessing a given state of mind will dispose you to behave in a particular way only given other states of mind. The behaviorist dream of "analyzing away" the mental is unattainable.

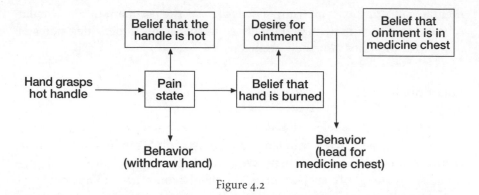

Figure 4.2

Functionalists embrace this observation in regarding states of mind as functional states, states characterizable by their place in a complex causal network. Pains, for instance, might be characterized by reference to typical causes (tissue damage, pressure, extremes of temperature), their relations to other states of mind (they give rise to the belief that you are in pain, and a desire to rid yourself of the source of pain), and behavioral outputs (you move your body in particular ways, groan, perspire). Consider your being in pain as a result of your grasping the handle of a cast-iron skillet that has been left heating on the stove (figure 4.2).

Here, your being in pain is a matter of your being in a particular state, one that stands in appropriate causal relations to sensory inputs, to output behavior, and to other states of mind. These other states of mind are themselves characterizable by reference to their causal roles. Figure 4.2 provides a hint of these relationships.

## Characterizing functional states

The example suggests that functional characterizations of states of mind are in danger of succumbing to circularity. If behaviorism fails in attempting to provide non-circular accounts of states of mind, accounts that do not themselves require mention of further states of mind, in what sense is functionalism immune to the same difficulty? The functionalist says that your being in pain is a matter of your being in a state that occupies an appropriate causal role in your psychological economy. But can this state be characterized informatively? Can we specify it without mention of further states of mind the characterization of which requires mention of still further states of mind, and so on until we eventually loop back to the states with which we began?

One preliminary response to this worry is to point out that functionalism does not aim to "analyze away" states of mind. As figure 4.2 makes clear, the functionalist regards states of mind as perfectly real. Indeed, states of mind are taken to occupy nodes in a causal network. Neither pain, nor any other state of mind, can exist in the absence of such a causal network. Minds, unlike stone walls, are not built by putting together self-sufficient elements, but by creating an arrangement of elements that exhibits the right kind of causal structure. The elements making up the structure – states of mind – owe their identity to their relations to other mental elements. The presence of one state of mind, then, requires the presence of many.

Precisely this feature of the mental encourages worries about circularity, however. If a state of mind owes its character to relations it bears to other states, how could any state have any character? Try to imagine the economy of a community in which everyone makes their living by taking in someone else's washing.

David Lewis has provided one line of response to this worry. The functionalist holds that states of mind are characterizable by reference to their place within a causal network. If this is so, it should be possible to characterize this network as a whole without mention of any particular state of mind. Imagine that minds are representable by flow charts of the sort illustrated in figure 4.2. Such flow charts would be complex, indeed. They might, for instance, include indefinitely many boxes sprouting indefinitely many connections to other boxes.

Imagine that we have managed to specify an entire mental network, we have constructed a dense flow chart along the lines of figure 4.2. Suppose now that we erase the labels inside each box, and replace these with neutral expressions: thus, we might replace "pain state" with "$F_1$," "belief that the handle is hot" with "$F_2$," "desire for ointment" with "$F_3$," "belief that ointment is in the medicine chest" with "$F_4$," and so on (figure 4.3). Because they involve no mental notions, we can leave the specification of sensory inputs and behavioral outputs as they are. (In fact, as we noted in our examination of behaviorism in chapter three, you might doubt that

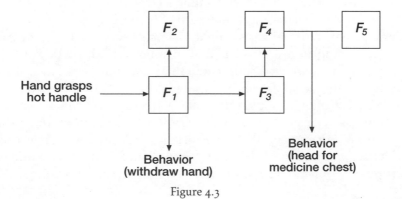

Figure 4.3

inputs and outputs could be given the sort of neutral specification envisaged. In the interest of clarity and simplicity, however, I shall ignore this complication.) Call the resulting flow chart a total functional description. A state of pain, then, is a state that occupies the place of $F_1$ in any system that possesses the causal architecture exhibited by the total functional system.

The idea is that, because the identity of every state depends on relations it bears to other states, we cannot characterize mental items piecemeal, but only all at once. Think of points in a co-ordinate system. Every point is distinguished only by its unique relations to every other point. This does not mean that talk of individual points in a co-ordinate space is invariably circular. It means, rather, that we must characterize the system as a whole. We cannot start by characterizing a single independent element or collection of elements and use these to build up a conception of the remaining elements. Of course, once the system is in place, we can perfectly well speak of individual points within it.

In the same way, once we have in place a mental grid, we can speak of individual places on that grid, individual pains, wants, and beliefs. How do we arrive at such a grid? Perhaps we acquire it in learning, as children, to talk of pains, wants, and beliefs. And, although we acquire the ability to do this over time, we do not acquire it piecemeal. As Wittgenstein puts it, "light dawns gradually over the whole" (1969), § 141.

If this still seems overly mysterious, reflect on a child's acquisition of a complex skill – riding a bicycle, for instance. Riding a bicycle requires the co-ordination of myriad component micro-skills. A child does not learn these individually or in isolation, however. Rather, the skills are mastered together; the mastery of each depending to some degree on mastery of the others. After practice, the child comes to possess the skills as a unit. Once possessed, they can be refined and extended indefinitely.

Functionalists, then, unlike behaviorists, apparently have resources to characterize states of mind without circularity. Of course, behaviorists might make use of the same trick. After all, our total functional system is anchored to behavioral inputs and outputs. Does this mean that functionalism is, at bottom, just a gussied-up form of behaviorism?

Perhaps not. A behaviorist might characterize your being in pain as your responding to a particular kind of input with a particular kind of behavior, and use our specification of a total functional system as a way of spelling out the usual "other things equal clause." In taking this route, however, a behaviorist would interpret the nodes in our functional specification, not as designating internal states of agents to whom the specification applied, but merely as empty calculational devices that provide an appropriate connection of behavioral responses to external stimuli. Thus interpreted, a functional specification would be merely a complex algorithm, a method of inferring behavioral outputs from descriptions of inputs.[1]

Functionalists, in contrast, take the nodes in a functional specification to designate genuine causally efficacious internal states of systems whose causal architecture mirrors the architecture spelled out in our total functional specification.

## Total functional systems

Return for a moment to the notion of a total functional system, and consider just two categories of mental state: beliefs and desires. Although we are alike in many ways – all of us have beliefs and desires – human beings need not share all their beliefs and desires. Two total functional systems differ, however, if they differ with respect to any of their beliefs and desires. Indeed, because your own beliefs and desires are constantly changing, the total functional system that constitutes your mind at one time is likely to differ from the system constituting your mind at some earlier or later time. Now, imagine the set – an infinite set, no doubt – consisting of every total functional system possible for an adult human being. If functionalism is on the right track, then every possible human mind is exhaustively characterizable by reference to elements in this set.[2]

This holistic picture suggested by talk of total functional systems needs qualification. We might imagine that adult human beings, by and large, exhibit broadly similar total functional systems. In contrast, the functional architectures of infants and non-human creatures must be decidedly simpler. Does this mean that infants and non-human creatures lack minds: that they cannot entertain thoughts, harbor desires, or feel pain?

A functionalist might respond by conceding that infants and non-human creatures differ functionally from adult human beings. Even so their respective functional architectures overlap that of adult human beings in significant ways. Thus, the total functional systems of infants and non-human creatures incorporate states that play the role of pain states ($F_1$ in figure 4.3) with respect to inputs and outputs. Their systems are attenuated only with respect to assorted mediating states, those occupying nodes corresponding to beliefs and desires, for instance.

---

[1] It would be open to a behaviorist to interpret the nodes in a functional specification as designating non-mental, material states. This option calls to mind the Armstrong–Lewis brand of functionalism.

[2] For those who care about such things, another way of making the same point would be to allow that the possession of any state of mind is characterizable by a conjunction of conditional (if–then) statements, the antecedents (if-clauses) of which include descriptions of inputs and specifications of total functional architectures, and whose consequents (then-clauses) include outputs (behavioral and otherwise).

This suggests that there could be borderline cases, cases in which, owing to diminution of complexity, we should not know what to say. Do primitive creatures, earthworms, for instance, or paramecia, feel pain? Such creatures draw away from aversive stimuli, and in that regard exhibit their possession of states that bear an important resemblance to our pain states. But the total functional architecture of primitive creatures may be such that it is just not clear what we should say about them. In this regard, functionalism may mirror our own natural tendency to remain undecided about such cases. Indeed, we might imagine a continuum of total functional systems, ranging from those exhibited by adult human beings, to those possessed by infants, all the way down to those of single-celled organisms. Drawing a line on this continuum, one that marks a clear-cut boundary between creatures capable of feeling pain, and creatures lacking this capacity, could be largely a matter of decision rather than principle.

## The Representational Theory of Mind

Consider an alternative way of specifying a total functional system, one, in some respects, more in keeping with the flow chart model deployed in the characterization of computer programs. Again, for convenience, let us focus on beliefs and desires. Rather than conceiving of beliefs and desires individually, think of the mind as including a "belief box" and a "desire box" (figure 4.4).

The idea is that your forming a belief that the window is open is a matter of a symbol expressing the proposition that the window is open being deposited in your belief box. In the same vein, your wanting the window to be open is your having such a symbol in your desire box. Your belief box and your desire box are connected in distinctive ways to the rest of the system constituting your mind. If a symbol representing the proposition that the window is shut is in your desire box, for instance, this might – in conjunction with the presence of appropriate symbols in your belief and desire boxes – lead you to walk across the room and lower the window. The presence of the same symbol in your belief box (assuming

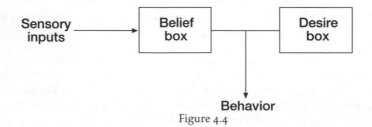

Figure 4.4

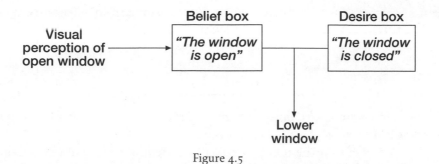

Figure 4.5

that it is absent from your desire box) might – and, again, in conjunction with the presence of other symbols in your belief and desire boxes – lead to very different behavior (see figure 4.5).

This way of thinking of total functional systems enables us to see more clearly how creatures with very different beliefs and desires might nevertheless be seen as functionally on a par. You, an infant, and I might all fit the highly simplified model in figure 4.4. We differ, however, with respect to the symbols apt to appear in our respective belief and desire boxes.

This conception of mind, the Representational Theory of Mind, has long been defended by Jerry Fodor. The Representational Theory of Mind requires the postulation of a system of symbols that function as "mental representations." These symbols make up what Fodor calls a language of thought, a biologically fixed code analogous to the "machine code" hard-wired into an ordinary computing machine. Your forming a belief that the window is open is a matter of a sentence in the language of thought corresponding to the English sentence, "The window is open," acquiring an appropriate functional role – or, as we put it earlier, a matter of this sentence's slipping into your belief box.

## Semantic engines

Fodor and his allies have expended considerable energy arguing that the Representational Theory of Mind (and with it the language of thought hypothesis) is "the only game in town." The Representational Theory of Mind provides a way of understanding how minds, higher-level entities, could systematically affect and be affected by bodily goings-on. Until someone produces a serious competitor, the theory wins by default. Or so it is claimed.

But how is all this supposed to work? What could it mean to speak of sentences in the language of thought occupying belief and desire boxes? Notice first, that the focus is on "sentence tokens." A sentence token – a particular inscription – is a concrete entity, something that could have a causal role. A sentence token is to be distinguished from a sentence type. To appreciate the distinction, consider the box below.

> Babar is king.
> Babar is king.

How many sentences does the box contain? The box contains two instances or tokens of a single sentence type.

I shall not clutter the text by explicitly signaling when I am discussing sentence tokens and when I am discussing sentence types. The context makes clear which is intended. When proponents of the Representational Theory of Mind speak of sentences occupying belief boxes, for instance, or sentences having parts in causal processes, it is clear they are speaking of sentence tokens, not types – individual entities, not kinds or types of entity.

Think of the sentences on this page. Each one is the result of an ordinary material causal process. And each one produces ordinary material effects: it reflects light in a particular way, for instance. To see why this is important, let us distinguish sentences from propositions they express (or propositions they are used to express). When we encounter sentences in our native language, their meanings, the propositions they express, leap out at us. But of course, we may encounter sentences without having any sense of what they mean. This happens whenever we confront sentences in a language we do not understand.

Now imagine a device that could manipulate sentences without regard to their meanings, but that did so in a way that coincides with the way those sentences would be manipulated by someone who knew their meanings. Such a device – what John Haugeland dubs a "semantic engine" – would perfectly mimic the performance of a native speaker, but would do so without relying, as a native speaker would, on the meanings of the sentences it manipulated. Those sentences might express propositions (at least they express propositions when used by ordinary speakers), but the device would care only about their shapes, their "syntax." (Syntax concerns the purely structural features of sentences; "semantics" concerns their meanings.) The device we are imagining, a semantic engine, operates on purely syntactic principles and "formal" relations among sentences, relations definable solely by reference to the syntactic characteristics of sentences.

Is such a device possible? Not only are semantic engines possible, they exist already, and in large numbers! An ordinary computing machine is a semantic engine. We design and program computers so that they manipulate symbols in accord with purely syntactic and formal principles. The symbols are meaningful – to us – but the machines that deploy them care nothing about this. They operate on uninterpreted symbols, but in a way that honors semantic constraints. (This is just a fancy way of saying that computing machines manipulate symbols in a way that makes sense – to us – in light of their meanings.)

How is this possible? How can syntax mirror semantics? If you have ever studied logic, you have already encountered an important example of a system that makes use of purely syntactic or formal principles in the manipulation of symbols, but in a way that honors semantic relations among those symbols. Ordinary rules of inference refer only to shapes of symbols. Take the rule commonly known as *modus ponens*:

$$p \supset q$$
$$p \; / \therefore \; q$$

(In English: where "$p$" and "$q$" are arbitrary sentences, "If $p$ then $q$," together with "$p$," implies "$q$.")

The rule tells us that, if you have a particular configuration of symbols (here, $p \supset q$ and $p$), you are permitted to write a new symbol (in this case, $q$). (Think of the $\supset$ as expressing an English conditional – "if . . . then . . ." – construction.) In formulating the rule, I have used variables ($p$ and $q$) that range over sentences. The rule, in effect, says that whenever you have a $\supset$ flanked by sentences together with a sentence that matches the sentence on the left of the $\supset$, you are permitted to "detach" the sentence to the $\supset$'s right.

For our purposes, what is significant about the *modus ponens* rule is that it is formulated and deployed without regard to semantics, without regard to the meanings of sentences to which it applies. Even so, applications of the rule make sense; they conform to the semantics of inference. If you accept the sentence

If it's raining then I'll need an umbrella,

and the sentence

It's raining,

Then you are entitled to infer the sentence

I'll need an umbrella.

This is something any English speaker, anyone who understands English, knows. Systems of formal logic mirror this kind of semantic knowledge in rules the application of which requires no semantic knowledge.

Well and good. But what has this to do with minds? Imagine that our aim is to explain the human mind by supposing that minds manipulate mental representations, sentences in the language of thought. It might seem that there is an obvious objection to this project. If minds manipulate sentences, symbolic representations, then this would seem to require a "sentence understander," some component of the mind that interprets the symbols. This would mean that we are explaining the mind by positing within it another mind: an homunculus, a little intelligent agent whose job requires that he understand sentences in the language of thought. And an explanation of this kind is no explanation. The point is perfectly general. You and I are watching a machine that sorts and wraps candy bars. You are impressed, and ask how the machine works. "Simple," I reply. "There is a device inside it that controls its operations."

Against this background it is easier to appreciate the relevance of the notion of a semantic engine. A semantic engine is a device that performs symbolic operations – manipulates symbols – in a way that reflects semantic relations holding among these symbols, but does so exclusively by means of formal and syntactic principles – that is, without regard to the meanings of those symbols. We can suppose, then, that minds process mental representations, without having to suppose that minds contain components – little men, homunculi – that understand the meanings of those representations. Ordinary computing machines are realizations of semantic engines. Perhaps brains are as well. If so, and if the brain has an appropriate functional organization, then it would seem that we have gone a long way toward explaining how minds work.

You might think that there is an obvious problem with this view. When we open up the brain, we see nothing that resembles symbols or sentences in a language of thought. What could it be for brains to contain sentences?

Think of an ordinary computing machine. It is regarded as uncontroversial that computing machines process symbols. Yet, were you to examine the inside of a computing machine while it is engaged in symbol manipulations, you would see nothing resembling symbols. Nor, incidentally, would you see any 0's and 1's, the basic ingredients of a computing machine's symbolic repertoire. The electronic items that function as symbols in a computing machine need not resemble our pencil-and-paper representations of those symbols. Nor could you expect to read off symbols as they are manipulated by a computing machine any more than you could hope to read off a musical score by closely examining deflections in the groove of a phonograph record or the track of a compact disk.[1]

---

[1] This is not to say that you could not learn to do this. But learning it would require learning a complex rule that takes you from electrical events, or patterns of deflections, or magnetic patterns, to familiar symbols or musical notation.

If the mind is a semantic engine realized by the brain, if mental operations include the manipulation of symbols, sentences in the language of thought, then the embodiment of those symbols in the brain need not resemble the symbols we write with pencil and paper. They might involve subtle electrical or chemical states; they might be embodied in connections among neurons; they might be widely distributed in networks of neurons. In any case, there is no reason to imagine that such symbols could be read off the brain in the way you read words off this page. If there is a language of thought, its sentences may well be invisible from the point of view of an observer examining the micro-structure of a brain.

## The Chinese Room

The Representational Theory of Mind depicts the mind as a semantic engine, a device that operates on purely formal and syntactic principles, but in a way that honors semantics. This means, roughly, that although mental operations are blind to the semantics of the symbols they manipulate, their manipulations are indistinguishable from those that might be performed by someone who understood the symbols. When you tell your desktop computer to print a document by means of a typed or voiced command, the device does not first interpret the input, then act on the basis of its understanding of that interpretation. The mechanisms that process your command care nothing for its meaning. Yet the machine is programmed in such a way that its syntax reflects its semantics: it operates just as though it understood your command.

For proponents of the language of thought, this is all there is to understanding. You understand the sentences on this page. But the mechanisms responsible for your understanding do not themselves understand. If we thought they did, we would not have explained what it is for you to understand the sentences. We would merely have pushed the problem back; we would now need to account for those mechanisms' understanding.

But is this all there is to understanding? John Searle has argued that it is not. Searle's argument is based on a widely discussed thought experiment. Imagine, he says, that you are seated in a cramped windowless room. At your feet is a large basket of plastic Chinese characters, although you have no idea that this is what they are. You are ignorant of Chinese, and for all you can tell the items in the basket might be plastic decorations of an abstract design: squiggles. Periodically, through a slot in the wall, you receive a batch of Chinese characters. Although these mean nothing to you, you are equipped with a manual that tells you that, when particular sequences of plastic squiggles come through the slot, you are to pass out other sequences from your supply in the basket. Suppose you become adept at this. When a sequence of squiggles is input, you can quickly output a sequence called for by the manual. We might even imagine that, in time, you learn the manual by heart, and so your manipulations of squiggles become virtually automatic.

Now, outside the room, and completely unknown to you, is a group of Chinese scientists. These scientists can read the characters that are passed into and out of the room. The strings of squiggles they pass into the room amount to questions in Chinese, and the strings of squiggles you pass back out amount to answers to those questions. (We can ignore the fact that, for the answers to make sense in light of the questions, the manual will need to be very complicated indeed.) It looks to the Chinese scientists as though you understand Chinese. But, says Searle, clearly you do not. You are behaving as though you understand, indeed you are operating as a semantic engine, yet you understand no Chinese. At best you are simulating a Chinese speaker.

Searle's Chinese Room thought experiment is best interpreted in light of a test proposed in 1950 by A. M. Turing (1912–54), an influential mathematician whose work on the theory of computation underlies the operation of modern computing machines. Turing was interested in the question whether it might be possible to build an intelligent machine. After reviewing failed attempts to define "intelligence" (and, for that matter "machine"), Turing proposed to define intelligence "operationally" and in that way bypass altogether the vexed question of what exactly constitutes intelligence. An operational definition takes the form of a test for determining whether the defined term applies. Turing's test is designed to insure that whatever passes the test qualifies as intelligent.

The Turing test is based on a game Turing dubs the "Imitation Game." The Imitation Game is played by three ordinary people. One, an interrogator, puts questions to two players, a man and a woman, and tries to guess which is which. One of these players must answer honestly, the other tries to mislead the interrogator. To avoid inappropriate visual or auditory clues, the players are placed in a separate room and communicate with the interrogator by means of a teletype. By asking clever questions, the interrogator will sometimes win the game, but will sometimes lose as well. Let us imagine that the interrogator wins – that is correctly discovers which player is which – about 30 percent of the time.

Now, says Turing, suppose we substitute for one of the players a computing machine. If a machine can fool a clever interrogator about as often as a human player can, then we should say that it passes the test: it is intelligent. (If this seems too easy, you might reflect on the fact that no existing or currently contemplated computing machine comes remotely close to exhibiting the kind of resourcefulness and wit required to fool a moderately competent interrogator.)

Searle's Chinese Room can be seen as a variant on the Turing test. We can imagine that the Chinese scientists assembled outside the room are taking the role of the interrogator in the Imitation Game, and that you (seated in the room with your manual and basket of Chinese squiggles) are standing in for the computing machine. (The other player, we might imagine, is an ordinary Chinese speaker seated next to you.) Suppose you fool the interrogators about as often as a native Chinese speaker would. What does this show? Searle argues that it shows only that you have been provided with an ingenious prop – a stunningly clever manual – that enables you to play the part of a Chinese speaker. But you neither speak nor understand Chinese. Because you operate just as a computing machine would (the manual constitutes your program), we should not say that a computing machine that passes the Turing test is genuinely intelligent or that it understands the sentences it receives as inputs or produces as outputs.

Searle hopes to draw a more general conclusion from all this. The brand of functionalism we have been discussing, the Representational Theory of Mind, is based on the idea that the mind is a semantic engine: mental processes consist of operations over uninterpreted symbols (sentences in the language of thought). But, contends Searle, the Chinese Room thought experiment makes it clear that there is more to minds than this. A device – a robot, perhaps – whose "brain" realized a semantic engine and thereby satisfied the requirements of the Representational Theory of Mind, would no doubt fool us: we should think it was intelligent, that it had a mind. But we would be wrong. At best the device would be simulating intelligence and understanding, in the way a computing machine might produce a simulated weather pattern or an instance of molecular bonding.

Some proponents of the Representational Theory of Mind have accused Searle of begging the question. Searle assumes that, in the Chinese Room, there is no genuine understanding. But, these theorists argue, there only appears to be no understanding because the thought experiment invites us to focus on just a single component – you, sitting in your chair sorting through a basket of Chinese characters – rather than the whole system of which you are but one component. Thus, while it is true that you understand no Chinese, the system that includes you, the room as a whole, does.

Uncommitted bystanders to this debate may feel pulled in different directions. On the one hand, Searle is apparently onto something important. On the other hand, there is some justice in the functionalists' complaint that the appeal of the Chinese Room stems from its tendency to make us focus on a component of a system rather than the system as a whole. I shall, however, leave the debate here, and move to consider the question how sentences in the language of thought come by their semantics. In due course (in chapter six), I shall suggest a way of reconciling these issues. Doing so, however, requires that we move beyond functionalism and the Representational Theory of Mind, and take a prolonged excursion into metaphysics.

## From syntax to semantics

Central to the Representational Theory of Mind is the idea that minds manipulate mental representations in the form of uninterpreted sentences in the language of thought. In this context, "uninterpreted" means that the processes whereby mental symbols are manipulated operate without regard to the meanings of those symbols. In this respect, mental processes are taken to resemble computational processes. They resemble as well your bravura performance in the Chinese Room.

But if mental symbols are uninterpreted, in what does their meaning reside? Reflect for a moment on the operation of ordinary computing machines. Suppose we program a computing machine to keep inventory in a supermarket. The program keeps track of bananas, cans of soup, and cartons of milk. We might say that the computing machine on which the program runs is storing information about bananas, cans of soup, and cartons of milk. The machine performs operations over symbols that designate these items, however, without regard to what they designate. Indeed, we might imagine that the very same program could be run on a different machine, or on the same machine on a different occasion, to keep track of items in a hardware store. In this case, the device would store information about nails, glue, and ant traps. We might even imagine that the very same symbols that, in the supermarket case, represent bananas, cans of soup, and cartons of milk, represent, in this machine, nails, glue, and ant traps, respectively.

What, then, gives a symbol manipulated by a computing machine its meaning: what makes it designate cartons of milk rather than ant traps? And, we might ask, what gives sentences in the language of thought their meaning – for, although it may be controversial whether states of a computing machine are in any sense meaningful, it is surely not controversial that our thoughts have meaning. The whole language of thought project is predicated on the assumption that thoughts are meaningful, and that this is something that calls for explanation.

Note first, that a devotee of the Representational Theory of Mind assumes (as most philosophers nowadays assume) that the meaning of a symbol is not intrinsic to that symbol. What a symbol signifies is not built into that symbol, but depends rather on how the symbol is deployed by agents (or systems) that deploy it. The symbols processed by a computing machine owe their significance to the use to which they are put by agents who program and enter data into the machine for particular purposes. When you type "bananas" into the machine and this inscription is converted into a pattern of magnetic deflections, this pattern of magnetic deflections, insofar as it functions as a symbol, designates bananas because this is what you mean by "bananas."

We can say that the meanings of symbols processed by an ordinary computing machine are derivative of the meanings given those symbols by agents making use of the machine and its program. But this cannot be the explanation of the meanings of symbols in the language of thought. Your thoughts do not mean what they do because you assign those meanings; your mental concepts do not designate what, if anything, they designate because you decide what they designate. The language of thought is supposed to explain how we can have meaningful thoughts. If the meanings of expressions in the language of thought require that we assign those expressions meaning, then we have explained nothing. The assignment of meanings is an activity that presupposes meaningful thought. If we are to account for the semantics of the language of thought, we must do so without assuming what we hope to explain.

What, then, is the source of meaning for the language of thought, to what does it owe its semantics? We can exclude the possibility that expressions in the language of thought possess intrinsic, built-in significance. And we can exclude the possibility that meanings of those expressions depend on the interpretive activities of thinkers. What options remain?

Perhaps this: expressions in the language of thought owe their significance to causal relations those expressions bear to goings-on in our surroundings. Thus, a particular term in the language of thought might designate bananas (and so mirror the English word "banana") because it is evoked by the presence of bananas. Another term might designate cans of soup (mirroring the English expression "can of soup") because instances of it are brought about by agents' causal contact with cans of soup.

This sketch is, to be sure, oversimplified. The point, however, is that it is open to a proponent of the Representational Theory of Mind to advance a broadly causal account of the semantics of the language of thought. Such an account would be complex, and would include non-causal elements. The so-called logical terms, for instance, those corresponding to the English expressions "all," "some," "and," "or," "not," "if . . . then . . ." might be explicable purely by reference to relations sentences in the language of thought bear to one another. But the fundamental idea is that the semantics of thought is fixed by the context of thinkers. In this respect, too, ordinary agents resemble computing machines. The significance of symbols processed by a given computing machine depends on the context in which the machine is deployed.

I shall have more to say about these and related issues in chapters five and six. Meanwhile, let us return to our examination of the ontology of functionalism.

## The layered view of the world

Fodor appeals explicitly to the computer model of the mind. Mental operations are operations performed over symbols, sentences in the language of thought. The science of psychology aims to work out the programs controlling our behavior. These can be represented, just as computer programs can be represented, by means of flow charts that specify the causal structure of systems they characterize. Psychology, on this model, is a "higher-level science," one that abstracts from lower-level implementational details.

One advantage of such a view is that it enables us to see how minds might fit into the material world, and how minds are related to brains. Minds are related to brains in something like the way computer programs are related to the hardware in which they are implemented. Minds are not identifiable with or reducible to brains for just the reasons that programs or computational operations are not identifiable with or reducible to the hardware on which they run. Brains realize minds much as computing machines realize particular programs. And just as, in describing the operation of a computing machine at the program level, we are describing its causal structure in abstraction from its hardware, so in describing mental operations, we are describing the causal structure of intelligent agents in abstraction from their biological hardware.

All this seems to demystify the mind. We can understand how attempts to reduce minds to material entities are bound to fail, without thereby embracing the dualist notion that minds are immaterial substances. Perhaps, however, this demystification goes too far. You might worry that a computational conception of mental processes threatens to turn us into rigidly programmed robots, beings altogether lacking in spontaneity or free will.

The functionalist idea, however, is not that we blindly follow formal routines that we are powerless to alter. Intelligent behavior is principled behavior. And we can think of the principles we adopt (or cultivate, or learn, or inherit along with our biological constitution) as core ingredients in our mental program. And this is perfectly consistent with most conceptions of free will.

## Taxonomic levels and the special sciences

Return, for a moment, to the notion that the operations of an ordinary computing machine can be described on different levels. An electrical engineer or a physicist might describe the operation of a given machine at the hardware level. In so doing, the engineer or physicist employs a characteristic array of concepts. A computer programmer describing the operations of the very same machine makes use of a very different conceptual repertoire.

Fodor speaks in such cases of distinctive "taxonomies," distinctive ways of classifying and organizing explanations of phenomena. Lower-level and higher-level sciences "taxonomize" phenomena very differently. Taxonomic categories that specify entities of interest at higher levels need not, and typically will not, be definable in terms of categories found at lower levels. In the computer case, we cannot define computational operations in terms of material transactions in the hardware that realize those operations. One obvious problem with attempts to do so stems from the fact that computational operations are multiply realizable: the very same operation can be realized in very different sorts of material system. You might think that we could define higher-level operations by means of a disjunction of lower-level goings-on. Thus, the summing operation might be characterizable as either a particular kind of brass gear and cog operation (in a Babbage machine), or a particular kind of operation in a device made with vacuum tubes, or a particular kind of transistor-based operation, or. . . .

Functionalists like to point out that such a strategy faces an obvious difficulty. The dots at the end of the model disjunctive specification indicate that we shall need to add descriptions of further lower-level operations if we are to provide an exhaustive lower-level accounting of our higher-level category. It would seem, however, that there are endless lower-level ways of realizing any complex higher-level operation. The prospects of reducing higher-level categories to lower-level categories, even long disjunctions of lower-level categories, are not encouraging.

Even if we allowed a systematic mapping of higher-level categories onto long – perhaps infinitely long – disjunctions of lower-level categories, however, the reductive strategy seems to fly in the face of scientific and everyday practice. Suppose we distinguish physics (or "basic physics"), the fundamental lower-level science, from the various higher-level sciences. Physics provides us with an inventory of basic particles and laws governing the behavior of those particles. Higher-level sciences deploy higher-level taxonomies. While physicists speak of quarks and fundamental forces, chemists focus on atoms and molecules, and biologists take up complex molecular structures: living organisms. At still higher levels, psychologists, sociologists, and economists ply their trades.

Each of these sciences is distinguished by the way it carves up reality. The categories definitive of a given higher-level taxonomy divide reality in ways that, from the perspective of lower-level sciences, would seem arbitrary. Consider a simple analogy. When you play chess, you move chess pieces in particular ways. Considered from the perspective of chemistry or physics, the range of appropriate moves (those permitted by the rules of chess) would appear entirely unprincipled. Patterns and regularities exhibited in games of chess appear only at a higher level. Biological categories, seen from the perspective of physics, must appear similarly arbitrary. Biology divides up the world in ways that, so long as we remain at the level of quarks and electrons, look contrived. Similarly for psychology: psychological concepts – pain and belief, for instance – circumscribe boundaries invisible at lower levels.

The idea here is that the sciences operate within a hierarchy of levels, with physics at the bottom, chemistry and biology occupying intermediate levels, and psychology and the social sciences at the highest levels. Each science imposes a system of categories, a taxonomy, on the world. The categories definitive of a given science mark off boundaries that are largely invisible within sciences at lower levels. This is why there is, in general, no prospect of reducing a higher-level science to a science at some lower level. Doing so would require a systematic way of drawing higher-level distinctions using lower-level categories. And this is just what would seem to be hopeless.

You might suspect that a conception of this sort goes too far. If physics is the science of everything, then why do we need the others? If the special sciences are not reducible to physics, then why should we accord them any legitimacy?

The answer given by functionalists sympathetic to Fodor is that it is precisely because higher-level sciences make use of categories not reducible to those of lower-level sciences that the higher-level sciences are vindicated. As we explore the world, we discover important regularities that are, from the point of view of physics, quite invisible. These regularities hold among objects in virtue of properties possessed by those objects that correspond in no principled way to properties of interest to the physicist. To ignore such things, however, would require that we ignore endless interesting and important regularities.

To see the point, think again of the operation of a computing machine. Suppose we describe the operation of a computing machine at the most basic hardware level, in terms of electron fluctuations inside transistors. If we limited ourselves to such descriptions, let alone descriptions framed in terms of the categories of physics, we should miss important generalizations that appear only when we consider the machine at the level of its program. We can, for instance, understand common features in the behavior of two machines with very different material compositions running the same program: both machines are doing sums, for instance, or sending files to a printer. At the ordinary hardware level, or at the level of physics, such commonalities disappear – in the way the pattern formed by arrangements of flowers in a floral clock vanishes when we look at individual plants.

## Laws and properties: levels of reality

Someone skeptical about this line of reasoning might object that it shows at most that we require higher-level sciences, and the categories they deploy, only as a matter of convenience. Higher-level sciences provide us with what from the point of view of physics or chemistry are hopelessly crude accounts of goings-on in the world around us. As it happens, these crude accounts are perfectly adequate for certain of our purposes. Moreover, finer-grained accounts would require an investment of time and energy that we could ill afford. By keeping to the program level, I can understand, explain, and manipulate the behavior of my desktop computer in a way that is perfectly adequate for my purposes. Those purposes aside, however, the real story is to be had only by descending to the hardware level and, ultimately, to the level of micro-physics.

We might compare here the use of familiar rules of thumb in predicting the weather: "Red sky at night, sailor's delight; red sky in morning, sailor take warning"; "Ring around the sun or moon, snow or rain is coming soon." Such rules of thumb are useful, no doubt, perhaps even practically indispensable. Even so, they merely approximate much more complex and fine-grained pronouncements whose home is in the lower-level sciences, meteorology and climatology, for instance, and, ultimately of course, in physics. We might see psychology in the same light. Psychology provides us with a stock of rough and ready generalizations that serve our purposes when we interact with one another. But these at best approximate truths at lower levels. As we descend from psychology, through neuropsychology, to neurobiology, to chemistry, we refine these approximations until we reach bedrock: physics.

Fodor is adamant that this way of depicting the relation of higher-level to lower-level sciences is misconceived. The categories embedded in a higher-level science, psychology, for instance, designate genuine properties of objects. These properties are not reducible to properties found in sciences at lower levels. "Being in pain" and "believing that it is raining" designate such higher-level properties. If these properties are not found among the properties inventoried by lower-level sciences, we should not conclude that they are in some way less-than-perfectly-real. On the contrary, this is just what we should expect if psychology is an authentic higher-level science.

What makes a property genuine? On the view we are considering, a genuine property is one that makes a causal difference to objects possessing it. If being red is a genuine property, then objects possessing it, red objects, will behave differently than objects lacking it. Functionalists in Fodor's camp most often put this in terms of causal laws. A genuine property is one that figures in some causal law. The special sciences are in the business of formulating causal laws governing objects falling under them. Genuine properties, then, are revealed by causal laws uncovered as we investigate our world. If we discover causal laws in neurobiology, or psychology, or economics, laws that govern higher-level objects, and if these laws range over higher-level properties, then these higher-level properties must be genuine. Of course we could be wrong about what the laws are, hence mistaken as to the genuine properties, but that goes without saying.

Two features of this view are worth emphasizing.

First, its proponents are committed to a layered conception of reality. The world contains levels of objects and properties governed by levels of causal laws. Although objects at higher levels are made up of objects at lower levels, it is nevertheless true that higher-level objects and their properties have a kind of life of their own. They are not reducible to, not "nothing but," arrangements of objects and properties at lower levels.[1] Hearts are made up of cells, and ultimately of quarks and electrons. But hearts are not just assemblages of electrons and quarks, and properties of hearts are not properties of electrons and quarks or assemblages of electrons and quarks. (The reasoning here parallels the reasoning, discussed in chapter two above, that leads us to doubt that boats are just the collections of planks that make them up.)

Second, higher-level laws are taken to be laws that hold only *ceteris paribus*, only "other things being equal." In this respect, they differ from the laws governing the fundamental entities studied in physics. Laws governing the fundamental entities are exceptionless. In contrast, laws governing entities at higher levels are only approximate, they apply *ceteris paribus*. Do not confuse *ceteris paribus* laws with probabilistic laws of the sort mentioned in chapter two. The fundamental laws might turn out to be probabilistic. Their application is none the less universal and exceptionless.

---

[1] The supervenience relation is standardly invoked to explain the relation of higher-level objects and properties to those at lower levels. The idea, roughly, is that, while higher-level objects and properties "depend on and are determined by" lower-level objects and properties, they are nevertheless distinct from lower-level objects and properties.

The laws we might hope to discover in psychology, or economics, or even neurobiology, in contrast, are irreducibly "hedged."

I mention this second point because you might be wondering about laws of psychology, laws governing the operation of the mind. Consider a law that you might think governs beliefs and desires:

> $(L_\psi)$ If an agent, $S$, wants $x$ and believes $y$ is needed to obtain $x$, then $S$ wants $y$.

If you want to take the subway and believe that, in order to take the subway, you must buy a token, then you will want to buy a token. Although $(L_\psi)$ governs many instances of desire formation, it is not difficult to imagine exceptions. If you believe, for instance, that you have no money, then your belief that you must buy a token to ride the subway might lead you to cease to desire to ride the subway – or to a desire to panhandle.

More significantly, you could fail to form the desire to buy a token because you are, at the instant it occurs to you that you need to buy a token, knocked unconscious by a slab of falling plaster. Note that, in this case, we encounter a kind of intervention that involves entities and processes that fall outside the purview of psychology. Things fail to go right at the psychological level owing to occurrences at the neurobiological level. But psychological laws are necessarily silent about such occurrences: this is what makes psychological laws psychological laws.

The example can be extended to the laws of every special science. Each special science carves up the world in a particular way and endeavors to discover laws governing the entities falling under its special categories. These entities are made up of lower-level entities. Goings-on affecting these lower-level entities can have higher-level consequences. Changes in the molecules of your brain, for instance, can have dramatic repercussions for your brain and for your state of mind as well. But the laws of each special science concern only entities at the level appropriate to that science. Psychological laws contain no mention of molecules, though molecular events can affect psychological processes. So long as we regard the laws of a special science like psychology to be autonomous, so long as we take them to be irreducible to laws governing lower-level entities, we can be assured that the laws must fail to be exceptionless.

## Layered ontology

Where does all this leave us? I have taken us on a rather a long detour through issues in the philosophy of science in order to motivate the metaphysical conception of mind that has been most influential in functionalist circles. I do not mean to suggest that all functionalists subscribe to this picture. Nevertheless, the picture has been widely influential, both in philosophy and in allied disciplines in the cognitive sciences, so it is worth spelling out. Most importantly, it provides a rationale for the view that the world is layered, that minds are higher-order entities, and that mental properties are higher-level properties. This is a central tenet of virtually all versions of functionalism (although the Armstrong–Lewis brand of functionalism mentioned earlier is an apparent exception).

We are left with the following picture of the mind. Mental expressions – "being in pain," "believing that bears are furry" – designate functional properties of entities to which they are ascribed. Functional properties are ultimately realized in material systems by non-functional properties of those systems. When you possess a particular mental property, the property of being in pain, for instance, that property is realized in you by some material property of your brain. In another kind of creature, an octopus, say, or an Alpha Centaurian, that same mental property, being in pain, might be realized by a very different material property. You, an octopus, and an Alpha Centaurian all possess the property of being in pain. In you this property is realized by a particular kind of neurological process, in an octopus it is realized by a very different sort of neurological episode, and in an Alpha Centaurian it is realized by a non-neurological, silicon-based process.

Pain, like any other functional property, is multiply realizable. It is anyone's guess as to what the limits are on realizers for pain. Might a computing machine be programmed to feel pain? If a computing machine could be given the right sort of functional organization, then, according to the functionalist, it could feel pain: the property of being in pain would be realized by transfers of electrons across transistors – or, in the case of a Babbage machine, by some sequence of rotations of brass cogs and cylinders.

We shall look more closely at the notion of multiple realizability – and the associated idea that the world consists of levels of entities and properties – in chapter six. Meanwhile, let us consider an important line of criticism of functionalism that focuses on an aspect of the mind that functionalists are often accused of ignoring: the qualitative aspect.

# "Qualia"

Suppose we accept the functionalist's depiction of states of mind as functional states. This means that you possess a given state of mind, you are in pain, for instance, just in case you are in a state that satisfies a particular job description, a state that plays a particular kind of causal role. Among other things, you are in a state brought about by tissue damage, or pressure, or extremes of temperature, and one that brings about a range of characteristic "pain responses," behavioral and mental: you cringe, you form the belief that you are in pain, and you acquire a desire to take steps to alleviate the pain.

All this seems quite right, as far as it goes. The trouble is, it seems not to go quite far enough. When you are in pain you are in a state that undoubtedly has a range of causal or dispositional properties. (What state does not?) But could this be all there is to your pain? Surely, when you experience pain, your experience has a characteristic "feel." As we saw in chapter three, philosophers like to call attention to this feel by noting that "there is something it is like" to be in pain – to have a blinding headache, for instance. And this "what it's like," the qualitative dimension of pain, is apparently missing from the functionalist's story. In having a headache, you undergo a kind of conscious experience, an experience with certain salient qualities. Philosophers often refer to these qualities as "qualia." Qualia are just those qualitative features of our mental life we focus on when we contemplate what it is like to be in pain, or view the sun setting in the Pacific, or bite into a jalapeño pepper.

A functionalist need not deny that when you are in pain, your being in pain has a characteristic feel. Functionalists sometimes do deny this, apparently because they can find no place in the world for the qualities of experience. What a functionalist must deny, however, is that the qualitative dimension of pains is what makes pains pains. A functionalist might grant that pains are invariably accompanied by feelings of certain sorts, just as rock stars are invariably accompanied by fans clamoring for mementos. But what makes a given state a state of pain is not what it is like for the creature in the state, but its causal role in the creature's psychological economy.

## Zombies

One apparent upshot of a view of this sort is that it might be possible for a creature to be in pain, yet experience none of the qualitative "feels" that so occupy us when we are in pain. Let us be clear about the case. In imagining a creature that satisfies the functionalist's conception of pain, yet lacks qualitative "feels," we are not imagining a creature anesthetized. An anesthetized creature is not in pain on anyone's view. We are rather imagining a creature who behaves just as we do when we are in pain. The creature complains, takes steps to alleviate the pain, and appears to be suffering just as we would. The causal connections, hence appropriate pain behavior, are all present. What is missing is the inner side of pain, the qualitative side.

You might doubt that there could be such creatures. The idea, however, is not that creatures of the kind in question – "zombies" – are possible given the laws of nature. Is it possible that pigs could fly? Well, not given the laws of nature. But (it is often said) the laws of nature are contingent: they could have been different. And if we allow that the laws of nature could have been different, then, we can allow that the world could have been such that pigs fly. And similarly, those who regard the zombie possibility as a live one declare, zombies are possible given differences in the laws of nature.

Why should we care about such a bizarre possibility? Well, the mere possibility of zombies seems to imply that conscious qualities are not essential to minds – or, at any rate, they are not essential if functionalism is correct. Zombies satisfy all the functionalist criteria for possessing a full complement of states of mind. Yet zombies lack anything like the qualitative "feel" that permeates our conscious experiences. It follows that you could have been just as you are now with your full complement of psychological states (including the belief that you are not a zombie!), your same psychology, and yet have altogether lacked conscious experience. Were that so, you would inhabit a world undetectably different from the actual world from the outside, but, from the inside, dramatically different – a world without an inside.

Some critics of functionalism regard the zombie possibility as sufficient grounds for rejecting functionalism. Such critics take the qualitative aspect of our mental lives to be central and essential to what it means to possess a mind. How, they ask, can functionalists seriously contend that a creature could be in pain, yet utterly lack anything resembling what we regard as the conscious feeling of pain?

One functionalist response to the zombie story is simply to contend that, despite appearances, zombies are not in fact possible. The kind of complex functional organization required for a creature to be in pain would not be possible unless the creature underwent conscious experiences with the kinds of experiential qualities that are salient when we are in pain. To be in pain is not merely to produce appropriate pain behavior under the right circumstances. It is, as well, to form beliefs that one is in pain, that the pain has certain qualities (it is dull, or sharp, or stinging). A creature capable of experiencing pain is capable as well of picturing pain and empathizing with other creatures. And all these activities – reflecting on one's pain, picturing the pain of another – would seem out of reach for zombies. If that is so, then zombies would differ from us functionally, and there would be no compulsion to regard them as possessing minds.

Other functionalists have thought that a response of this sort is not in keeping with the spirit of functionalism. Functionalism reduces mental properties to causal powers. If qualia – the qualitative dimension of conscious experiences – resist reduction, we are faced with a choice. Either we reject functionalism, or we bite the bullet and accept that conscious qualities are not, after all, essential to states of mind.

## Biting the bullet

Perhaps consciousness in all its qualitative splendor is a natural, although strictly inessential, accompaniment of mental goings-on. The laws of nature guarantee that any creature like us in material composition and organization will be like us with respect to conscious experience. (David Chalmers goes further, contending that our laws of nature guarantee that anything like us functionally, irrespective of its material composition, must be like us with respect to conscious qualities.) But there is no deeper necessity in the connection between the qualities of conscious experience and the properties of material systems. There could be a world, precisely resembling ours in every material detail, but entirely empty of consciousness. A world of this sort, a zombie world, would, if functionalism is correct, be a world in which agents have beliefs, desires, pains, and emotions. It is just that, in the zombie world, these familiar states of mind lack the inner, qualitative dimension they happen to exhibit in our world.

If, like me, you find talk of alternative worlds off-putting, consider the implications of functionalism for the actual world. According to the functionalist, minds are complex arrangements of functional states, states that bear the right kinds of causal relation to one another and to inputs and outputs. Now, it would seem that we could create a system that satisfied this requirement, and so, on functionalist criteria, a mind, while lacking conscious experiences.

Ned Block is the source of a much-debated thought experiment designed to bring home this possibility. Imagine the population of China linked together and to the outside world by telephones, and organized in a way that corresponds to the way that, according to functionalists, a human mind is organized. A functionalist seems obliged to say that this system is a mind: that it perceives, has beliefs and pains, and perhaps that it is conscious. But this strikes most people as wildly implausible. The individuals making up the system are conscious, certainly, but not the system as a whole.

A functionalist might try denying that the population of China could be organized in a way that mirrors the organization of the human mind. If, however, all there is to the mind is an appropriate functional arrangement, then it is hard to see what could motivate this denial. If the population of China is inadequate, include the population of the entire planet, or the insect population, or the cells making up your digestive tract. Providing these are arranged in the right way, providing they satisfy a system of the sort illustrated in figure 4.3, they must count as minds (and perhaps even conscious minds). Fanciful examples are not required. It would not be especially surprising if the so-called "brain in the gut," or even the auto-nomic nervous system (that portion of the nervous system dedicated to the control of non-voluntary bodily functions like respiration, heart rate, and body temperature), matched a significant portion of the functional organization of the mind – if not the mind of an adult human being, then the mind of an infant or the mind of some non-human creature.

Functionalists can bite the bullet here, and simply accept this con-sequence as one counterintuitive result of an otherwise plausible theory. If you are not already committed to functionalism, however, you may find this a compelling reason to conclude that functionalists have missed the boat.

## Dispensing with qualia

Perhaps a more satisfying functionalist response is available. Imagine that you are now looking at a nearby fir tree. You are, we may suppose, under-going a conscious visual experience of the tree. What are the qualities of this conscious experience? As we noted in chapter three, it is a mistake to confuse qualities of an object you perceive with qualities of your perceiv-ing. The tree is forty feet tall and green. Your perceptual experience of the tree is neither. Indeed, as we have had occasion to note already, it is dif-ficult to say with any precision what the qualities of your perceptual experience of the tree might be.

Seizing on the point, a functionalist might contend that experiences themselves lack qualities of their own, qualities identifiable independently of the qualities of objects experienced. Or, more cautiously, although an experience might have qualities, these are not qualities we are in any sense aware of in undergoing the experience. If your experiences are realized in your brain, then the qualities of your experience will be neurological qualities. Such qualities pose no special problem for functionalism.

Let us take a slightly different tack, however. Suppose that the qualities available to us in conscious experiences – qualia, so-called – are just those qualities we represent objects as having. These are to be distinguished from qualities of representations. My representation of a fir tree two paragraphs ago is a representation of something tall and green, but the representation is neither tall nor green. The representation has qualities, but not these qualities. Representations of the very same object – representations of something tall and green – can have endless different qualities depending on the medium of representation. I represent the tree by using a printer to inscribe sentences on white paper with black ink. A painter represents it by means of colored paints on canvas. And an electronically inclined designer might represent it by creating a pattern of colored pixels on a computer screen. Although each of these depictions represents a fir tree, each differs in its intrinsic qualities from the others.

Suppose we agree with the functionalist that experiencing a tree is a matter of representing the tree mentally. In visually experiencing a tree, you represent the tree as having various visually detectable qualities. Your representation has, as well, certain intrinsic qualities of its own. These will be qualities of the neurological processes in which your representation is realized. It is a safe bet that you know nothing of these qualities. Certainly you know nothing of them solely on the basis of your visual experience of the tree. But now consider the qualities we represent the tree as having. Perhaps these qualities – or rather our representations of them – are enough to satisfy those who harp on qualia. If so, we have uncovered a way of reconciling what are misleadingly called "qualities of conscious experience" and functionalism. Qualities of experiences themselves, the functionalist contends, are not present in ordinary awareness. But that is no loss, that poses no problem for functionalism. Your becoming aware of the qualities of an experience would require that you experience your experience – by observing the operation of your surgically exposed brain in a mirror, for instance.

What of those qualities that seem purely mental, qualities that seem to have no place in the material world? Suppose that your dreaming that you are watching a greenish alien or your hallucinating a greenish alien is a matter of your representing the presence of a greenish alien. Your representation itself is not greenish – any more than the words on this page that represent the alien are greenish. Indeed, in these cases, nothing at all need be greenish. Greenishness drops out of the picture. Now think of your experience of a throbbing pain in your left big toe. Your having this experience is (we are supposing) a matter of your representing a throbbing, aversive occurrence in your big toe. As we noted in chapter two, the experience – the representing – need not itself be in your big toe. If you are tempted by functionalism, you will locate it – or its realizer – in your brain. Further, although in the normal case your experience of a pain in your toe will be an experience of an actual physiological occurrence in your toe, it need not be. This would be so if your experience were hallucinatory, or if you were suffering a "phantom pain."

What of the throbbing quality? It seems unlikely that this is a quality of anything in your toe. When we examine the toe, we do not discover anything throbbing. Is the throbbing a quality of your experience, then? This too seems unlikely. When we cut open your brain, no throbbing qualities are discovered. Perhaps the throbbing is like the greenishness we represent the alien as having. It is not a quality possessed by anything. We represent certain occurrences as throbbing, but nothing in fact throbs. If functionalism dispenses with such qualities, then, it is not dispensing with anything we should miss. These are qualities we represent objects as having, but it does not follow that anything actually has them – any more than, from the fact that we can represent mermaids, it follows that mermaids exist. What anti-functionalism describes as qualities of conscious experiences – qualia – are qualities of nothing at all. They are rather qualities we mistakenly represent objects and occurrences as having.

Opponents of functionalism regard this line of argument as a kind of sleight of hand. We can accept the distinction between qualities of experiences and qualities experienced objects are represented as having. It is much less obvious, however, that the qualities of our experiences are not available to us except in the indirect way envisaged earlier – via observations of our own brains. Accepting for the moment that experiences are representational, a veridical visual experience of a tomato, a visual hallucination of a tomato, and a visual image of a tomato are alike representationally: they all represent a tomato. But they surely seem to be alike qualitatively as well. Hallucinating a tomato, for instance, resembles – qualitatively – visually perceiving a tomato. And the qualitative similarity between imagining and perceiving a tomato is what gives imagery its point.

A functionalist might respond that the similarities in question are all intra-representational. Your visual perception of a tomato, your hallucination of a tomato, and your tomato imagery all include similar representations – representations of a tomato. But this is not enough. A painting and a written description of a tomato both represent a tomato. They do so in very different ways, however; they involve qualitatively different representational modes. Hallucination and imagery resemble ordinary perception not merely representationally but also, and crucially, qualitatively. Or so it seems.

## The mystery of consciousness

One catch-all functionalist response to worries of this sort is to point out that consciousness is deeply mysterious on anyone's view. We have no idea how to accommodate consciousness to the material world, no idea how to explain the phenomenon of consciousness. That being the case, we are in no position to tar functionalism with what appear to be its implausible consequences. Until we have a better idea of the roots of consciousness, who is to say what is or is not implausible?

If we hope to venture an informed opinion on such topics, we shall need a firmer grasp on the metaphysical issues that underlie the debate. Before delving further into metaphysics, however, let us examine an alternative approach to minds and their contents, an approach that focuses on the practice of ascribing states of mind to agents. This practice, it is argued, is warranted by the fact that it enables us to make sense of one another. Agents possess minds if we can find a place for them within a particular kind of interpretive scheme. And this, in the end, is all there is to possessing a mind. Approaches of this kind will occupy us in chapter five.

## Suggested reading

John Haugeland provides an excellent introduction to computers and computation in *Artificial Intelligence: The Very Idea* (1985). Ned Block's "What is Functionalism" (1980b) provides an indispensable introduction to functionalism. See also Sydney Shoemaker's "Some Varieties of Functionalism" (1981) and William Lycan's *Consciousness* (1987).

D. M. Armstrong and David Lewis have both advocated versions of functionalism according to which functional properties are identified with their realizers. See Armstrong's *A Materialist Theory of Mind* (1968); and see Lewis's "An Argument for the Identity Theory" (1966), and "Mad Pain and Martian Pain" (1980). I have not discussed the Armstrong–Lewis brand of functionalism in part to keep the discussion as simple as possible, and in part because few functionalists have embraced it. The essays by Block and Shoemaker mentioned above discuss Armstrong–Lewis style functionalism and argue that it is defective. For a reply, see Lewis's "Reduction of Mind" (1994).

The holistic strategy for characterizing states of mind, to which most functionalists are beholden (and which is illustrated in figure 4.2) is spelled out by Lewis in "Psychophysical and Theoretical Identifications" (1972).

The foremost proponent of the Representational Theory of Mind (and the language of thought) is Jerry Fodor. See *The Language of Thought* (1975). See also Kim Sterelny, *The Representational Theory of Mind: An Introduction* (1990). John Haugeland discusses the notion of a semantic engine in "Semantic Engines: An Introduction to Mind Design" (1981b).

Searle's discussion of the Chinese Room originally appeared in "Minds, Brains, and Programs" (1980). Alan Turing's appeal to the Imitation Game to explicate the concept of intelligence can be found in "Computing Machinery and Intelligence" (1950). A convenient summary of the Turing Test can be found in Haugeland, *Artificial Intelligence: The Very Idea* (1985), pp. 6–9.

Fodor sketches a reasonably accessible account of the semantics of the language of thought in his *Psychosemantics* (1988). A more recent version of the same story is told in *The Elm and the Expert: Mentalese and its Semantics* (1994). Accounts of the semantics of interior states that attempt the same thing in different ways can be found in Fred Dretske, *Explaining Behavior: Reasons in a World of Causes* (1988); and in Ruth Millikan, *Language, Thought, and Other Biological Categories: New Foundations for Realism* (1984); see, as well, Millikan's "Biosemantics" (1989). Fodor discusses laws, properties, and the special sciences in both the volumes mentioned above.

The best-known discussion of the ineliminability of the "what it's like" question is Thomas Nagel's much-cited "What is it Like to be a Bat?" (1974). Nagel's concerns applied to functionalism have yielded complex debates over the status of "qualia," the qualities of conscious experiences.

Ned Block's Chinese nation case appears in his "Troubles with Functionalism" (1978). Sydney Shoemaker defends functionalism from the "qualia" threat in "Functionalism and Qualia" (1975). See also "Absent Qualia are Impossible – A Reply to Block" (1984b). A different line of response to Block can be found in Lycan's *Consciousness* (1987), chaps 4 and 5. The functionalist account of qualia discussed in this chapter is a hybrid of views advanced by Gilbert Harman, "The Intrinsic Quality of Experience" (1990) and Fred Dretske, *Naturalizing the Mind* (1995), chap. 3.

Zombies, in the special sense associated with functionalism, are the invention of Robert Kirk. See his "Zombies vs. Materialists" (1974). Kirk's more recent views on the subject are spelled out in *Raw Feeling* (1996), especially chap. 3. The philosopher most impressed by zombies is David Chalmers. Chalmers, in a much-discussed book, argues that zombies, though "nomologically impossible," are logically possible, and so make consciousness deeply mysterious; see *The Conscious Mind: In Search of a Fundamental Theory* (1996), especially §II, "The Irreducibility of Consciousness."

For an accessible account of the "brain in the gut" by a journalist, see Sandra Blakeslee's "The Brain in the Gut" (1996). The live possibility that the autonomic nervous system satisfies functionalist criteria for the mental is eloquently defended in D. T. Ryder's "Evaluating Theories of Consciousness Using the Autonomic Nervous System for Comparison" (1996).

# CHAPTER 5
# Interpretational theories of mind and eliminativism

# Interpretational theories of mind and eliminativism

pproaches to the mind we have considered thus far are "realist" in character. All assume that minds and their contents are real features of the world standing alongside tables, stones, and electrons. It is possible, however, to regard minds as constructs. To ascribe thoughts to agents, on such a conception, would be like ascribing a latitude and longitude to a place on the surface of the Earth. We should err in imagining that latitudes and longitudes are kinds of entity, however, components of the world resembling rivers, canyons, and mountain ranges. A child looking at a globe who mistakes the equator for a feature on the Earth's surface would be confusing a characteristic of our descriptive apparatus for a characteristic of the planet.

Now, it might seem hard to believe that anyone could be tempted to suppose that minds are like co-ordinate systems. After all, we seem intimately acquainted with our own minds, and this acquaintance appears not to be a matter of our imposing any co-ordinate-like system on ourselves. Further, and perhaps more seriously, it is hard to see how any such theory could possibly work. Suppose, for a moment that ascribing states of mind resembles the imposition of a co-ordinate system on a region of space. This imposing is something we do, something that evidently depends on our having thoughts, intentions, and a broad range of distinct states of mind. But this suggests that every mind would depend for its existence on a pre-existing mind. If being a mind depends on the imposition of a co-ordinate-like system, then this pre-existing mind, too, must depend for its existence on some further mind. And we are thus led to a regress of minds, each depending on the prior existence of some distinct mind.

Let us bracket this regress worry for the moment, however, and look in more detail at attempts to make out what I shall label "interpretive" accounts of the mind. Once we are clear on what such accounts amount to, we shall be in a position to evaluate the seriousness of the envisaged regress. My plan is to look at the work of two widely influential philosophers, Donald Davidson and Daniel Dennett, both of whom offer interpretive conceptions of mind. We shall see that the issues are less straightforward than my sketch of the regress problem above might suggest.

# Davidson and the propositional attitudes

Davidson's focus is exclusively on what philosophers call the propositional attitudes: beliefs, desires, hopes, fears, intentions, and the like, insofar as these are taken to have "propositional content." Davidson is silent on the nature of sensation and imagery, for instance. Because Davidson's work has done much to set the agenda in the philosophy of mind, some philosophers have embraced the view that minds are to be understood solely as congeries of propositional attitudes. Other facets of our mentality are taken to be analyzable in terms of the propositional attitudes or ignored. None of this is part of Davidson's program, however. Indeed, as I shall try to show, that program is unthinkable in the absence of a host of "nonpropositional" states of mind.

Let us set to one side such considerations and explore Davidson's account of the propositional attitudes on its own terms. As a first step, consider the traditional conception of a propositional attitude. Your having a belief, the belief that it will rain, for instance, is a matter of your taking up a particular sort of attitude – belief or acceptance – toward a particular proposition – the proposition that it will rain. You might harbor the same attitude toward a distinct proposition, in which case you have a different belief; or you might have some other attitude toward the same proposition: you might believe, desire, hope, fear, or, if you are a rain-maker, intend that it will rain.

I know of no simple way to characterize propositions. At an intuitive level, we might distinguish propositions from sentences. Thus, the sentences below could be said to express the same proposition.

> It's raining.
> Il pleut.
> Es regnet.

So considered, propositions are "abstract entities." In this regard they resemble numbers – as distinct from numerals, labels we use (like "five," "cinq," "5," and "v") to designate numbers. Philosophers have also identified propositions with a variety of other exotica, including sets of possible worlds and states of affairs. Some philosophers who speak of the propositional attitudes, including Davidson, contend that talk about propositions can be rephrased and replaced by talk about something else. For purposes of discussion here, the notion of a proposition can be left at an intuitive level: a proposition is what a sentence expresses. (For the record: anyone who takes propositions to be abstract entities owes the rest of us an account of how human beings could interact with such things.)

## Semantic opacity

One notable feature of the propositional attitudes is their fine-grainedness or definiteness. Your believing that Socrates is wise differs from your believing that the husband of Xanthippi is wise, even though Socrates is the husband of Xanthippi. Beliefs inherit this feature – "intensionality" (spelled with an "s") – from the propositions: the proposition that Socrates is wise differs from the proposition that the husband of Xanthippi is wise. You may believe that Socrates is wise, but never having heard of Xanthippi, fail to believe that the husband of Xanthippi is wise – or even that the husband of Xanthippi is not wise. The (somewhat technical) point here is that belief and the other propositional attitudes possess "semantic opacity." A capacity for belief includes a capacity for thoughts that differ, not merely in what they represent, but also in how they represent.

Davidson contends that any account of belief must honor semantic opacity. This means that it could make sense to ascribe beliefs to a creature only when it makes sense to suppose that the creature in question has a capacity to represent states of affairs in different ways. Does the neighbor's dog, Spot, have such a capacity? Can we sensibly suppose that Spot can, as we can, represent his master or his food dish in different ways? Or are representations we are inclined to ascribe to Spot "semantically transparent," are they merely simple devices for pointing at the world?

Such questions raise a host of issues that we shall need to set aside for the moment. Looking ahead, I shall simply note that, on Davidson's view, there is an intimate connection between the capacity to use a fully-fledged language and a capacity for what I have called representing the world in different ways. If Davidson is right, then only creatures capable of language are capable of thought. You may find this consequence unpalatable. Surely Spot has beliefs! Surely prelinguistic infant human beings think! If this is your response, then you should carefully evaluate Davidson's approach to the topic and consider where you think he goes wrong.

## Radical interpretation: background issues

According to Davidson, an understanding of beliefs, desires, intentions, or any other propositional attitude, must include a grasp of what is required for the interpretation of speech. Think of what might be involved in your understanding what I say when I utter some sentence. If you and I share a language, then you interpret my utterance unthinkingly and automatically. Nevertheless, your capacity to understand what I say, as opposed to merely hearing my utterance as patterns of sounds, as an infant might, includes a complex ability, one not shared by those unfamiliar with our language. We can think of this ability as the possession of a technique, a collection of principles that allow you to associate a meaning with each of my utterances.

Before venturing further, I should note that, in speaking of "meaning" here, I am speaking of what, for lack of a better term, might be called "literal meaning." We can distinguish literal meaning from "speaker meaning." The distinction is illustrated by a case in which I utter "The grass needs cutting," meaning that I want you to cut the grass. The literal meaning of my utterance is that the grass needs cutting. In uttering this sentence, however, I mean for you – by way of your understanding of the sentence's literal meaning – to recognize that I want you to cut the grass. You understand the literal meaning of my utterances when you understand the sentences I utter. Whether you understand what I might hope to accomplish in uttering those sentences, what I might be driving at, or whether you have a grasp of the "deeper" meaning, if any, I might have in mind is a different matter.

Let us focus for a moment on simple declarative sentences. Declarative sentences ("The grass needs cutting") are to be distinguished from interrogative sentences ("Does the grass need cutting?"), imperative sentences ("Cut the grass!"), and the like. A long tradition has it that declarative sentences are fundamental, at least in the sense that our understanding of any sentence depends on our understanding of its declarative root. Now consider what it is to understand a declarative sentence, to understand what such a sentence says. One possibility is that you understand what a sentence says when you understand its "truth-conditions": what is the case if the sentence is true (and what is the case if it is not true). The notion of a truth-condition is intended to correspond to what I earlier called "literal meaning."

How does any of this help? Well, we are looking for an accounting of what is involved in your understanding my utterances. At the very least this would seem to include your being able to associate a truth-condition with sentences I produce. According to Davidson, this ability is constituted by your possession of a "theory of truth" – what I shall call a "*T*-theory" –

for those utterances. A *T*-theory, a theory of truth, is not, despite its name, a theory about the nature of truth. *T*-theories assign truth-conditions to sentences a speaker utters or might utter. Far from explicating truth, such theories presuppose a prior grasp of the concept of truth. You are in a position to deploy a *T*-theory only if you already understand what it is for sentences to be true (or fail to be true).

*T*-theories are modeled on theories of truth devised by Alfred Tarski for "formal languages" of the sort deployed by logicians. If you have studied logic or computer programming, you have encountered examples of formal languages. A *T*-theory generates, by means of finite sets of rules, a "*T*-sentence" for every sentence in the language. *T*-sentences have the form

(T)  *S* is true if and only if *p*,

where *S* is a description of a sentence uttered (or one that might be uttered), and *p* expresses that sentence's truth-conditions.

You might think that such a procedure would be hopelessly crude. Consider the sentences below:

Jocasta is running.
Oedipus's mother is running.

"Jocasta" and "Oedipus's mother" are co-referring, so these sentences have the same truth-conditions. They do not, however, have the same meaning. How then could we hope to use a theory that focuses on truth-conditions to make clear what we do when we interpret – that is, understand – the meanings of utterances?

The gap between what we ordinarily regard as a sentence's meaning and the conditions under which it is true is narrowed, however, when we recognize that a theory of truth yields truth-conditions systematically for every sentence in a language. Natural languages encompass an infinite number of sentences, and theories of truth are finite. As a result, a theory of truth must make use of the compositional structure of language. Sentences are made up of elements – words – that appear in other sentences. The truth-conditions (or meanings) of sentences depend on these elements and their arrangement. If it is possible to give a Tarski-style truth theory for a natural language (a big *if*), *T*-sentences implied by that theory should mirror, or at least approximate, native speakers' judgments about meaning.

These cryptic remarks should become clearer when we look at examples of *T*-sentences. We shall discover that the *T*-sentences – sentences that specify the truth-conditions – for "Jocasta is running" and for "Oedipus's mother is running" are different. The moral: a *T*-theory does more than merely associate sentences and truth-conditions; it does so in a way that distinguishes sentences that differ in meaning yet are true or untrue under the same circumstances. This result is assured by the requirement that *T*-theories incorporate finite sets of rules.

What is the significance of this talk of "finite sets of rules"? The formal languages deployed by logicians, as well as natural languages like French, Urdu, and English, include an infinity of sentences. We who use these languages, however, are finite beings. This suggests that whatever our understanding of a language comes to, it cannot merely be that we have learned to associate a particular meaning or truth-condition with every sentence. It appears, rather, that we learn the elements of our language together with a relatively small set of principles for combining these elements into meaningful sentences. Your understanding of the words "tiger" and "warble," together with your grasp of rules for combining these words, enables you to understand the sentence "Tigers warble," although it is most unlikely that you have encountered this sentence before.

The rules at issue here are not rules you consciously entertain or apply. In this respect they resemble rules you learn when you learn to play a game by playing it. We learn the rules of checkers and tic-tac-toe this way. Although we may be competent at both these games, most of us would be hard-pressed to spell out the rules we follow when we play them. You can get a sense for their complexity by trying to imagine programming a computing machine to play checkers or tic-tac-toe. In doing so, you would be obliged to make the rules utterly explicit.

The idea, then, is that we can provide an account of what is included in your understanding my utterances, if we can make explicit a finite collection of rules that associate a meaning or a truth-condition with each sentence I might utter. One implication of a view of this sort is that understanding a sentence in a language requires understanding the whole language. If this seems implausible, consider: there is something puzzling about the notion that someone could understand the sentences "Birds warble" and "Tigers growl," and yet have no idea what the sentence "Tigers warble" means.

Think of a word as analogous to a chess piece. You grasp the significance of a chess piece – a rook, for instance – when you understand all the moves it can and cannot make. Similarly, to understand a word is to understand its role in sentences, the contribution it makes to the meaning of sentences in which it occurs. If understanding a sentence requires understanding the words that make it up, and an understanding of those words requires understanding their role in all the sentences, then understanding the elements of a language must include understanding the whole language – the language made up of those elements.

But wait. Surely someone could understand the French sentence "Il pleut" ("It's raining"), without understanding other French sentences.

The issues here are delicate, and a satisfactory resolution of them would take us far afield. The idea, however, is that you can understand an utterance of "Il pleut" without understanding other French sentences only because you can be confident that this sentence bears a relation to the speaker's actual and potential utterances that mirrors the relation borne by the sentence "It's raining" to sentences of English. Your confidence is based on collateral information you possess concerning human beings and their use of language. Note, however, that you could be wrong in this case. The person uttering "Il pleut" might not be speaking French at all, but some other language containing a sentence that sounds like the French sentence, but means something altogether different.

One way to factor out extraneous information and thus to see what is involved in understanding utterances is to imagine that you are in the position of interpreting the utterances of a speaker whose language is entirely unfamiliar to you. All you have to go on are the speaker's utterances, the context in which they are uttered, and the speaker's non-linguistic behavior – his gestures, the direction of his gaze, and the like. And we could say that an account of what is included in anyone's understanding of any utterance must appeal only to resources available to such a "radical interpreter." To move beyond these is to assume part of what it is we are trying to explain. This, at any rate, is Davidson's idea.

## *T*-theories

When you understand a particular utterance, according to Davidson, you associate that utterance with a truth-condition. Suppose you understand an utterance of "Il pleut." Your understanding amounts to your recognizing that the sentence uttered is true if it is raining, and false otherwise. And this is reflected in the "*T*-sentence"

   ($T_o$) "Il pleut" is true if and only if it's raining,

which is an instance of the schema introduced earlier:

   ($T$) $S$ is true if and only if $p$.

Again, $S$ is a description of a sentence uttered (or a possible utterance), and $p$ is an expression of $S$'s truth-conditions.

We must distinguish the language in which *T*-sentences are formulated (your language), from the language you are interpreting. Philosophers call the latter the "object language" and the language you an interpreter use the "metalanguage." If you speak English, and you are interpreting utterances produced by a French speaker, then English is the metalanguage, and French is the object language. If we imagine your French respondent interpreting you, then, for that interpretation, French is the metalanguage, and English the object language.

Suppose, now, that you and I are both speakers of English. I utter a sentence, "It's raining," and you understand my utterance. In what sense do you need to interpret me? If we share a language, and if we know this, then your understanding my utterances will, on the whole, amount to your taking those utterances at face value. (On the whole, but not always. I may misspeak, or use words slightly differently than you do. You might discover, for instance, that in uttering "She's intolerant" I meant that she is intolerable.) In this case the metalanguage and the object language coincide. When this is so, the truth-conditions of a sentence uttered can be specified by using the sentence itself. If, for instance, you advance a T-theory in English for utterances I, a fellow speaker of English, produce, you might express the truth-conditions for my utterance of "Tigers are striped" by using that very sentence:

$(T_1)$  "Tigers are striped" (uttered by J. H.) is true if and only if tigers are striped.

In this case, T-sentences will consist of a sentence inside quotation marks, followed by "is true if and only if" followed by the sentence itself, "disquoted."

Do not be put off by the apparent triviality of $(T_1)$. A T-theory must include resources for generating every sentence of the language to which it applies. Your knowing the truth-conditions of some sentence involves your having mastered (albeit quite unselfconsciously) a theory that implies a theorem of the form $(T)$, a T-sentence, for that sentence. Such a theory implies indefinitely many T-sentences, however. You understand my utterance of a particular sentence only if you are in a position to understand my utterance of indefinitely many sentences. On this view, your appreciating the meaning of a sentence requires not only that you appreciate the meanings of many sentences, but also that you grasp systematic relations among sentences of the sort captured by rules used to generate T-sentences.

## From T-theories to I-theories

Davidson contends that to interpret my speech you must be in a position to associate meanings or truth-conditions with my actual and possible utterances, and to do so systematically. But this is possible, he thinks, only

if you are simultaneously in a position to decipher my propositional attitudes: my beliefs, desires, and intentions. I utter a sentence with a particular intention – to inform, to deceive, to amuse, to threaten – because of
what I believe, what I take the sentence to mean, and what I hope to
accomplish in uttering it. A theory of interpretation, what I shall call an
"*I*-theory," provides an accounting of all these attitudes at once. To understand my speech you must understand what I believe and desire; and a
grasp of my beliefs and desires requires that you understand my utterances.[1] How might it be possible to break into this circle?

Davidson's suggestion is that interpretation depends on the primitive
attitude of "holding true" applied to sentences. (Here, and in what follows,
sentences are taken to be sentences uttered on particular occasions, utterances, or potential utterances.) Without prior knowledge of my language
or my beliefs and desires, you might ascertain that I hold a particular
sentence true. This does not presuppose that you know what I mean in
uttering this sentence, or what I believe. For this reason, your discovery
that I hold some sentence true can constitute evidence for any hypothesis
you might venture as to what I mean and what I believe. I will hold true
the sentence "Tigers are striped" just in case I believe that tigers are
striped, and I take the sentence to mean (or to be true if and only if) tigers
are striped. In interpreting my speech, then, you begin with guesses about
what I believe and what my utterances mean, and check these guesses
against sentences you take me to hold true.

Think of sentences held true as vectors, the products of two forces:
beliefs and meanings (figure 5.1). Suppose, for instance, I hold true the
sentence "Pythagoras is peculiar." I do so because of what I believe (among
other things, that Pythagoras is peculiar) and what I take the sentence
"Pythagoras is peculiar" to mean (namely, that Pythagoras is peculiar).
(See figure 5.2.)

*Pace* some theorists, this does not imply that, if you are to interpret me,
I must be truthful. You might, for instance, discover that, for any sentence,
$p$, in general I hold true not-$p$ when I utter $p$. In this respect, it is useful to
distinguish the philosopher W. V. Quine's notion of "assent" to sentences
from the attitude of holding true; we can and do assent to what we do not

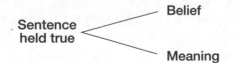

Figure 5.1

---

[1] One consequence of such a view (foreshadowed earlier) is that only creatures capable of
linguistic utterances could be subjects of propositional attitude ascriptions: thought
requires talk.

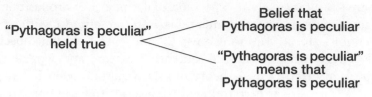

Figure 5.2

hold true. So long as you have some way of discovering what sentences I hold true, you have a way of testing hypotheses about what my utterances mean – in conjunction with what I believe. (If this strikes you as an impossible task, think of puzzles in which you are required to interrogate informants, some of whom tell the truth and some of whom are chronic liars, in order to discover the answer to some question.)

The envisaged interpretive technique is based on an insight afforded by decision theory. Decision theory provides a formal account of choice or preference in terms of probabilities and utilities. The guiding idea is that an agent's preference for one course of action over one or more competitors depends on the relative desirability (for the agent) of the actions' outcomes and the probabilities associated (by the agent) with these outcomes (figure 5.3).

You must choose between going to the movies or taking a hike. The outcomes of these choices could have different values or utilities for you, and these values or utilities may be affected by a variety of possible circumstances. You might enjoy hiking more than the movies, for instance, but not if it rains. Your overall preference is determined by the relative utility or desirability of outcomes weighted by their probability. If the chance of rain is small, you opt for the hike; otherwise you choose the movies.

Probabilities and utilities are expressible numerically, and decision theory can be given a precise formal characterization. One consequence of the theory is that, given an agent's preferences for various courses of action, it is possible to derive a unique assignment of probabilities and utilities for that agent. This makes it appear that decision theory is a straightforward empirical theory: we hypothesize probabilities and utilities – beliefs and desires – and test our hypothesis by noting agents' preferences.

The appearance is misleading. Decision theory might be thought of as

Figure 5.3

providing a framework within which we can depict important structural features of human decision making. In this respect it resembles co ordinate systems or familiar systems of measurement – about which I shall have more to say presently. For the moment, I shall note only that, on Davidson's view, a theory of interpretation, an *I*-theory, includes two components: (1) a Tarski-style theory of truth, a *T*-theory, and (2) a decision theory. Evidence for a theory of interpretation consists of agents' attitudes toward sentences uttered, most particularly the attitude of holding true. Just as in the case of orthodox decision theory, agents' beliefs and desires (construed as probabilities and utilities) are taken to determine their preferences, on a theory of interpretation, agents' beliefs, desires, and meanings (truth-conditions associated with sentences) are taken to determine what sentences those agents hold true. In interpreting me, you in effect advance a theory that ascribes to me a universe of beliefs, desires, and meanings, and is constrained by sentences you take me to hold true.

## Charity and indeterminacy

The *I*-theory you develop assigns "contents" simultaneously to my utterances and to my propositional attitudes. You can adjust for apparently anomalous utterances by supposing that you are wrong about what I mean, or that I have a desire to deceive you, for instance, or that I am being ironic, or by supposing that I harbor a false belief. This might suggest that an *I*-theory need answer only to a requirement of consistency: if your theory results in an implausible prediction as to what I hold true, you are free to adjust the theory – by changing what you take me to believe or mean – to secure a more acceptable prediction.

Imagine that you are taking me on a tour of London, we enter the City, and I remark "It's wonderful to see so many people in bowling hats." You are momentarily baffled: bowling hats? Then you realize I meant that it was odd to see so many people in bowler hats – bowlers. In so doing, you engage in a bit of radical interpretation. You have evidence that I hold true the sentence "It's wonderful to see so many people in bowling hats." What do I mean? Well, one possibility is that I believe we are surrounded by people wearing bowling hats and take "bowling hats" to mean bowling hats. Another possibility is that I mean by "bowling hats" (what you mean by) bowlers, and that I (in effect) believe that we are surrounded by people wearing bowlers. Either hypothesis is consistent with your evidence. Does this mean that both hypotheses are equally satisfactory?

Davidson does not think so. According to Davidson, propositional attitude ascriptions are governed by a Principle of Charity: you must count me right in most things. If you are attempting to discover what I believe and what my utterances mean, you cannot but suppose that my beliefs are largely true. Without this assumption, any consistent *I*-theory might be as good as any other. An *I*-theory must optimize the truth of my beliefs, then, while simultaneously making sense of my utterances.

In the present case, this means that you will interpret my talk of "bowling hats" as talk of bowlers. To do otherwise, to imagine, for instance that I mean by "bowling hat" just what you would mean by the term, would oblige you to suppose that I had a host of false beliefs, including the belief that bowlers are worn for bowling. Charity requires that you adjust your *I*-theory in a way that optimizes the truth of my beliefs.

Astute readers may have guessed that, even given the Principle of Charity, there is no guarantee that there is a unique theory of interpretation for any speaker. It is possible for there to be wildly divergent *I*-theories for a given speaker that are compatible with all actual and possible evidence. Suppose that you and a companion, working independently, construct *I*-theories for me. Both theories fit all the evidence either of you has or could have, both enable you to make sense of my utterances, and to converse with me on endless topics. On comparing notes, however, you discover that the two theories systematically assign different meanings to my utterances! In the extreme case, you interpret my utterance of a particular sentence as meaning "Tigers have stripes," and your companion interprets the same utterance as meaning "Tigers do not have stripes." What has gone wrong here? Which of you is right – if either is right? And how would you decide?

We are face to face with the notorious doctrine of the indeterminacy of interpretation. Quine, a forerunner of Davidson on these topics, has argued that every utterance is susceptible to endless, perfectly adequate, but incompatible interpretations – or "translations." (In discussing Quine, I shall speak as he does, not of interpretations but of translations. The distinction, although important, does not affect the present point.) These translations can be compatible with all a speaker says, or would say. You might think this means that it would be difficult or impossible for us to tell which of a pair of competing translations is right. But Quine's idea is more startling: all there is to what a speaker means is spelled out in a translation that fits everything a speaker says or would say. The possibility of competing but equally adequate translations shows that there is no further "fact of the matter" as to what speakers mean.

Quine distinguishes (what he calls) the "indeterminacy of meaning" from the kind of "underdetermination" we encounter in evaluating scientific theories. Two scientific theories can fit all the evidence, indeed all the evidence we can imagine, yet one theory can be correct, the other not. In science, theories purport to capture an independent reality. But, when it comes to meanings, Quine thinks, there is no independent reality, no reality beyond speaker's dispositions of the sort captured in systematic translations of their utterances. This does not imply that translations cannot be wrong. On the contrary, some translations may fail to mesh with actual and possible observations of agents' speech behavior. But every translation that does fit such observations can equally lay claim to capturing speakers' meaning.

Davidson agrees with Quine that indeterminacies of this sort are inevitable. He differs from Quine, however, in suggesting that indeterminacies that turn up in *I*-theories are entirely benign. Two equally charitable *I*-theories that are consistent with all an agent's preferences amount to no more than "notational variants" of one another. The situation resembles that in which temperature is assessed in Fahrenheit or Celsius. I say that water freezes at 32 °F, you contend that it freezes at 0 °C. Which assessment is correct? The question assumes what is false, namely that there is some definite feature of the world concerning which the two assessments might differ. Rather they are simply two ways of capturing the same fact. In this respect, Davidson's conception of radical interpretation is to be distinguished from Quine's conception of radical translation. Radical translation leaves open the prospect of more far-reaching substantive indeterminacies. The reasons for this are technical and need not concern us here. Our goal is to develop a feel for Davidson's special conception of mind.

## The omniscient interpreter

I have described Charity as mandating that we ascribe beliefs to agents so as to optimize the truth of those beliefs. In practice, this means that you ascribe beliefs to me in such a way that they come out mostly true by your lights: you make my beliefs consistent with your beliefs as nearly as possible. But now we confront an apparent difficulty. There is an obvious and important difference between what is true and what any finite agent believes to be true. Suppose that many – or most – of your beliefs were false. Then, your charitable interpretation of many of my beliefs would make my beliefs false as well.

Davidson argues, however, that this way of thinking about the matter misses an important feature of Charity. Consider your beliefs. The beliefs you actually have are those that would be ascribed to you by an interpreter who knew all there was to know about you and your circumstances, an interpreter in possession of all the evidence, an "omniscient interpreter." This is just to say that your beliefs must in fact be optimally true. And if your beliefs are of necessity optimally true, then there can be no deep difference between your ascribing beliefs to me in such a way that they are optimally consistent with yours and your ascribing beliefs to me in such a way that your ascription optimizes truth.

Could this possibly be right? Perhaps so long as we take seriously Davidson's perspective on belief ascription. The object of a particular belief – what that belief is a belief about – is, Davidson supposes, fixed in part by its cause. Your belief about a tree concerns a particular tree because it is caused by that tree. We ascribe beliefs, then, partly by reference to their causes. We can of course be wrong about these, we can misascribe beliefs. But it cannot be the case that an ascriber's beliefs are mostly false. They concern their causes, quite independently of what anyone, including the believer, takes these causes to be.[1] This is just a more prosaic way of saying that the beliefs you, as ascriber, possess are those that would be ascribed to you by an omniscient interpreter.

How plausible is it to imagine that beliefs concern their causes? It is surely possible for a bump on the head to cause me to believe that Napoleon died in battle. The cause of this belief is a bump on the head, yet my belief concerns, not the bump, but Napoleon.

It is central to Davidson's view, however, that beliefs, like meanings, cannot be ascribed singly. In ascribing a particular belief to me, you implicitly ascribe a world of other beliefs, those beliefs, namely, implied by the *I*-theory you invoke. It is this holistic edifice that must satisfy Charity and the demand that the objects of belief are fixed by their causes. A correct theory of interpretation can accommodate false belief against a background of largely true belief. All things considered, then, an *I*-theory that depicts me (on the basis of what I say and do) as having acquired a belief about Napoleon as a result of a bump on the head could easily be more charitable than a theory that ascribes to me a belief about a bump on the head.

## Interpretation and measurement

Consider what is involved in the explanation of a phenomenon or domain of phenomena. Explanation takes many forms. An explanation purports to make clear, or make sense of, or facilitate our grasp of something we hope to understand. One familiar sort of explanation is decompositional: we come to understand complex entities by seeing how their parts fit together and interact. You come to understand heat by recognizing that heating an object agitates its constituent molecules, and this agitation is transmitted to adjacent molecules – from the hot sand on the beach to the soles of your

---

[1] This way of putting it is slightly misleading. Every belief has endless causes. *The* cause of a belief, the cause that fixes its content, depends on which cause is, or would be, salient to an interpreter. This is one reason the interpreter is ineliminable in Davidson's theory.

feet. You grasp the operation of a clock, or a machine that wraps candy bars, or a cold front, or liquidity by discovering the mechanism responsible for the behavior of clocks, candy-wrapping machines, cold fronts, and liquid substances. In these cases you come to understand the mechanism by seeing how it works, how its parts interact with one another and with their surroundings to produce a particular kind of outcome. Mechanistic explanation of this sort is common in the sciences, and in engineering, medicine, and in everyday life.

Another sort of explanation, a sort much beloved in psychology and the philosophy of mind, is functional explanation. In giving a functional explanation, I abstract from physical details of a mechanism and consider it exclusively in terms of the causal roles of its constituents. We can describe the operation of a steam engine, or a computing machine, or the digestive tract of a human being without concern for the "physical implementation" or "realization" of these things.

A very different way of understanding a domain of objects is to devise a perspicuous description of the domain's structure. This can be accomplished by overlaying the domain with another domain whose structure is antecedently well understood. We employ calibrated yardsticks, pan balances, and thermometers in describing the lengths, weights, and temperatures of objects. Similarly, we comprehend the layout of the surface of our planet by imposing a co-ordinate structure on it. Once in place, this system of co-ordinates enables us to specify areas, distances, and the relative locations of objects and occurrences on the planet's surface. It enables us, as well, to offer certain sorts of prediction. If you know the velocity of an object moving across the surface of the planet and you know its location at a time, you can predict its location at some future time. If you know the location of an object and its distance and direction from another object, you can fix the location of the second object.

Co-ordinate systems represent a special case of measurement, the application of the domain of numbers to a domain of objects or properties. When we describe an object as 12 feet long or as weighing 110 pounds, what features of the object correspond to these numbers? The question is misleading. Ordinary physical objects in ordinary settings exhibit a relatively enduring structure that lends itself to description via well-understood systems of numbers. The structure of these descriptive systems, the relations among their elements, is crucial; the particular elements that make them up are in one respect arbitrary. We can express weights in pounds or kilograms, length in feet or meters. What is important is that the numbers we choose, and the axioms governing their combinations, exhibit an appropriate structure.

Consider again the use of a co-ordinate system in mapping the surface of the Earth. Your choice of a system is, in part, arbitrary. You might use a

Mercator projection or a spherical projection, for instance. Notice that a geographical region appearing in a Mercator projection can look very different from the same region represented in a spherical projection. I can recall being baffled as a child by the apparent difference in the relative size of Greenland on the globe in the front of my fourth grade classroom and on the large map on the wall above the blackboard. On the one, Greenland seemed to be only a little larger than Texas; on the other, it appeared nearly as big as the whole of North America. I wondered how large Greenland was really; both maps could not be right. (My teacher's explanation: the wall map was larger than the globe.) But of course both maps were right. My mistake was to compare objects on one map with objects on another without taking into account that the mapping systems, though "structurally isomorphic," were different.

The example provides a nice illustration of what, according to Davidson, indeterminacy of interpretation amounts to. Distinct I-theories might appear to ascribe different beliefs or meanings to an agent, yet each theory could be correct. It need not follow that there is no "fact of the matter" as to what the agent believes, however, any more than it follows from differences in maps of the sort illustrated above that there is no fact of the matter as to the relative size of Greenland. The appearance of mystery comes from comparing items across systems without taking into account the systems in which those items are embedded.

Let us say, then, that the structure and point of I-theories is analogous to that of co-ordinate systems. We know in advance that anything describable by means of such a system must have certain properties. In the case of a co-ordinate system, if one object, A, is to the northwest of B, and B is to the northwest of C, then A is to the northwest of C. Objects that fail to satisfy such conditions cannot usefully be represented in such systems and could not be said to have straightforward locations. In the case of an I-theory, if an agent prefers A to B and B to C, then the agent prefers A to C. Creatures who failed to satisfy this condition – not in the sense that they exhibit intransitive preferences, but in the sense that they fail to exhibit anything identifiable as an appropriately transitive repertoire of choices – would not satisfy an I-theory and could not be said to have straightforward preferences. (Preferences can change, of course, and so can the locations of objects. The simplifying assumption here is that we are considering only "time-slices" of domains: those domains at particular times.)

If we are to avoid confusion, we must distinguish internal constraints on an I-theory (or a co-ordinate system) and descriptions of agents (or geographical regions) in terms of the theory (or co-ordinate system). In deploying a co-ordinate system, you make use of a well-behaved geometrical structure, the features of which can be described quite independently of features of the world on which it is imposed. Similarly, in deploying an *I*-theory, we make use of a framework that can be characterized abstractly and independently of its applications. In applying co-ordinate systems or *I*-theories, we overlay one domain of objects with a structure that reveals structure in the target domain. The target domain itself exists independently, as do the objects and properties that make it up. Nevertheless our description of this domain reflects both those independent features and features of the co-ordinate system or *I*-theory in terms of which those features are described. And we must not mistake features of the one for features of the other. To do so would be like mistaking latitude and longitude lines on a map for physical features of the terrain. If Davidson is right, then imagining that talk of the propositional content of beliefs, desires, and intentions is talk about mechanistic components of agents is to make a mistake of this sort.

Consider a simple geographical truth, Milwaukee's being north of Chicago. This truth depends on the application and orientation of a co-ordinate system and on system-independent features of a particular region of our planet. Imagine now that you correctly ascribe the belief that tigers are striped to me. The truth of this ascription turns on the application of an *I*-theory and on theory-independent features of me, ultimately my dispositional makeup. On Davidson's view, I possess beliefs with settled propositional contents in something like the way cities possess locations. We do not imagine that locations have distinctive physical "realizations" (or that they are "multiply realizable"), nor are we tempted to suppose that if locations are not physical, they must be non-physical. The same holds for the propositional contents of beliefs, desires, and intentions.

We ascribe propositional attitudes to agents whose behavior (actual and potential) accords with those ascriptions. One possibility is that it so accords because the ascriptions, if correct, pick out components of a mechanism responsible for the behavior. (This is the kind of picture promoted by the Representational Theory of Mind. Beliefs and desires are sentences in the Language of Thought occupying "belief boxes" and "desire boxes.") But, if Davidson is right, there may be no need to suppose this. Propositional attitude ascriptions and the *I*-theories that license such ascriptions need not provide quasi-mechanistic explanations of behavior any more than talk of the location of a city or the direction in which it lies from some other city provides a geologically illuminating assessment of the terrain.

If this is so, then the kind of explanation of agents' intelligent behavior we obtain in reckoning their beliefs, desires, and intentions is not a functional, mechanical, or decompositional explanation, but one the success of which stems from its exposing and describing in a systematic way the structure of a complex phenomenon. Such explanations have predictive force, not because they reveal hidden mechanisms, but because they apply to potential utterances and deeds, as well as to actual utterances and deeds. More precisely: propositional attitude explanations illuminate, and thus partly explain, the structure of certain sorts of dispositional system. These explanations work, not because they pinpoint the gears and levers in the underlying mechanism or because they uncover an isomorphism between interpretive elements and components of the mechanism; they work because they reveal a structured system of dispositions describable by means of an antecedently well-understood domain, a domain plotted in theories of truth and decision theories.

Putting all of this together, we can say that, to the extent that we can be subjects of propositional attitude ascriptions, our behavior, or rather the dispositional basis of our behavior, accords with a particular sort of theory. Its so according yields a kind of explanation of it. The explanation is not mechanical, or decompositional, or functional, however; it differs in kind from such explanations. A mistake made by many philosophers of mind and by some psychologists is to imagine that an *I*-theory describes a mechanism, perhaps at a functional level, components of which correspond to elements of the theory.

## Mental causation and the propositional attitudes

A difficulty remains. On the view I have pegged to Davidson, explanations that appeal to the propositional attitudes are non-mechanistic. Such explanations illuminate human behavior by invoking a structure defined by an appropriate *I*-theory. But if this, or something like it, is right, it would seem to be at odds with another idea of Davidson's, the idea that reasons are causes: beliefs, desires, and intentions explain actions only insofar as they are causes of those actions.

Suppose your flipping the light switch is explained by your desire to illuminate the room together with your belief that by flipping the switch you will illuminate the room. Suppose, as well, that the success of an explanation of this sort does not depend on the identification of an internal mechanism responsible for your flipping the switch. Although the success of the explanation undoubtedly depends on your neurological condition (and on much else besides), its success need not depend on there being a simple correspondence between components of your explanation, particular propositional attitudes, and particular kinds of neural state or event. Even if the explanation is correct, then, this implies nothing about the character of the mechanisms responsible for your behavior – other than that they must be such that they are capable of producing behavior of this sort.

Still, the explanation includes an important causal ingredient. It is part of the explanatory framework invoked when we appeal to beliefs, desires, and intentions that an agent can have a reason, $R$, to perform a particular action (where a reason consists of a belief–desire pair), and perform the action for a reason, but not perform the action for reason $R$. In this case, $R$ does not account for the agent's behavior because it is not part of the agent's reason for doing what he does.

Imagine that you want to eat a healthy breakfast, and believe that you can eat a healthy breakfast by eating the steaming bowl of Brussels sprouts on the table in front of you. Suppose, in addition, that you want to learn self-discipline and believe that your eating a bowl of Brussels sprouts for breakfast will contribute to this end. In this case you might act in order to eat a healthy breakfast: you eat the bowl of Brussels sprouts because you want to eat a healthy breakfast, and not because you want to learn self-discipline. And it is hard to understand the "because" here non-causally. Indeed, as Davidson himself has emphasized, the role of propositional attitudes in explanations of behavior appears to be through-and-through causal: propositional attitude explanations of actions are explanations in terms of reasons, and reasons are causes.

Suppose this is right. Its being right need not be due to belief and desire ascriptions – ascriptions of reasons – picking out pieces of the causal mechanism responsible for your doing what you do. What you do depends on the dispositional character of your body. This dispositional character is what ultimately licenses ascriptions of beliefs and desires. As we have seen, according to Davidson, the ascription of propositional attitudes involves the application of something like a theory of interpretation, an–$I$-theory. This theory provides a perspicuous description of a complex dispositional system.

How does this help reconcile Davidson's view of propositional attitude ascription with our conviction that propositional attitudes figure in causal explanations of actions? Reflect for a moment on the implications of the idea that $I$-theories hold of agents in virtue of the dispositional structure of those agents. Dispositions can exist, can come and go, without being manifested. An object can possess distinct dispositions the manifestation of which in the object's behavior would be indistinguishable. One of these dispositions could be manifested without the others being manifested. An object might possess two distinct properties, $P_1$ and $P_2$, each of which, in concert with the object's other properties (and properties of objects nearby) disposes the object to turn green when heated. When the object is heated and, as a result, turns green, this might be due to its possessing $P_1$, or to its possessing $P_2$, or to its possessing both $P_1$ and $P_2$. We may have trouble deciding whether $P_1$, or $P_2$, or both $P_1$ and $P_2$ are responsible for the change of color, but that is a separate issue.

Now, what of action? I explain an action, your ingesting a bowl of

Brussels sprouts, by citing your desire to learn self-discipline. In so doing (as we are supposing), I explain your behavior by imposing a framework provided by a theory of interpretation, an *I*-theory. Your behavior satisfies this theory. But note: an *I*-theory according to which you act on your desire to learn self-discipline differs from an *I*-theory according to which you act on your desire to eat a healthy breakfast. True, your behavior here and now, your eating the Brussels sprouts, accords with either theory. But this is only part of what the theories address. *I*-theories range over dispositional systems. And the dispositional makeup of an agent whose behavior accords with the first theory differs from the dispositional makeup of an agent whose behavior accords with the second theory. To be sure, there is an epistemological hurdle to be negotiated in discovering which theory is correct. But, as in the case of ordinary, non-mental dispositional systems, that is a separate issue.

Explanations that appeal to propositional attitudes are sensitive to dispositional, hence causal, differences in agents whose behavior they endeavor to explain. This need not, if Davidson is right, depend on the presence of anything like a one–one correspondence between propositional attitudes and bodily components. In the ordinary case, your desire to act in a particular way explains your so acting only if you would not have acted as you did had you lacked the desire. This is because, were you such that you lacked the desire, were you such that an *I*-theory ascribing the desire to you would not be correct, your dispositional condition would have been such that you would not have behaved as you in fact behaved.

What of a case like that of your eating a bowl of Brussels sprouts, in which you have two reasons, either of which would account for your behavior? In such cases, it might well be false that, had you not possessed one of the reasons, you would not have eaten the Brussels sprouts. Had you lacked the one reason, you might still have had the other. And this reason might have accounted for your behavior. The example provides a reminder that the use of counterfactual and subjunctive conditional locutions to capture dispositional characteristics of objects yields at best partial results. We must appeal to actual dispositional differences between the two cases.

Consider a pair of agents, Wayne and Dwayne, both of whom harbor the desires discussed earlier: the desire to eat a healthy breakfast and the desire to learn self-control. Both Wayne and Dwayne believe that they can satisfy these desires by eating a bowl of Brussels sprouts, so both have reasons to eat the Brussels sprouts. Imagine that Wayne and Dwayne each eat a bowl of Brussels sprouts: Wayne does so because he wants a healthy breakfast, and Dwayne does so because he wants to learn self-control. Although Wayne and Dwayne are both disposed to eat a bowl of Brussels sprouts, they nevertheless differ dispositionally: the dispositional basis of Wayne's action differs from the dispositional basis of Dwayne's action. And it is in virtue of these differences that Wayne and Dwayne satisfy distinct *I*-theories.

If Wayne and Dwayne have the same desires, why should we imagine that they satisfy distinct *I*-theories? Desires differ in intensity. You and I might both crave a Whopper, but your craving might outweigh mine, at least in this sense: your desire has greater motivational force within your psychological economy than my desire has within mine. We need not consider the question of whether desire strength can be compared across agents. All that matters here is that, within an agent, the relative strength of desires may vary considerably. This is built into our concept of desire. And it is reflected in decision theory by the utilities assigned to outcomes of actions, the objects of desire.

Another part of the conceptual apparatus associated with desire is the principle that, when agents act deliberately, they do what they most desire. It is possible, then, for Wayne and Dwayne to have identical desires, but for those desires to differ in their respective levels of motivational strength for each agent. When this is so, different desires can "call the shots": both Wayne and Dwayne eat a bowl of Brussels sprouts, but Wayne does so on the basis of his desire for a healthy breakfast, and Dwayne does so on the basis of his desire to learn self-control. Decision theory provides a way of distinguishing Wayne and Dwayne, and this is reflected in the *I*-theories we deploy in interpreting their behavior. Both are grounded in the dispositional systems that underlie Wayne's and Dwayne's actions.

## The regress problem

We have been examining Davidson's idea that ascriptions of propositional attitudes and the explanation of behavior by reference to propositional attitudes is a matter of superimposing a metric on a complex domain in a way that makes salient a structural component of that domain. In this respect, the ascription of beliefs and desires resembles our ascription of temperature, or length, or location. In each case, we invoke a descriptive framework whose structure is fine-grained, orderly, and antecedently well-understood. In the case of temperature and length, we make use of the properties of numbers organized in simple axiom systems. In the case of the propositional attitudes, we exploit semantic features of the sentential structure of our language in concert with a theory of rational choice.

Like explanations generally, explanations that appeal to the propositional attitudes are projective, hence predictive. If Davidson is right, this is due not to their mapping components of a mechanism responsible for behavior, however, but to their applying to agents in virtue of those agents' overall dispositional structure. We are apt to be misled by our everyday practice of explaining the behavior of an agent on a particular occasion by ascribing to that agent individual beliefs, desires, and intentions. This makes it appear as though distinct components of the agent correspond to each of these. (Thus the attraction of Fodor's Language of Thought and the Representational Theory of Mind.) On Davidson's view, however, individual propositional attitude ascriptions are grounded in an implicit theory of interpretation. An ascription of a belief, desire, or intention is correct just in case it is implied by an *I*-theory satisfied by the agent. This suggests a parallel with measurement and our use of co-ordinate systems. In measuring the lengths of particular objects, we import a system of numbers; in locating objects in space, we impose a system of co-ordinates. We can make nothing of lengths or locations independently of such systems.

The practice of ascribing propositional attitudes is sometimes labeled "folk psychology." Folk psychology, like folk medicine, is useful, even indispensable. Neither folk practice, however, aims to reveal details of the underlying mechanism. Nor does the apparent success of either practice depend on its revealing such details. This need not mean that folk psychology is ripe for replacement (or elimination) by neuroscience. Folk psychology and neuroscience are not competitors, any more than cartography and geology are competitors.

Is this the end of the story? Have we provided a total theory of mind? Surely not. Davidson's theory is silent about the sensory aspect of our conscious lives. Even if we focus on our intentional characteristics – our thoughts, for instance – it is clear that Davidson's story cannot be the whole story. Indeed, this is implicit in the story itself. On Davidson's view, agents' enjoying propositional attitudes (beliefs, desires, reasons for action) depends on their being interpreted. Just as a co-ordinate system is something we impose on a region of space, so an agent's possession of beliefs and desires is tied to the imposition of an *I*-theory on that agent. The activity of interpretation itself, however, evidently involves interpreters' possessing propositional attitudes themselves. And this points toward a regress foreshadowed at the outset of our discussion of Davidson: my propositional attitudes depend on your interpreting me; your propositional attitudes depend on someone interpreting you; that someone's propositional attitudes depend on some further someone; and so on. How could such a process get off the ground?

Two responses to this worry are worth mention. First, Davidson's idea is that the practice of deploying *I*-theories and ascribing propositional attitudes requires a community of ascribers. Consider a two-person com-

munity consisting of you and me. The idea is not that I have propositional attitudes courtesy of your invoking an *I*-theory to account for what
I do, and that you possess your propositional attitudes from some third
source. Rather, we interpret one another. We engage in practices that, once
they reach an appropriate level of sophistication, constitute the application
of *I*-theories.

Although agents' possession of propositional attitudes depends on their
being interpreted, the sense of dependence in play here is not the causal
sense. The relationship between your deployment of an *I*-theory for me
and my possession of propositional attitudes, is not a causal relation. It is
not causal any more than the application of a co-ordinate system to the
earth's surface is a matter of causing the earth to possess new features.

If it sounds excessive to insist, as Davidson does, that your possession of
propositional attitudes depends on your place in a community of interpreters, consider an analogy. Imagine a world that includes no conscious
agents. In that world is anything 3 feet long? Well, you might be tempted
to say, in one sense, yes, and in another sense, no. A world lacking conscious agents could contain objects that would, if placed beside yardsticks in our world, align perfectly. Still, something's being 3 feet long
depends on the presence of a measuring convention and this presupposes
intelligent agents. Suppose the system of feet and inches we now use
had never been invented. Is it so clear that objects that we now describe
as 3 feet long would have been 3 feet long? And is it so clear that a
molecule-for-molecule duplicate of you languishing in a world lacking
other similar agents could possess just the propositional attitudes that you
possess?

A second response to the regress worry pushes us beyond Davidson. It
is clear that there is more to thought than the having of propositional
attitudes – in the strict Davidsonian sense. Davidson may be right about
the propositional attitudes, but it may also be true that the kinds of
capacity required to have beliefs, desires, and reasons for action include a
host of important non-propositional mental capacities. Although much of
our thinking has a linguistic flavor, much of it does not. A carpenter building a cabinet makes use of spatial imagery to see how parts will fit
together. This imagery is evidently non-propositional and non-verbal. It
resembles qualitatively a range of visual and tactile experiences familiar to
the carpenter.

My suggestion is that "non-propositional" thought of this sort undergirds intelligent action generally, and, more particularly, the kinds of linguistic practice on which Davidson focuses. It is easy to lose sight of such
things when we set out to write about or discuss such topics. You use
language – what else? – to tell me what you are thinking and to describe
my thoughts. It need not follow, however, that your actual thoughts, or

mine, are linguistic or "propositional" in character. Even when our thoughts are explicitly linguistic – when we talk to ourselves – this is arguably at bottom a form of imagery: verbal imagery.

I shall have more to say about imagery and "non-propositional" thought in the next chapter. The point here is merely to suggest that the interpretational practices Davidson discusses float on the surface of a sea of mentality about which his theory is silent. We should err were we to interpret this silence as denial. Davidson restricts the scope of his inquiry, but we need not follow him in that. And if we hope to acquire a grasp of the mind as a whole, we had better not follow him.

## Dennett and the intentional stance

Daniel Dennett advocates an approach to the mind that, at first glance, might appear similar to Davidson's. That appearance, as will become evident, is misleading. Dennett's concern is to advance a scientifically informed account of the mind. Like Davidson, he insists on distinguishing practices of propositional attitude ascription from systematic attempts to understand the mechanisms responsible for intelligent action. Unlike Davidson, however, Dennett regards the ascription of propositional attitudes – beliefs, desires, intentions – as constrained only by a weak requirement of "rationality." We can correctly and legitimately ascribe propositional attitudes to any system – animal, vegetable, or mineral – whose behavior could be construed as rational in light of the system's "ends." The result is a deliberately "instrumentalist" approach to the mind. (The significance of all this will emerge in the discussion to follow.)

### The intentional stance

According to Dennett, a creature's having a mind is strictly a matter of our usefully regarding the creature as having a mind. This amounts, in practice, to our treating the creature as "one of us": a being with certain (mostly true) beliefs about the world and desires for certain states of affairs, a being who acts reasonably in light of those beliefs and desires. You observe a robin hunting worms in the garden. You explain – that is, make sense of – the robin's behavior by supposing that the robin is hungry and so seeking food. The robin believes that worms are food, believes that worms are to be found in the garden, and in consequence desires to hunt worms in the garden. The robin, in sum, acts in light of its beliefs and desires.

In explaining the robin's behavior by reference to beliefs and desires, you are adopting what Dennett calls the "intentional stance." The stance is one we take up in order to make sense of and predict the behavior of any creature. Why is that octopus emitting a black inky substance? Because the octopus believes it has been spotted by a predator, wants to protect itself, believes it can do so by placing a dark cloud between it and the predator, and believes that by emitting an inky fluid, it will cause a dark cloud to come between it and the predator. Why is this white blood cell enveloping that microbe? Because the cell wants to destroy invaders, believes the microbe is an invader, and so wants to destroy it. For its own part, the microbe wants to invade a red blood cell, believes that it is likely to find a red blood cell by swimming about randomly in the bloodstream, and so swims randomly.

Do robins, octopodes, and white blood cells really have beliefs and desires? Do such organisms really behave rationally? Or do they merely behave as if they had beliefs and desires (and acted reasonably in light of these)? Dennett regards questions of this sort as wrong-headed. Having beliefs and desires amounts to nothing more than being explicable via the intentional stance. If we can make sense of the behavior of a microbe by taking up the intentional stance toward its activities, then the microbe does indeed have beliefs and desires, hence reasons for what it does.

You might object. If this is what having beliefs, desires, and reasons amounts to, then plants must have beliefs, desires, and reasons, too. This elm sinks its roots deep into the soil because it wants to find water and believes that water is likely to be found at greater depths. More startlingly, perhaps, on a view of this sort what is to prevent artifacts – your desktop computer, or even a lowly thermostat, from having beliefs and desires? Your desktop computer is displaying a "Printer is out of paper" alert because it believes that the printer is out of paper, and wants to let you know. The thermostat turns on the furnace because it believes that the room temperature has dropped below 68 °F, and it wants to increase the temperature to at least 68 °F.

You might concede that, although we do talk this way on occasion, we do so merely as a matter of convenience. We can see single-celled organisms, plants, and artifacts as analogous to human beings in certain ways. Thus we speak of them as if they were like us in those ways. But of course they are not really like us. They operate on simpler principles. To imagine that they have – really have – beliefs and desires, to suppose that they have – really have – reasons for what they do, is to confuse the metaphorical with the literal.

Dennett insists, however, that ascriptions of beliefs and desires to single-celled organisms, plants, and artifacts are no more metaphorical than is the ascription of beliefs and desires to our fellow human beings. All there is to an entity's having beliefs and desires, all there is to an entity's acting on reasons, is the entity's behaving as if it had beliefs and desires and acted on reasons. In ascribing beliefs, desires, and reasons to organisms or objects, we take up the intentional stance. The intentional stance enables us to make sense of and predict the behavior of whatever falls under it. But it will do this quite independently of whether those entities have minds like ours.

A view of this sort construes the propositional attitudes "instrumentally." That is, the correctness of an attribution of beliefs, desires, and reasons for action lies, not in its corresponding to some independent fact or state of affairs, but to its serviceability. To the extent that the practice of ascribing propositional attitudes serves our interests – enables us to make sense of and predict the behavior of objects with which we interact – it is fully justified. To expect anything more, to take a "realist" line on beliefs, desires, and reasons for action is to miss the point of the practice.

## From intentional stance to design stance

Your having beliefs, desires, and reasons for action, then, is simply a matter of your being susceptible to descriptions framed in terms of beliefs, desires, and reasons. In deploying such descriptions, we take up the intentional stance. We find this unavoidable in the case of our fellow human beings, and equally unavoidable in attempting to come to terms with the exploits of non-human creatures as well. In the case of simple organisms, plants, and inanimate objects, we may find that we can dispense with the intentional stance and explain their behavior by grasping their design. In so doing, we move to what Dennett calls the "design stance." We make sense of the behavior of objects by regarding them as having been designed or engineered in a particular way to achieve a particular end.

You may describe the behavior of your desktop computer by attributing various beliefs and desires to it. But a programmer is in a position to make sense of the device's behavior by reference to its program. In the same way, a biologist can explain the behavior of a white blood cell by reflecting on its design from an evolutionary perspective. The design of a desktop computer has a human origin. The design of a white blood cell, or the circulatory system of a frog, or the mechanism that controls the growth of a plant reflects the hand of Mother Nature. Evolutionary pressures insure that badly engineered mechanisms, those that prove maladaptive, are weeded out.

The design stance does not replace the intentional stance. When we arrive at a "design-level" understanding of a white blood cell or the behavior of a bird protecting her nestlings by feigning an injury, we do not falsify claims made from the intentional standpoint. On the contrary, we merely offer a deeper, more fine-grained explanation of why such claims hold. Such explanations in many ways resemble functional explanations. But our capacity to deploy the design stance in particular instances does not, according to Dennett, mean that beliefs, desires, and reasons for action are, at bottom, functional states. We adopt the intentional stance when our interest in understanding or explaining the behavior of some entity is largely action-oriented – when we have an interest in predicting, quickly and without expending much effort, how that entity is likely to behave. If this is our aim, the intentional stance is wonderfully efficient and cost-effective. We resort to the design stance only when our interests change and when circumstances make it possible (or desirable) to examine more carefully and systematically mechanisms controlling an entity's activities. An ethologist adopts the design stance in explaining the behavior of a particular species of bird, but a hunter need not, and typically will not.

Psychologists, psychobiologists, sociobiologists, and, in general, cognitive scientists adopt in their various ways the design stance toward human beings. Once again, this is not a matter of undermining the intentional stance we take up in order to make sense of one another's behavior by appealing to beliefs, desires, and reasons. Nor, on Dennett's view, is it a matter of discovering that beliefs, desires, and reasons are at bottom functional states responsible for behavior. The beliefs, desires, and reasons for action ascribable to us are so ascribable, perhaps because we have the functional architecture we have. But beliefs, desires, and reasons are not causally potent components of that architecture.

What, then, would a design-level description of a human being look like? You can get some idea by reflecting on what scientific investigators tell us about, for instance, the mechanisms of vision, or memory, or language-processing. Explanations of such things involve appeals to details of our nervous system – components of the retina and optic nerve, for instance – in a way that regards these as subserving particular systemic ends. Examples of the design stance taken toward human and non-human creatures' capacities abound in psychology and biology textbooks.

As noted earlier, this design-level approach is to be distinguished from the line taken by functionalists. Functionalists regard terms designating states of mind appealed to in the intentional stance as, at bottom, designating functional states of creatures to which the terms apply. But in adopting the design stance we in effect take up the intentional stance toward mechanisms we take to underlie creatures' behavior. We see these mechanisms (as opposed to the creature as a whole) as having ends, and working to achieve them. You might worry that this imports an unwarranted anthropomorphic element into our fine-grained accounts of creatures' inner workings. You might worry as well that the strategy bogs down in a kind of regress: we explain complex states of mind by positing mechanisms that possess the very features we had hoped to explain. To what extent are these worries well-founded?

## From design stance to physical stance

Dennett's idea is that we account for mental phenomena by locating neural mechanisms capable of a design-level description, one that, true enough, involves seeing those mechanisms as working to achieve certain goals. The explanatory process need not stop here, however. We move to explain these mechanisms by discovering simpler mechanisms that make them up. The retina is taken to perform a particular intelligent function, and this is explained by discovering that the retina consists of rods, cones, and assorted other cells that themselves perform intelligent, but more limited, narrowly-directed functions. As we analyze systems into component systems in this way, we eventually arrive at a level at which the constituent mechanisms are acutely focused or single-minded. At this level of analysis, we might expect to find, for instance, individual cells that do nothing more than detect the presence or absence of a particular chemical substance and notify neighboring cells accordingly.

When we reach this level, we have in effect "discharged" the design stance, and moved to the physical stance. We can see how the imagined cell performs its function by examining its chemistry. In this way our investigations are grounded in the non-mental, and the threat of circularity is deflected. Intentionality, that feature of thoughts in virtue of which they are of or about one thing or another, is seen to stem from the biochemistry of organisms enjoying it.

Before taking up Dennett's account of conscious experience, it might be useful to pause and review the theory as it has been developed thus far.

## From the mental to the physical

Functionalists regard it as a genuine empirical question whether creatures – or artifacts – to which we commonly and unhesitatingly ascribe beliefs, desires, and reasons for action, do in fact have beliefs, desires, and reasons. The question is one that might be resolved for a given creature by discovering whether that creature was sufficiently like us functionally. Dennett thinks this is a red herring. The having of beliefs and desires is a matter of being so describable. When we regard it as more than that, when we imagine that in ascribing beliefs, desires, and reasons we are identifying components of mechanisms causally responsible for behavior, we run the risk of anthropomorphizing and thereby missing the gulf between the minds of human beings and the minds of other creatures.

The idea is straightforward. In taking up the intentional stance – in ascribing beliefs, desires, and reasons for action – we deploy a system of categories that enables us to sort out and predict the behavior of creatures, artifacts, and natural systems. The justification of this practice depends, not on its successfully cataloging gears and levers responsible for the operation of whatever it is we hope to explain, but on its utility. For a great many purposes, it is all we need. You explain to a companion what your desktop computer is doing by noting that it *wants* to print a document, *discovers* that the printer is out of paper, and *hopes* to attract your attention by beeping.

The italicized words in the preceding sentence are not, if Dennett is right, used metaphorically: they hold literally of your desktop computer; you are using them in exactly the sense you would use them in describing the behavior of a fellow human being. You would err, however, if you imagined that what goes on inside your desktop computer resembles – functionally or otherwise – what goes on inside a human being. Understanding what makes us tick requires that we descend to the design stance. And when we do this, we begin to notice vast differences between desktop computers, human beings, and other creatures.

In taking up the design stance we, in effect, extend the intentional stance to components of intelligent systems. The project is saved from a bottomless regress by the fact that it is premised on the possibility that we can successively analyze intelligent systems into subsystems until we arrive at a systemic level the operation of which is trivial from the design point of view, though perhaps physically complex. Here we move to the physical stance and "discharge" our higher-level talk of beliefs, desires, and reasons for action. Our arriving at this level, our achieving the physical stance, does not falsify or replace our higher-level intentional stance and design stance assessments, however. To imagine that it does is to lose sight of the utility and economy afforded by the intentional and design stances. This utility and economy provide all the justification we need for deploying them.

## Second-order representation

Like most theorists who see themselves as cognitive scientists, Dennett accepts the idea that human beings and non-human creatures process information and internally manipulate representions of their surroundings. It is one thing for a creature's behavior to be guided by representations, however, and quite another matter for a creature to appreciate that this is what it is doing. Moreover, there is, Dennett contends, not merely a difference in degree, but a difference in kind between a capacity for representation (something arguably possessed by single-celled organisms) and a capacity for second-order representation: the representation of representations or representation of oneself as representing. Only creatures capable of surveying their own representations (and recognizing these representations as theirs), only creatures capable of taking up the intentional stance toward themselves, deserve to be described as "thinking." Sea slugs and single-celled creatures represent aspects of their limited worlds, but they do not think. What of beagles, or dolphins, or chimpanzees? Again, a case can be made for saying that such creatures represent their surroundings. Do they think? They do so only if they represent self-consciously, only if they possess a capacity for second-order representation, a capacity to appreciate, hence represent, their representations as representations.

This latter capacity, Dennett believes, emerges only with the advent of language. If we accept Dennett's earlier suggestion that thinking includes an ability to manipulate representations self-consciously, then it would follow that thought requires language. This is not because language is needed as a medium for thought. (This is the view of proponents of the Language of Thought.) Thinking need not be linguistic or language-like. Thought could be pictorial. The connection between thought and language is less direct. Evolutionary pressures for self-conscious representation are absent until the birth of co-operative communication. Communication provides a way to share information. More importantly (from an evolutionary perspective), communication provides a way for creatures to turn the possession of information not possessed by others to their own advantage. If I know something you do not know and are unlikely to know unless I tell you, I can trade my information for some benefit, or, if it serves my interests, mislead you.

If we look at the evolutionary paths of non-human species, we see that members of those species typically inhabit surroundings in which information obtained by one individual is likely to be obtainable by every other individual. When this is not so, we may find that practices of deception emerge (as when chimpanzees take steps to prevent fellow chimpanzees from discovering a hidden morsel of food). Such practices mandate a degree of representational sophistication that constitutes what might be called "proto-thought." This is a stage on the evolutionary road to fully-fledged thinking.

Infants and young children may lack the kind of reflective capacities that Dennett considers necessary for genuine thought. In one experiment, a child is shown a puppet hiding a toy in a particular place. The puppet goes away and, during its absence, the experimenter, in full view of the child, moves the toy to a new hiding place. The child is then asked where the puppet will look for the toy when it returns. Three-year-olds may say that the puppet will look in the new hiding place; older children reply that the puppet will look where the toy was originally hidden. One possible explanation for this disparity is that younger children represent the world, but are unable to represent representations of the world. They are, in consequence, in no position to represent the puppet's imagined representations of the world, and so are unable to regard the puppet as falsely representing the toy's location. Predicting that the puppet will look in the new hiding place does not, or so it is claimed, require the child to represent the puppet as having a true representation, hence does not require the child to represent the puppet as representing anything.

The argument implicit in Dennett's line of reasoning is founded not on purely philosophical or a priori considerations concerning what suffices for thought. It is rather that, when we look below the surface at how other creatures do what they do, we are not tempted in the slightest to imagine that they engage in self-conscious thinking in anything like the sense in which we do. A philosopher or a pet owner might point out that it is still possible that infants, or chimpanzees, or dolphins, or beagles engage in elaborate, but secret cogitations. This impression, Dennett suggests, is just the result of taking the intentional stance too far.

Once we realize this, once we descend to the design stance, we learn that nature has provided much more elegant solutions to problems posed by the environment. Were you to set out to build a nest, you would no doubt first plan a course of action and keep this plan in mind – modifying it as necessary – as you proceeded with the task. Encouraged by the intentional stance, you might imagine that a bird building a nest operates in much the same way. When we begin to study the behavior of birds more carefully, however, we discover that their elaborate, and in many cases ingenious, solutions to the nest-building problem are not the result of elaborate and ingenious thoughts but of simpler mechanisms. The mechanisms are ingenious certainly, but the ingenuity is Mother Nature's, not the birds'.

## Kinds of mind

Although we are within our rights to describe infants, chimpanzees, dolphins, beagles, sea slugs, even thermostats as having beliefs, desires, and reasons for what they do, we do well to reserve the notion of thought for creatures who, like us, have evolved a capacity for self-conscious representation, a capacity to entertain representations of representations. Does this mean that only creatures like us have minds? Not according to Dennett. Having a mind is a matter of being guided by representations. And we have ample evidence that the activities of infants, chimpanzees, dolphins, beagles, and sea slugs are governed by representations of their goals and circumstances. Perhaps this is so even for the lowly thermostat.

Conceding that sea slugs and thermostats have minds, however, is not to concede very much – at least not if Dennett is right about minds. We can still identify vast qualitative distinctions among kinds of mind. Dennett envisages a hierarchy. At the basic level are primitive "Darwinian" minds, those hard-wired to respond in optimal ways to their environment. Darwinian minds are possessed by the simplest creatures, those that have evolved clever solutions to problems posed by their circumstances. In the case of Darwinian creatures, the steps from the intentional stance to the design stance and from the design stance to the physical stance may be relatively abbreviated.

At a rung above Darwinian creatures are those possessing "Skinnerian minds" (named in honor of the behaviorist psychologist, B. F. Skinner). These are possessed by creatures capable of learning via operant conditioning – trial and error. A Skinnerian creature exhibits a degree of mental "plasticity" not possessed by simpler Darwinian creatures. A Skinnerian creature can adapt its behavior to changes in its circumstances. In this way it has a hand in shaping itself to fit its environmental niche. For Darwinian creatures, this role is played exclusively by Mother Nature: such creatures are shaped wholly by evolutionary pressures.

"Popperian minds" belong to creatures who have managed the trick of representing their environment in a way that enables them to test likely outcomes of distinct courses of action "in their heads," and so to learn without the attendant risk of potentially lethal errors. (Popperian creatures operate on principles reminiscent of those the philosopher Karl Popper believes to lie at the heart of scientific rationality. According to Popper, the success of science as a rational enterprise hinges on scientists' willingness to engage in "conjecture and refutation." Theories are conjectured and tested against the evidence. A theory is accepted only insofar as it survives rigorous testing.) A Skinnerian learns from experience, trial and error; a Popperian can learn by anticipating experience. Rats are evidently Popperian. A rat allowed to explore a maze may later put its knowledge of the maze to use in attaining a particular reward. The rat does so (according to psychologist E. C. Tolman) by constructing a "cognitive map" of the maze. Once constructed, this "map" can be put to advantage in negotiating the maze to obtain a food pellet.

> Skinnerian creatures ask themselves, "What should I do next?" and haven't a clue how to answer until they have taken some hard knocks. Popperian creatures make a big advance by asking themselves, "What should I think about next?" before they ask themselves, "What should I do next?" (It should be emphasized

that neither Skinnerian nor Popperian creatures actually need to talk to themselves or think these thoughts. They are simply designed to operate *as if* they had asked themselves these questions.)

(Dennett, 1996, p. 100)

At the top of Dennett's hierarchy are Gregorian creatures (named, not for the Pope, but for the psychologist, Richard Gregory). A Gregorian creature, like its Popperian forerunners, is capable of testing hypotheses in its head. The difference is that Gregorian creatures are capable of representing self-consciously. This opens up new horizons and possibilities, not available to Popperians.

Human beings, endowed as we are with language, are Gregorian creatures. We are also, in some measure, Darwinian, Skinnerian, and Popperian. The human nervous system bears the marks of its evolutionary history, exhibiting Darwinian, Skinnerian, Popperian, and Gregorian elements. Any complex action requires the co-ordination of all of these. We should not, then, confuse kinds of mind with kinds of creature. The brain of a Skinnerian creature, for instance, a creature capable of learning, incorporates Darwinian – hard-wired – mechanisms, as do sophisticated mammalian brains. A Gregorian creature, one capable of self-reflection, is not non-Darwinian, or non-Skinnerian, or non-Popperian. Rather, Gregorian creatures – among terrestrial species, human beings – have evolved additional capacities that distinguish their minds from the minds of creatures lacking self-consciousness.

The vast differences between Gregorian creatures and the rest are largely invisible so long as we rest content with the intentional stance. We ascribe beliefs, desires, and reasons for action in a way that, wrongly interpreted, makes the minds of non-Gregorian creatures appear to resemble ours. So long as our interest is merely in interacting with and predicting the behavior of such creatures, this attitude is justified. But when we pursue a deeper understanding of what makes other creatures tick, when we seek to refine our understanding and increase our prospects of predicting and manipulating their behavior, we are bound to look below the surface. When we do, when we descend to the design stance, we discover that differences swamp similarities.

Most notably we discover that the intelligence of non-human creatures is, in comparison to our own, rigid and "gappy." Spot, whose behavior exhibits considerable intelligence in many domains, is unable to arrive at a solution to the problem of how to unwind his leash from a tree. It seems not to occur to dolphins (regarded by some enthusiasts as our intellectual equals) to try to escape tuna nets by leaping over them, although this is something any dolphin might easily do. These gaps appear puzzling only so long as we imagine that other creatures think as we do. The results of careful experimental work suggest otherwise. Thus, impressive as they are, tool-using chimpanzees and ants that engage in "farming" fungus harvested for food all fall short of the Gregorian plateau. Reports of chimpanzees (and other apes) engaging in apparently deceptive practices might suggest that this assessment is overly pessimistic: perhaps chimpanzees have a "theory of mind" that they put to use in deciding how to interact with their fellows. Dennett discourages this interpretation. The intelligence displayed by chimpanzees and other non-human creatures does not call for the Gregorian solution. Indeed, if we interpret chimpanzees as thinking as we do about matters that concern them, then their inability to generalize this thinking in obvious ways appears baffling.

## Consciousness

What of conscious experience: consciousness? According to Dennett, obsession with the "what it's like" problem has prevented philosophers from appreciating a solution to the mystery of consciousness that is ready to hand. Representations play an important role in the production of behavior in even the simplest creatures. Consciousness, however, emerges only with the capacity to reflect on these representations, and, as we have seen, this capacity is, according to Dennett, linked to the ability to deploy language. Strictly speaking, then, thought and consciousness are possible only for linguistically endowed creatures. For such creatures, conscious states of mind are not those exhibiting distinctive qualitative or "phenomenological" features, or those located in some central chamber of the mind, but those that, in competition with other representational elements, assume control of behavior.

Why should this feature suffice for consciousness? Surely more is required for a representation to take on the characteristics of a conscious experience.

> Such questions betray a deep confusion, for they presuppose that what *you* are is something *else*, some Cartesian *res cogitans* in addition to all this brain and body activity. What you are, however, just *is* this organization of all the competitive activity between a host of competencies that your body has developed.
>
> (Dennett, 1996, pp. 155–6)

Does this mean that other creatures – chimpanzees, dolphins, beagles – are "zombies," that they do not feel pain, for instance? No; such creatures have pains and assorted other sensory states. What they lack is an additional capacity to reflect on these states. And this lack, Dennett suggests, means that, although they may be said to feel pain, they do not "suffer." Attempts to model their pains on ours are invariably misleading.

Dennett is aware that, in advancing such a view, he is opening himself to attack from pet owners and animal rights activists. He argues, however, that our moral obligation to refrain from needlessly harming other creatures stems not from their possession of a capacity to suffer as we do, but merely from the fact that they, like us, can be in pain. A capacity for pain, however, is to be distinguished from a higher-level capacity, your capacity to reflect that you are in pain. A creature lacking this capacity cannot dwell on its pain, or dread its onset, or be haunted by painful memories. And a capacity for such things underlies the capacity for suffering.

How could one's possession of the capacity for self-reflection affect the feeling of pain, the qualitative dimension of an experience of pain? Dennett contends that this is the wrong question to ask. Experiential qualities – "qualia" – are dubious entities, artifacts of an outmoded and discredited Cartesian conception of the mind. We can account for the apparent prominence of these qualities by recognizing that when you are in pain, for instance, you are in a particular kind of state, one that, among other things, leads you to believe that you are in a state with particular qualities. Creatures lacking language lack a capacity for second-order thought, hence for thoughts of this sort. Such creatures can be in states functionally resembling our pain states, but they lack the wherewithal to reflect on those states.

Does this imply that such creatures feel nothing when they are in pain? The question presupposes what is false, namely that pain states or episodes possess intrinsic qualitative features. They do not – at least not if Dennett is right. But this does not mean that non-human creatures do not undergo pain, or that their pains are less intense or distressing than ours. To think that it does, is to assume – falsely – that pains are what they are – pains – in virtue of their intrinsic qualitative character. But nothing possesses an intrinsic qualitative character. The fact that pain states lack it, then, is entirely unremarkable.

You may find a view of this sort wildly implausible. To his credit, however, Dennett takes seriously the problem of reconciling the apparent qualitative nature of conscious experience with the character of the material states and episodes that seem to "underlie" such experiences. As many philosophers like to point out, it is hard to see how these could be reconciled without accepting some form of dualism. Dennett's strategy is to analyze the qualities of conscious experience in terms of states of mind that themselves lack such qualities. Just as, when you experience a round reddish-orange after-image, nothing material in your vicinity – and certainly nothing in your brain – need be round and reddish-orange, when you experience a pain as throbbing, nothing need be throbbing. Perhaps this is no more mysterious than our entertaining thoughts of dragons or mermaids when there are no dragons or mermaids.

## Searle's objection

One response to such attempts to analyze away the qualities of conscious experience is to argue, as John Searle has, that the move merely represses a problem without solving it. The argument is simple. Suppose you hallucinate a tangerine-colored geranium on the table in front of you. There need be nothing tangerine-colored or geranium-shaped in your vicinity. But now consider your hallucination itself. We seem to have removed a tangerine-colored or geranium-shaped item from the public material world, and placed it inside your mind. The qualities you seem to find in the "external world" exist, perhaps, but only in your mind. Nevertheless, they indisputably exist there: in your mind. And this is no help at all if our aim is to advance a fully materialist conception of mind.

Recalling a point encountered in chapter one, we commonly distinguish appearance from reality. When it comes to the mind, however, appearance is reality. Suppose we agree that something's merely appearing pink is a matter, not of its being pink, but of your being in a particular state of mind. We banish the perceived pinkness to the mind. Dennett seems to want to make the same move with respect to experienced pinkness. But how is this supposed to work? Perhaps the experienced pinkness is "merely apparent." This means that your experience of pinkness is just a matter of your taking yourself to be experiencing pinkness. And this just seems to shift the troublesome "phenomenal quality" from a first-order perceptual experience to a second-order experience (just as the quality was originally moved from the external world into the mind). This does not remove the troublesome quality, however. It merely shifts it from one part of the mind to another.

From this it seems to follow that attempts to analyze away the qualities of conscious experiences by attaching them to second-order mental states – your beliefs about the pain you now feel, for instance – are bound to fail. We eliminate the troublesome qualities from your pain state only by depositing them in your representations of your pain state.

We broached these issues in chapters three and four. There I noted that it is vital to distinguish qualities of objects experienced from qualities of experiences. Your visual experience of a red tomato in bright sunlight has a distinctive qualitative character. We can designate these qualities by mentioning their causes: brightly illuminated red tomatoes. But we must not confuse qualities of the cause with those of the effect. An experience of a red tomato need not be red. In fact, an experience, unlike a ripe tomato, is not the sort of thing that could be red. When you hallucinate a red tomato, or for that matter, experience a vivid reddish-orange after-image, you undergo an experience something like the experience you undergo when you see a red tomato in bright sunlight. And again, although your experience is "of" a round, reddish-orange object, your experience is not itself round or reddish-orange.

The point of all this is to suggest that Searle's contention that, when it comes to the mind, appearance is reality is scarcely a straightforward doctrine. If Searle means that when you undergo a reddish-orange after-image, when something appears reddish-orange to you, then something is reddish-orange – if not something outside you, then a mental something – the contention is unwarranted. If, however, we interpret Searle as saying something weaker, namely that when you experience something, your experience has a distinctive character, then it is not clear how deeply it cuts against Dennett.

To be sure, Dennett denies that experiences have any qualitative character at all. As we shall see in the next chapter, however, there are good reasons for thinking that everything has qualities, hence some qualitative character, so this denial seems implausible on the face of it. Suppose we interpret Dennett – charitably – to be denying that experiences have the qualities of experienced objects. A vivid visual experience of a brightly illuminated red tomato need not itself be red. Then Searle's complaint that Dennett cannot account for the appearances is misguided.

Searle's attack is on the right track in one respect, however. If we distinguish carefully the qualities of objects (hallucinatory or otherwise) from the qualities of our experiences of those objects, then there is no particular incentive to introduce second-order states of mind – beliefs about one's pains, for instance – to account for the qualities of conscious experience. If your having a conscious experience is a matter of your being in a particular state with particular qualities, then no philosophical sleight of hand is required to accommodate conscious qualities.

In any case, the move to second-order states ought immediately to arouse suspicion. Suppose you believe that France is hexagonal. Your having this belief is, on most views, Dennett's included, not a matter of your undergoing a conscious experience. Now imagine that you come to believe that you believe that France is hexagonal. Your having this belief is a matter of your being in a particular second-order state, your having a belief about a belief. But if your first order belief is not conscious, why should the addition of a second-order belief-about-a-belief result in a conscious state? It is not to the point to note that self-reflective thoughts are often conscious. The question is whether consciousness depends on second-order thought. Surely you are conscious of many things – your surroundings, for instance, or the disposition of your limbs – without being aware that you are aware of these things. Second-order states of mind, although undoubtedly important, seem ill-suited to marking off the boundary between "conscious" and "non-conscious."

## Eliminativism

Before moving on, I propose to consider very briefly the view that there really are no intentional states: no beliefs, no desires, no intentions, no reasons for actions. This view – eliminative materialism, or eliminativism, for short – has been defended by Patricia and Paul Churchland, among others. Eliminativism is worth mention for two reasons. First, it represents one natural extension of Dennett's thoughts on the intentional stance. Dennett holds that the ascription of familiar psychological states – beliefs, desires, and reasons for action, for instance – is just a way of making sense of complex systems. If, however, we want to understand exactly how those systems operate, we must abandon the intentional stance, move to the design stance, and eventually to the physical stance. This makes it appear that conventional talk of minds and their contents represents, at bottom, a kind of pretense, one that, were our concern solely an accurate plumbing of reality, we could live without.

A second reason for taking up eliminativism is that someone might be tempted to describe the kind of position I develop in the next chapter as eliminativist. I shall argue that it is not. It will be useful, then, to have a clear view of what exactly eliminativism amounts to if only to distinguish it from its competitors.

### Theories and theory reduction

According to the Churchlands, talk of minds is merely a time-honored way of trying to come to grips with the complexities of intelligent behavior. When we look at what makes intelligent creatures (including human beings) tick, however, we discover intricate neural mechanisms. The principles on which these mechanisms operate bear scant resemblance to the platitudes of "folk psychology," the commonsense theory of mind encoded in our language, enshrined in our social and legal institutions, and refined in the social and behavioral sciences. The Churchlands conclude that most psychological categories and modes of explanation are either "reducible" to more fundamental neurobiological categories, or apply to nothing, hence are expendable.

Why should this be so? Psychology provides us with a theory of mind founded on intentional categories (belief, desire, and intention, for instance). Like any theory, this one could turn out to be inadequate in light of the emergence of a new and better theory. Suppose neuroscientists develop a theory of mind that does a significantly better job of predicting and explaining the activities of intelligent creatures than do conventional psychological theories. Suppose, further, that neuroscience does so without recourse to familiar mental concepts: beliefs, desires, images, and the like. (Imagine that, in the new theory, such things are never mentioned, only neurons, synapses, ganglia, and neurotransmitters.)

When we look at the history of science, we discover that when a new theory threatens to replace an existing theory, two outcomes are possible. First, an old theory might be shown to be "reducible to" the new theory. Second, a new theory could wholly displace the older theory.

Consider, first, theory reduction. Reduction occurs when the concepts of the old theory are mirrored by concepts in the new theory. In that case, the older concepts can be said to designate "nothing but" what the new concepts designate. "Temperature" turns out to be nothing but mean molecular energy of molecules; lightning is nothing but an electrical discharge. Theories in which the concept of temperature figures, then, are reducible to more fundamental physical and chemical theories. Reduced theories can be seen as "special cases" of the theories to which they are reduced. Further, we are inclined to regard entities and properties included in the reduced theory as being illuminated by the reducing theory. Temperature, we now see, is mean molecular kinetic energy of molecules; lightning is a stream of electrons.

Although the history of science includes important examples of theory reduction, it is more common for a new theory simply to replace an older theory. Heat was once explained by postulating an impalpable fluid, "caloric," thought to flow from heated bodies to adjacent colder bodies. Caloric, although weightless, was taken to occupy space. The passage of caloric into a cold body caused the body to swell, thus accounting for the expansion – without an accompanying gain in weight – observed in bodies when they were heated. With the coming of the chemical revolution, belief in caloric was abandoned, replaced with the notion that heat was, not a substance, but a kind of energy. Caloric was not reduced to anything more fundamental, but eliminated.

According to the Churchlands, it is this latter, eliminative fate that awaits our ordinary intentional mental concepts. Neuroscience will not illuminate our mental categories but replace them. Thoughts, beliefs, imagery, and the like will turn out not to be complex neural goings-on, but, like caloric, to be non-existent. We might, of course, continue to talk as we do, just as we continue to talk of the sun's rising and setting, although we know better. If our aim is an accurate view of matters, however, we shall be obliged to admit that it is simply false that anyone has beliefs, desires, or reasons for action; false that any creature is guided by imagery; and false that anyone has ever thought of anything.

## Is eliminativism self-refuting?

Some philosophers have argued that this conclusion is self-refuting. If no one believes anything, then how could we – or its proponents – believe the eliminativist thesis? If no one thinks, if no one has reasons for action, how can eliminativists expect us to accept their arguments? Accepting an argument is a matter of accepting certain statements as providing good reasons for belief in a particular conclusion. But none of this seems to make any sense if eliminativism is correct.

One need not be a proponent of eliminativism to doubt the cogency of this response. Surely a hypothesis could be such that its truth is inconsistent with its being asserted – or even believed – to be true, yet for all that nevertheless be true. Consider the hypothesis that all assertions are false. Pretend for a moment that the hypothesis is true: every assertion is false. Were this so, it could not be asserted! There would be something self-defeating, then, about someone's insisting that every assertion is false. But it does not follow from this that every assertion is not false. We might think of eliminativists as pointing out a possibility by using terminology that would be empty were that possibility actual. From this, however, it does not follow that the possibility in question is not actual. It does follow that, in "asserting" his thesis, the eliminativist asserts nothing. But that is a consequence of the theory, not an objection to it!

In this context, it might be useful to cite a famous passage from Wittgenstein's *Tractatus Logico-Philosophicus* (1922/1961, § 6.54). The *Tractatus* concerns (among many other things) the conditions required for thoughts to "picture" the world. For complicated reasons we can ignore here, the position Wittgenstein takes would, if true, make it impossible for anyone to entertain thoughts concerning the relation of thoughts and the world. Yet this is apparently a central topic in the *Tractatus*! Does this mean that Wittgenstein's thesis is self-refuting? Not according to its author:

> My propositions serve as elucidations in the following way:
> anyone who understands me eventually recognizes them as
> nonsensical, when he has used them – as steps – to climb
> beyond them. (He must, so to speak, throw away the ladder
> after he has climbed up it.)

> He must transcend these propositions, and then he will see
> the world aright.

The sentences used to formulate the thesis succeed indirectly: by "show-ing" the reader what is intended, rather than by "saying" it outright.

If eliminativism is correct, perhaps this is all a committed eliminativist can do. But whether it is or not, whether eliminativism cannot be reason-ably believed without assuming its falsehood, it would be hasty to imagine this shows that eliminativism is false. Pushing matters to an extreme, suppose that, if eliminativism were true, nothing we say makes any sense. Does it follow that eliminativism is not true, that the world is not as the eliminativist apparently describes it? I cannot see that it does.

These comments should not be taken as an endorsement of eliminativ-ism. As will become evident in the next chapter, there is no compelling reason to accept the eliminativist's conclusions – even if we embrace the idea that neuroscience might one day supplant psychology.

# Suggested reading

My discussion of Davidson's views draws on "Truth and Meaning" (1967), "Radical Inter-pretation" (1973), "Belief and the Basis of Meaning" (1974a), and "Reality without Refer-ence" (1977); see also "Psychology as Philosophy" (1974b). The omniscient interpreter is introduced in "A Coherence Theory of Truth and Knowledge" (1986). Those seeking for an introduction to Davidson's views might look at Simon Evnine's *Donald Davidson* (1991). Some components of my discussion of Davidson were introduced in an earlier attempt to explicate Davidson in *Perception and Cognition* (1983), chap. 7.

Tarski's discussion of truth is contained in his "The Concept of Truth in Formalized Languages" (1956). Quine's account of radical translation appears in the first two chapters of *Word and Object* (1961). Neither is a text for beginners or the faint of heart. Alfred Mele provides an explanation and defense of the distinction between desires' motivational strength and their evaluative standing in the psychological economy of agents. See his *Irrationality: An Essay on Akrasia, Self-Deception, and Self-Control* (1987), chaps 3 and 6.

For an account of dispositions and their relation to counterfactual and subjunctive con-ditional locutions, see C. B. Martin, "Dispositions and Conditionals" (1994).

In *The Hidden Life of Dogs* (1993), Elizabeth Marshall Thomas provides detailed descrip-tions of complex states of mind she finds in dogs. She does the same for cats in *The Tribe of the Tiger* (1994). Her cats, for instance "look up to" a particular dog, "believing that when cosmic troubles threaten, he'll know what to do." More remarkably, Stanley Coren, in *The Intelligence of Dogs: Canine Consciousness and Capabilities* (1994) claims to have decoded signals expressed by specific sorts of canine behavior (see especially chap. 6). When Spot sits with one paw slightly raised, for instance, he is thinking "I am anxious, uneasy, and concerned."

For more serious treatments of the mental lives of non-human creatures, see Fritz de Waal's *Chimpanzee Politics* (1982) and Dorothy Cheney and Robert Seyfarth's *How Mon-keys See the World: Inside the Mind of Another Species* (1990). The latter book is the subject of a *Behavioral and Brain Sciences* debate; see Cheney and Seyfarth, "Précis of *How Monkeys See the World*" (1992).

A good place to start for anyone interested in an introduction to Daniel Dennett's work is *Kinds of Minds: Toward an Understanding of Consciousness* (1996). Anyone wanting more details should consult *The Intentional Stance* (1987), and *Consciousness Explained* (1991a). See also "Real Patterns" (1991b). In *The Nature of True Minds* (1992), chap. 6, I explore an argument – very different from Dennett's – used by Davidson to establish that thought requires language. Davidson's own account of the relation of language and thought can be found in "Thought and Talk" (1975).

E. C. Tolman's discussion of rats' use of "cognitive maps" to negotiate mazes can be found in his "Cognitive Maps in Rats and Men" (1948). My depiction of an experiment designed to show that very young children lack a capacity for representing self-consciously is an amalgam of a number of experiments. See Heinz Wimmer and Josef Perner, "Beliefs about Beliefs: Representation and Constraining Function of Wrong Beliefs in Young Children's Understanding of Deception" (1983). See also Perner's *Understanding the Representational Mind* (1991). Related experimental work can be found in Alison Gopnik and J. W. Astington, "Children's Understanding of Representational Change and its Relation to the Understanding of False Belief and the Appearance–Reality Distinction" (1988), and Louis J. Moses and J. H. Flavell, "Inferring False Beliefs from Actions and Reactions" (1990). (I am grateful to Eric Schwitzgebel for these references.)

The line of argument I attribute to Searle against Dennett's notion that consciousness can be understood as a kind of second-order representation can be found in *The Rediscovery of the Mind* (1992), chap. 5, especially pp. 121–2. See also Searle's review of Chalmers's *The Conscious Mind: In Search of a Fundamental Theory* (1996) in "Consciousness and the Philosophers" (1997). Chalmers's reply to Searle, and Searle's response, appear in "Consciousness and the Philosophers: An Exchange" (Chalmers and Searle, 1997).

Eliminativism is defended by Paul Churchland in *Scientific Realism and the Plasticity of Mind* (1979); and in "Eliminative Materialism and the Propositional Attitudes" (1981). See also Patricia Churchland's *Neurophilosophy* (1986). Stephen Stich defends his own brand of eliminativism in *From Folk Psychology to Cognitive Science: The Case Against Belief* (1983). Lynne Rudder Baker (responding to Stich, among others) has argued that eliminativism is self-refuting; see her *Saving Belief* (1987), chap. 7, "The Threat of Cognitive Suicide." For an extended discussion of the question whether eliminativism is self-refuting, see my *The Nature of True Minds* (1992), pp. 5–11.

# CHAPTER 6
# Minds and their place in nature

**Metaphysical background**
Objects
Properties as particularized ways
The dual nature of properties
Dispositionality and causality
Complex objects
Emergence
Ontological layers
Predicates and properties
Properties, realism, and anti-realism

**Applying the view**
Multiple realizability
Is pain a property?
Pain as a second-order property
Causality and *ceteris paribus* laws
Levels of reality vs levels of description
Zombies
Qualities of conscious experience
"Privileged access"
Mental imagery
Uses of imagery
Intentionality

**Dénouement**
Dualism
The identity theory
Functionalism
Interpretationism
Concluding note

**Suggested reading**

# Minds and their place in nature

In the preceding five chapters, we have worked our way through a variety of distinct approaches to the mind. Each of these approaches was originally developed in response to a particular range of puzzles. Descartes, for instance, was struck by the apparent difference between properties of material objects and mental properties. He responded by arguing that the mental and the material are utterly different kinds of substance. Behaviorists, in contrast, were bent on making minds scientifically respectable subjects of empirical inquiry. On their view, this required showing that truths about minds and their contents could be paraphrased in terms of observable bodily motions and propensities to such motions.

Each of these various approaches can be seen as at least partly successful: each provides answers to questions regarded as especially pressing, each apparently solves certain problems. Notoriously, however, each leaves unanswered and unsolved a host of distinct problems as well. This is unsurprising. Theories of mind have been introduced to enable us to cope with particular issues that were, at the time of their introduction, considered to be central. To the extent that a theory is successful, the problems it solves recede into the background, and those it leaves unresolved become salient.

In this chapter I shall sketch an account of the mind that endeavors to make sense of what may strike us as plausible in each of the views discussed thus far, but without their attendant difficulties. I regard it as an important point in favor of the account that it encompasses core insights of a variety of distinct, even incompatible, theories. In philosophy there is a tendency to take doctrines with which we disagree and dismiss them entirely. But a view may be wrong without being altogether wrong. When we consider the historical development of theories in the philosophy of mind, we can see that the same difficulties cycle into focus again and again. One generation addresses the qualitative aspect of mentality, the next focuses on its scientific standing, its successor takes up the problem of mental content. The cycle then starts over, each generation rediscovering what had been invisible to its predecessor.

In this context, it would be foolish to claim originality for any view. Virtually every point I make in this chapter has been made before by other, more inventive philosophers. Chief among these is C. B. Martin. The position I advance here is a version of a position Martin has developed over a period of many years. (See "Suggested reading" for a listing of pertinent readings.) Martin himself borrows freely from Locke and Russell, and, although he would shudder at the thought, Descartes and Wittgenstein.

Throughout this volume, I have emphasized the importance of metaphysics and in particular, ontology – our best assessment of what there is – for the philosophy of mind. In this chapter, I endeavor to make good on this line. Certain important conclusions concerning minds and their place in nature follow from what I take to be an independently plausible ontology. I outline these in the sections that follow, although I do not try to defend them in depth. Many of these conclusions fall outside going conceptions of mind. That, I suggest, is all to the good.

Enough of this. The time has come to roll up our sleeves and get down to business.

## Metaphysical background

Nowadays the philosophy of mind includes a significant empirical component. Many philosophers of mind see themselves as "cognitive scientists" and make a point of distancing their pursuits from those of a philosophical tradition that distinguishes sharply between science and philosophy. The hope is that we can replace unconstrained metaphysical speculation with empirically informed theories. This need not be taken to imply that we are to set about providing empirical answers to longstanding philosophical questions. Rather, we should replace the questions and embark on an empirically informed investigation of the territory.

It is one thing, however, to take seriously the fruits of empirical labors, and quite another matter to imagine that the deep problems that beset the philosophy of mind will evaporate if only we formulate our concerns in a way that renders them susceptible to empirical resolution. As things now stand, even if we possessed a fully adequate empirical theory of consciousness, we should be in no position to recognize it as such. Our problem is not so much the lack of detailed information, but the lack of an adequate framework to make sense of whatever information we might obtain. We have much to learn about the brain. But, to take one currently prominent example, it is hard to see how any conceivable neurobiological discovery could account for the qualities of conscious experience.

My suggestion is that, before we can hope to advance an empirical theory of the mind, we must have a clear conception of the underlying ontology. This will give us, not an axiomatic system within which to deduce truths about the mind, but a suitable structure within which to locate empirical truths. The test of an ontology is, I believe, its power: its capacity to provide a sensible overall account of how things stand. This account should comport, at least broadly, with commonsense observation constrained by the sciences. It goes beyond the sciences, however, in providing a unifying framework within which claims issuing from the several sciences can be plotted: the sciences do not speak with a single voice.

## Objects

Let us start at the beginning. At a first approximation, the world comprises objects bearing spatial and temporal relations to one another. Some objects are complex, having objects as parts. Some objects are simple in this sense: they are not made up of other objects. I cannot offer a proof that some objects are simple. The denial that this is so entails that every object has objects as parts. I admit this as an abstract possibility, but I cannot see how it could work. (It evokes what E. J. Lowe has described as a "vertiginous feeling.") Complex objects depend for their existence on their parts, the objects that make them up. If every object is made up of other objects, however, there would seem to be nothing to ground the existence of any object.

I have described the world as comprising objects. I take it to be an empirical question – a question for science – what the objects are and what they are like. Objects might be corpuscular, particle-like, in the mold of the "atoms" envisaged by the ancient Greeks. Objects might, in contrast, be fields, points in or regions of space-time, or something stranger still.

If objects are fields or regions of space-time, then properties are properties of – not in – fields or regions of space-time. Motion of objects would then be only apparent motion: successive regions taking on and losing properties in a particular way. If you want a model, think of the motion of a scene displayed on a television screen or a train of lights moving round an old-fashioned movie marquee. Perhaps this is how it is quite generally. A billiard ball rolling across the table is really a succession of contiguous disturbances in space-time.

Corpuscular or not, objects are bearers of properties. When we consider an object we can consider it as a bearer of properties, itself incapable of being borne as a property, or we can consider its properties. This red billiard ball can be considered as something red, spherical, and having a particular mass. In so doing, we are reckoning the ball a "substance," a bearer of properties, itself unborne. But we can also consider the ball's properties: its redness, its sphericity, its mass. When we do this, we turn our minds to ways the ball is. Objects, then, even simple, non-composite objects, have structure. Properties are not parts of objects, however. The redness and sphericity of the billiard ball are not parts of the ball in the way its constituent molecules are parts of it. The ball is not made up of its properties.

So: an object is a bearer of properties. Although we can distinguish objects as property-bearers from properties they bear, these are separable only in thought, not in reality. An object cannot exist apart from its properties, nor they apart from it. An object can gain or lose properties, but this is not a matter of its properties moving elsewhere. A property is nothing more than an object's being a particular way. An object can cease to be one way and come to be some other way, but these ways cannot be transferred to other objects or "float free." Nor could an object exist, lacking properties, as a "bare particular," being no way at all.

In describing properties as I have, I mean to be distancing myself from the idea that properties are "universals." Some proponents of universals hold that universals are "transcendent" entities residing outside of space and time. Particular objects "participate in" or "instantiate" universals. Particular spherical objects might be thought to instantiate the universal sphericity. This conception of universals is associated with Plato. Another conception, perhaps stemming from Aristotle, but most recently defended by D. M. Armstrong, locates universals in their instances. The universal sphericity is taken to be wholly present in each of its spatially and temporally distinct instances. A universal is, in a certain sense, made up of its instances, although these instances are not its parts: the universal, remember, is wholly present in each of its instances.

Philosophers who regard properties as universals contend that, by so doing, we can solve the "one-over-many" problem. Consider a red billiard ball and a railroad warning flag. The billiard ball and the flag are the same in one respect and different in others. We may put this by saying that the ball and the flag *share a property* or that they possess *the same property*. A proponent of universals takes seriously the italicized phrases in the preceding sentence. If the billiard ball and the flag share a property, then there is some one thing, a property, they both possess. This property, redness, is common to all red objects. Similarities among objects are thus grounded in their shared properties. Differences are determined by properties they do not share.

You may find talk of universals mysterious. The mystery might be lessened slightly if you bear in mind that universals are meant to differ in kind from "particulars," concrete objects like warning flags and billiard balls. What holds for a particular need not hold for a universal. This helps only a little, however. It remains difficult to see what could be involved in an object's instantiating a universal (on the Platonic view) or what it could mean to say (as Armstrong says) that a universal is wholly present in each of its instances. I hope to bypass such puzzles by developing an account of properties that takes properties seriously but without a commitment to universals.

## Properties as particularized ways

Before looking more closely at the nature of properties, it might be worth asking why exactly we should imagine that the world contains such entities. Many philosophers have denied that properties exist. Talk of properties, they contend, should be replaced by talk of classes of objects. A red object is not an object that possesses the property of being red, but merely an object that belongs to a particular class: the class of red objects. Objects belong to this class, perhaps, because they are similar, but this similarity is an irreducible feature of the objects.

This is not the place to discuss such views in detail. Instead I shall merely call attention to two simple points. First, it is natural to wonder about the similarities of objects in virtue of which they belong to the class of red objects. These objects are similar in some ways, and different in some ways. Think of the red flag and the red billiard ball; these differ in shape, size, and mass, but are similar in color. This perspective on similarity pushes us back to ways objects are: objects fall into the class of red objects because they are similar in some respect. And it is hard to understand talk of "respects" here without taking it to refer to properties of objects, ways they are. If the point of introducing classes of objects, then, is to show that we might dispense with properties as ways objects are, the strategy appears to appeal to the very things it was designed to eliminate.

A second reason for suspecting that properties are more than merely classes of objects is just that it is difficult to see what could ground class membership if not shared properties. Simply put: objects belong to the class of red things because they are red; they are not red because they belong to the class of red objects.

I do not imagine that a staunch opponent of properties will be much moved by these observations. We are in a domain of philosophy where it is unreasonable to expect knock-down arguments. The most we can hope for is an account of matters that squares with our overall assessment of how things stand. In this context, we do well to remind ourselves of a simple point. Consider the sentences below:

(1) The ball is round.
(2) The ball is red.

Let us suppose that these sentences hold true of a particular billiard ball. Now it would seem on the face of it that there is something about the ball in virtue of which it is true to say of it that it is round; and something else about the ball in virtue of which it is true to say of it that it is red. In speaking of "something about the ball" we are, or surely seem to be, speaking about a way the ball is. And this is just to speak about what I have been calling a property.

I have distinguished this notion of a property – a particularized way an object is – from notions of properties as universals. Some philosophers have used the term "trope" as a label for what I am calling particularized ways. I resist this designation because it has become common for proponents of tropes to regard objects as "bundles" of tropes. This turns tropes into something too much resembling parts of objects for my taste. On the view I am advancing, objects are not made up of properties in anything like the way a billiard ball is made up of atoms or molecules. To repeat an earlier point: when we consider an object we can consider it as an unborne bearer of properties – a substance, in traditional parlance – or we can consider the properties it bears. On this view, then, an object is not a collection or bundle of properties; an object is a possessor of properties.

A simple object – an object that does not have objects as parts – is nothing more than an object possessing certain properties. Complex objects like atoms, molecules, and billiard balls are objects in a derivative sense: objects by courtesy. In just the same way properties of complex objects, to the extent that these are distinguishable from properties of their simple parts, are properties in a derivative sense. A complex object is made up of simple objects possessing particular properties and standing in particular relations to one another. The properties we find in complex objects are themselves "made up of" the properties possessed by the simple constituents in these arrangements. On this view, there is nothing more to a complex property than this. Complex properties do not "emerge"; they are nothing "over and above" the properties of the simple constituents duly arranged. (I shall have more to say about the notion of "emergence" presently.)

I might note in passing that the conception of properties I favor can accommodate ersatz universals: classes of exactly resembling properties. On this view, objects that might be thought to share a universal share, instead, membership in a class of objects possessing exactly resembling properties. The relation of resemblance these properties bear to one another is a primitive, "internal" relation. Objects resemble one another in virtue of their properties; properties – the basis of resemblance – resemble one another (when they do) *tout court*. Suppose properties $\alpha$ and $\beta$ are exactly resembling. Then this resemblance is intrinsic, built in to the properties. One consequence of this is that, if property $\chi$ exactly resembles $\alpha$, then $\chi$ exactly resembles $\beta$ as well.

Let me say a word about a matter that might worry some readers. I have described properties as ways objects are. This gives the impression that the properties are exhausted by the ways actual, existing objects are. There are, however, ways objects could be but no object is – or, for that matter, no object ever will be. Two kinds of particle could be such that, were they to collide, they would yield a third kind of particle possessing unique properties. (I discuss a case of this kind below.) This could be so even if the requisite collisions never took place. We might put this by saying that there are ways objects could be but no object is (or ever will be). Thus put, ways might appear mysterious, ghostly. We can avoid the mystery by noting that non-actual possible ways are prefigured in the ways actual objects are. Properties of existing objects are dispositional for (they are "directed to" and "selective for") manifestations – themselves properties, ways objects could be – that need never occur. The intrinsic "readinesses" of actual properties ground claims concerning non-actual, possible ways.

## The dual nature of properties

Properties are ways objects are. I regard this view as close to the commonsense conception. We distinguish the red of a billiard ball and the red of a railroad warning flag, even though these two objects may be precisely the same shade of red. There are two "instances" of red, one belonging to the ball, the other to the flag. Now it is time to look more closely at the nature of properties.

Every property, I contend (and here, as elsewhere in this chapter, I am merely following the lead of C. B. Martin), endows its possessor with both a particular disposition or "causal power" and a particular quality. Consider the property of being spherical. In virtue of its possession of this property a billiard ball has a particular quality, the quality we designate by the term "sphericity." But equally in virtue of possessing this property the ball possesses certain dispositions or causal powers. (I shall use these terms interchangeably although, because I take causality to be explicable by reference to dispositionality, I prefer "disposition" to causal power.) The ball is disposed to roll, for instance, when placed on an inclined surface.

In an effort to keep matters simple and in focus, I am oversimplifying here. The qualities and dispositionalities of any particular object result – at least – from the properties it possesses and relations these bear to one another. A ball's disposition to roll, for instance, depends both on its being spherical and on its being solid. Every property contributes in a distinctive way to the qualities and dispositionalities of objects possessing it. (I am streamlining the discussion in another respect as well. Throughout the chapter, I shall cite familiar features of objects as examples of properties – redness and sphericity, for instance. For various reasons, I doubt that either redness or sphericity is a genuine property. These serve well enough as illustrations, however, and they have the advantage of keeping the discussion from becoming hopelessly abstract. In any case, my use of such examples here does not affect the central argument of the chapter.)

The idea that properties have a dual nature is to be distinguished from the notion that there are two kinds of property: dispositional properties and "categorical" (non-dispositional) properties. On the latter view, it makes no sense to suppose that a property could be both dispositional and categorical. Every property is purely one or the other. A dispositional property, like the property of solubility possessed by a salt crystal, or the property of being fragile possessed by a delicate vase, is to be distinguished from categorical (that is, non-dispositional, purely qualitative) properties like being red or being warm. In virtue of their possession of dispositional properties, objects behave in particular ways, or would behave in particular ways under the right conditions. In virtue of their possession of categorical properties, objects exhibit particular qualities.

Under the assumption that dispositions and qualities are associated with distinct kinds of property, philosophers have been moved to advance a variety of theories. For some, the two kinds of property are irreducibly distinct. Others, however, noting that a property that endowed its possessor with no causal powers or dispositions whatsoever could make no difference at all in the world, have doubted the existence of non-dispositional, categorical properties. Such properties would be, for instance, undetectable – assuming that our detecting a property requires our being causally affected by it in some way. Moreover, as these philosophers point out, the usual examples of allegedly categorical properties are unconvincing. Take being red or being warm. Surely, an object's being red is what disposes it to reflect light in a particular way, and an object's being warm disposes it to affect the surrounding air differentially. And when we consider the properties ascribed to objects by the sciences, these seem invariably dispositional: having mass, for instance, or having negative charge, are characterized exclusively by reference to ways in which possession of these properties affects the behavior of their possessors. Considerations of this sort have convinced some philosophers that every genuine property is a dispositional property.

Another contingent of philosophers, however, appeals to the strangeness of the idea that properties could be purely dispositional. A world consisting exclusively of objects possessing dispositional properties would seem to be a world in which objects would be forever poised to act, but never act. An object's acting would be a matter of its dispositions being manifested. But if a manifestation were itself nothing more than a pure disposition, a disposition to be manifested in a particular way under the right circumstances, then the situation would resemble one in which a bank check is backed by a check, which itself is backed by a check, and so on indefinitely. Unless a check is ultimately backed by something other than a check, it is worthless; and, similarly, unless a disposition issues in something other than a pure disposition, nothing occurs.[1]

This point might be expressed slightly differently. A disposition is itself a manifestation. (I shall say more about the manifestation of dispositions presently.) If every manifestation were nothing more than a disposition for some further manifestation, the result would be an unwelcome regress. The world evidently contains actualities as well as potentialities – pure dispositionalities.

Aware of these difficulties, some theorists have suggested that dispositional properties must be "grounded" in non-dispositional properties. A dispositional property, on this view, might be a "second-order" property, a property had by an object in virtue of its possession of some first-order non-dispositional property. Consider the dispositional property of being fragile. This is a property an object – this delicate vase, for instance – might have in virtue of having a particular molecular structure. Having this structure is held to be a first-order non-dispositional property that grounds the second-order dispositional property of being fragile; the vase is fragile, not in virtue of having a dispositional property, but in virtue of having some non-dispositional structural property.

It is not easy to know what to make of this suggestion. It is hard to see, for instance, what more there is to an object's possessing a given second-order property beyond the object's possessing its first-order "grounding" property. Suppose, for instance, that being fragile is a second-order property had by this vase in virtue of its having a particular first-order property, a certain structure perhaps. In what sense exactly does the vase have two distinct properties here: a non-dispositional structural property, and a dispositional property? For that matter, in what sense is the vase's structure non-dispositional? Surely, it is its molecular structure that itself disposes the vase to reflect light in a particular way, to remain rigid at moderate temperatures, to make a particular ringing noise when tapped by a spoon, and, yes, to shatter when struck by a hard object. If having a certain structure is a property, then it would seem to be as dispositional as any other property one could imagine.

Of course, many objects with very different molecular structures could turn out to be fragile. This, however, ought not incline us to doubt that the property of being fragile possessed by this vase – this vase's fragility – is a

[1] For devotees of possible worlds, Simon Blackburn (1990, p. 64), puts the point this way: "To conceive of *all* the truths about a world as dispositional is to suppose that a world is entirely described by what is true at *neighboring* worlds. And since our argument was a priori, these truths in turn vanish into truths about yet other neighboring worlds, and the result is that there is no truth anywhere."

perfectly ordinary first-order property of the vase, perhaps the very property we have been discussing: having a particular structure. That would fit nicely with the view I have advocated. Properties have a dual nature: every property is both qualitative and dispositional, every property contributes in a distinctive way to the qualities and dispositionalities of objects possessing it. We can separate these natures only in thought – just as we can mentally separate a triangle's triangularity from its trilaterality – by considering the one without considering the other.

Locke dubbed this activity of mental separation "partial consideration." It is what enables us to consider an object's color without considering its shape, or its shape without considering its color, although every object with a shape must be an object with a color.

What relation does the dispositionality of a property bear to its qualitative nature? These are not merely necessarily connected, like triangularity and trilaterality. They are, rather, the selfsame property, differently considered. A relationship of this sort resembles that found in ambiguous figures. The drawing opposite (figure 6.1) depicts the face of an old lady and the profile of a young woman. The same lines make up both figures. We can distinguish the figures in our minds by shifting our attention. But one figure cannot be present without the other. In the same way, a property's intrinsic dispositionality and qualitative nature are separable only in thought.

In any case, the idea that objects' dispositional features are grounded in their structure appears to be a non-starter. As we have seen, structures themselves are dispositional as well as qualitative. More significantly, if we can so much as conceive simple objects, objects that lack parts – and hence lack structure in the relevant sense – we must conceive of those objects as possessing dispositionalities. They are capable of doing more than they in fact ever do. If there are elementary particles, then these particles are certainly capable of endless interactions beyond those in which they actually engage. Everything points to dispositionality's being a fundamental feature of our world.

The debate over whether properties are dispositional or categorical has had the following form. One side points out that the notion of a non-dispositional property is the notion of a property that would make no difference to its possessor. It is concluded that no genuine property is categorical (that is, in my terminology, qualitative). The opposing side focuses on the elusiveness of pure dispositionality, and concludes that no genuine property is dispositional.

Perhaps both sides' arguments are right in one respect and wrong in another. Perhaps the problem is only that inappropriate conclusions are being drawn. Suppose every property is dispositional. It does not follow that no property is qualitative. Similarly, if every property is qualitative, it

Figure 6.1

does not follow that no property (or no genuine first-order property) is dispositional. Neither of these conclusions follows because the arguments behind them are consistent with the position advanced here: every property has a dual nature, every property is both dispositional and qualitative.

Before moving on, I might point out the naturalness of this conception of properties. Consider a property like the property of being square. This property is a good example of what have standardly been regarded as categorical properties. And it is certainly true that the property of being square endows its possessors with a certain quality – the quality we associate with squareness. But it is equally true that being square endows objects with certain powers or dispositions. A square peg would pass through a square hole, but not a round hole (where the diameter of the hole matches the length of a side). A square would reflect light differently than a rectangle or a sphere. A square object would feel different to the touch than a spherical object. It is hard not to conclude that being square – squareness –

is simultaneously dispositional and qualitative. And in this it resembles every other property; or so I contend.

## Dispositionality and causality

If we are to take dispositionality seriously, then we must distinguish dispositions from their manifestations. A disposition can be perfectly real, wholly present here and now, yet remain unmanifested. A vase can be fragile without ever shattering, a substance can be soluble without ever dissolving.

Dispositions typically require for their manifestation suitable reciprocal disposition partners. If salt is soluble in water, then the dissolving of this crystal of salt is the mutual manifestation of the salt's solubility and the surrounding water's being a solvent for salt. Although a property's dispositionality is intrinsic to it, manifestations of this dispositionality may depend on the presence of appropriate reciprocal disposition partners. One and the same dispositionality can manifest itself differently depending on its reciprocal partners. Litmus paper turns pink in an acid, but the same paper turns blue in a base.

One further element is required to complete the picture. I have said that particular manifestations of many dispositions depend on the presence of appropriate reciprocal disposition partners. But they depend, as well, on the absence of disposition partners that block the manifestations in question. Salt dissolves in water, but not if an inhibitory agent is present; exposure to sunlight results in skin lesions, but not if a suitable "sun-block" is used.

Causal truths are ultimately grounded in the mutual manifestations of reciprocal disposition partners. Consider a simple causal sequence, a key's opening a lock. The effect, the lock's being open, is a mutual manifestation of dispositions possessed by the lock and the key. The cause, the key's turning, is itself the mutual manifestation of reciprocal disposition partners that include the key and the hand holding the key.

The dispositional model replaces the image of linear causal sequences or chains with a conception of the world as an inclusive dispositional network, what Martin calls a "power net." An advantage of this picture is that it enables us to dispense with misleading talk of causes versus "background" conditions. Consider a match igniting when it is struck. It is customary to think of the cause as the striking and the effect as the igniting. But the match would not ignite in the absence of oxygen. Is the presence of oxygen, then, a part of the cause? The presence of oxygen is not obviously part of the event – the striking – that we have identified as the cause. Perhaps the presence of oxygen is a "background" condition required for the cause to have the effect it has.

This way of looking at the matter requires that we distinguish causes from background conditions in a way that appears metaphysically arbitrary. If, in contrast, we see the match's igniting as the mutual manifestation of reciprocal disposition partners that include the surface on which the match is struck, the enfolding oxygen, and the chemical makeup of the match tip, we can assign equal credit to each of these contributing factors.

Another potential source of embarrassment for the prevailing view of event causation concerns the relative timing of causes and effects. A cause must precede its effects. But, as Hume noted, if a cause precedes its effect, there would seem to be a temporal gap or boundary between the occurrence of the cause and the onset of the effect. The causing event (or event component) would be over before its effect begins. But how can a completed event influence an event occurring now? If, in contrast, the causing event and its effect are temporally simultaneous or overlapping, it would seem that the portion of the causing event that occurs after the onset of the effect could not be implicated in the occurrence of the effect. Suppose you cause your car to move by pushing it. Do you first push the car and then the car moves? Your pushing and the car's moving are apparently simultaneous. Of course you set about pushing the car prior to pushing it and prior to its moving. The car is not moved by your setting about pushing it, however, but by your pushing it.

If we replace the traditional Humean picture of event-causation with Martin's "power net" conception, these worries recede. Events are mutual manifestations of reciprocal disposition partners. Reciprocal disposition partners do not stand in relations of succession to one another. The model is not that of links in a chain, but of two playing cards remaining upright by mutually supporting one another on a table top. (And note: the table top is a fully-fledged reciprocal partner, not a "background condition.")

What of "probabilistic" causation: causal relations in which causes apparently yield effects only with a certain probability? The quantum theory tells us that probabilistic causation is the rule rather than the exception. Philosophers who favor accounts of causation based on causal laws explain probabilistic causation by building probabilities into the laws. What might the analog be for a disposition-based account? Here is one possibility. Every property has a perfectly definite dispositionality. This dispositionality will manifest itself in a definite way given particular kinds of reciprocal disposition partner (and in the absence of "blockers"). It may be, however, that basic properties (or some of them) are oscillatory.

Consider an apparent case of probabilistic causation. $C$'s cause $E$'s 60 percent of the time and $F$'s 40 percent of the time under comparable conditions. Now, imagine two properties, $C_1$ and $C_2$, such that (1) $E$ is a mutual manifestation of $C_1$ and reciprocal disposition partner, $P$; (2) $F$ is a mutual manifestation of $C_2$ and reciprocal disposition partner, $P$; (3) $C_1$ and $C_2$

oscillate: $C_1$ alternates with $C_2$ in such a way that, in general, any object possessing $C_1$ or $C_2$ will possess $C_1$ (and not $C_2$) about 60 percent of the time, and $C_2$ (but not $C_1$) about 40 percent of the time; (4) it is built into $C_1$ and $C_2$ that they oscillate in this way.

It might seem that shifting the locus of probability from causal transactions (or disposition manifestations) to properties gains us nothing. I am not so sure. I grant that property oscillation is a surprising phenomenon. It strikes me as less surprising, however, than the idea that the very same properties, with the very same reciprocal disposition partners, manifest themselves differently on different occasions.

It is time to move on. I do not imagine that these brief remarks provide anything approaching decisive counterexamples to the prevailing view of event causation. I want only to indicate that the appealing simplicity of that view requires our complicating it in various unattractive ways. These complexities make perfect sense within the dispositional model. To that extent, at least, the model appears to be vindicated.

## Complex objects

The world, I have suggested, consists of a dynamic arrangement of objects. Objects may be simple or complex. A complex object has objects as parts. Simple objects have structure – a simple object is an object with properties – but no substantial parts.

This last statement requires amplification. Assume for a moment that simple objects are something more than space-time points. A simple object, although not made up of other objects, could nevertheless have spatial or temporal parts. A simple object might, for instance, have a top and a bottom half; these halves might have definite spatial dimensions. If a simple object persists through time, then we can speak of its temporal parts on analogy with its spatial parts. We could speak of the object-on-Tuesday, for instance, and distinguish this from the object-on-Wednesday. Spatial and temporal parts of an object are not, however, themselves objects. Although a sphere has two spatial halves, a sphere need not be made up of these two halves in the way a pencil is made up of a wooden shaft surrounding a cylinder of lead. (A different case would be that of a sphere made up by joining two hemispheres.) Unless otherwise noted, when I speak of parts of objects in what follows I shall not mean spatial or temporal parts, but substantial parts, parts that are themselves objects.

Complex objects have objects as parts. These parts may themselves be complex, but eventually we arrive at simple objects, those not made up of distinct objects. Let us say that complex objects are constituted by their constituent objects. Every object, then, is constituted by simple objects. Is there any more to complex objects than this? Many philosophers have thought so.

Think of a statue and the particles that make it up. (The example should remind you of the boat and the collection of planks that make up the boat discussed in chapter two.) Is the statue just the collection of particles? It would seem not. The collection of particles may change, and the statue remain. We can repair the statue and replace a piece that has broken off. When we do so, the result is a new collection of particles, but the same statue. More dramatically, we can destroy the statue by grinding it to dust without destroying the collection of particles. The statue and the collection of particles have distinct persistence conditions: the statue can continue to exist when the collection of particles does not, and the collection of particles can remain when the statue is destroyed.

Perhaps we could say that the statue is the collection of particles arranged in a particular way: the statue is the particles plus their arrangement. If the statue is ground to dust, its particles remain, but their arrangement is lost. However, it looks as though we could replace particles and the statue would remain, so long as we preserved the arrangement. Or we might alter the arrangement, thus modifying, but not destroying, the statue.

Considerations along these lines have led philosophers to the view that statues, and indeed complex objects generally, are distinct from arrangements of their constituent parts. True, they are, at any given time, made up of a collection of parts. But this just shows there is more to an object's identity than the objects that make it up and the relations these bear to one another. In the case of the statue, we might imagine two spatially overlapping objects: the statue (characterized by its identity conditions over time) and a collection of particles (characterized by its very different identity conditions over time).

The resulting picture is of a world consisting of "layers" of objects and properties. A statue, we might say, is a higher-level object; the particles that make up the statue, and perhaps certain collections of these particles, are objects at a lower level. Now it seems possible to explain the role of the special sciences. Physics is the science of objects at the basic level. Each special science – biology, for instance, or meteorology, or psychology – deals with some domain of higher-level objects. The world comprises, then, not objects, but a hierarchy of objects at distinct levels.

This layered conception of reality is widely accepted. I believe it is mistaken. Appeals to levels of reality, ontological hierarchies, leads to a distorted picture of how things stand and to a multitude of philosophical puzzles and mysteries.

Let us return to the statue. We have agreed that the statue is not to be identified with the collection of particles that make it up, nor even with the

collection of particles arranged in a particular way. In so agreeing, however, we are taking "collection" in an especially rigid sense. In this sense, a
collection is destroyed when it loses a single member, when a member is
replaced by a duplicate, or when a new member is added. I propose that we
consider a more relaxed notion of a collection. This relaxed notion is the
notion we deploy when we think of a stamp collection, or a collection of
baseball cards or paintings. In this relaxed sense, a collection can gain or
lose members, and yet remain the same collection. How many members
can a collection gain or lose, how much can a collection change and still
remain the same collection? This may be partly a matter of decision.

When we consider the statue as a collection of particles in this relaxed
sense, it is much more plausible to say that the statue is nothing over and
above, nothing other than, just this collection of particles appropriately
arranged. Still, this may not be not quite right. Arguably, statues are
artifacts, produced by intelligent creatures for particular reasons. An
appropriately arranged collection of particles that "fell from the sky" or
was produced by the random action of waves on a rocky outcropping
would not be a statue – although of course you might mistake it for one. A
statue, then, is not merely an appropriately shaped collection of particles.
In order to constitute a statue, a collection of particles must have the right
kind of causal history. This history must include intelligent creatures and
their states of mind.

Now suppose we build all this into our picture. That is, we take the
collection of particles (in the relaxed sense of collection) and add to it, not
merely relations these particles bear to one another, but also relations they
bear to other particles, themselves members of collections of particles. The
relations will be complex indeed, they will very likely exceed anything
encompassable by a finite human mind. Moreover, owing to our electing to
deploy "collection" and "appropriate arrangement" in a relaxed sense, the
possibilities for variation will be endless.

This is merely to say that there is no prospect of providing a definition,
or even a finite set of necessary and sufficient conditions, for something's
being a statue appealing only the vocabulary of particles and relations
among these. To regard this as a difficulty, however, is to miss the point.
My contention is not that talk of statues is translatable into, or analyzable
in terms of, talk of particles and their relations. The idea, rather, is that this
is all statues are; statues are nothing other than, distinct from, or over and
above collections of particles, where "collection" is taken in the relaxed
sense and includes relations these particles bear to one another and to
other collections.

Imagine that God sets out to create a world containing statues. He can
do so by creating simple objects and insuring that they bear the right
relations to one another. The creation of a single statue could well require

the creation of a dynamic arrangement of simple objects extending over time and taking in a sizable spatial region. If a statue requires the existence of intelligent creatures with particular thoughts, then other collections of simple objects with similarly extended spatial and temporal relations will need to be included as well.

Again, the thesis is not that "statue" can be defined or analyzed in terms of atoms or molecules and their relations. There is no hope of spelling out conditions of individuation or persistence in terms of constituent objects and their relations. Rather, the truth-makers for claims about statues are ultimately arrangements of simple objects: something is a statue in virtue of its being a collection (in the relaxed sense) of simple objects bearing appropriate relations to one another and to other collections of simple objects. There is no question of specifying these collections independently of our statue concept, nor is this required. The suggestion is not that we might reduce talk of statues to talk of electrons and quarks. The picture I am offering is an ontological picture, not a reductive account of the meanings of words.

Many philosophers find this picture hopelessly austere. It appears to them to deny reality to anything but the simple objects and relations these bear to one another. In the words of the ancient Greek atomist, Democritus (c. 460–c. 370 BC): only the atoms and the void are real. But this is to caricature the view. Statues exist, all right; it is just that they are nothing in addition to collections of simpler objects. Statues are not higher-level entities – except in the ontologically innocuous sense that they are complex entities made up of simpler constituents in complex arrangements. And this is so, as well, for every putatively higher-level entity, including ourselves, our social institutions, and the products of these.

A final point bears mention. The example of a statue and particles that make it up encourages the idea that the universe is grainy: complex objects are assemblages of simple objects that are themselves corpuscular. Although I admit this as a possibility, it is not the only possibility and, if physics is to be believed, it is not even an especially likely possibility. Imagine, for a moment, that simple objects are regions of space-time that themselves possess certain properties. Such objects are not particle-like, although we may well experience them as particle-like.

I do not think that this would affect anything I have said here. I have, to be sure, spoken of statues and their constituent particles, but this could be regarded as nothing more than a way of speaking about frighteningly complicated arrangements of disturbances in space-time. As it happens, the world is such that these disturbances are rarely isolated affairs. They tend to "clump together" in particular ways. This "clumping" gives rise to what we describe (to my mind, quite correctly) as statues and the particles making them up.

Although I remain officially agnostic on the question of whether objects are ultimately particles, or fields, or something else – this is not, after all, a question for a philosopher to decide – I shall continue to treat objects as "continuants," moving about in space and persisting over time. This is purely a matter of linguistic convenience. I am supposing that the truth-makers for claims about objects could turn out to be something that does not match our ordinary conception of objects as persisting, mobile, self-contained entities.

## Emergence

This compositional picture is meant to apply to properties as well as objects. Complex properties are properties of complex objects. (Which is not to deny that a complex object could have a simple property. As we noted earlier, a spherical object might be simple or complex.) A complex property is nothing over and above the properties of a complex object's constituent objects arranged as they are.

This conception stands in contrast to the view that properties of wholes are "emergent." The world consists of simple objects. Properties of these simple objects are simple properties. (It could turn out, and indeed it appears altogether likely, that there are, in fact, very few simple properties or kinds of simple property.) Every combinatorial possibility is written into the simple properties. These include possibilities that have never been manifested and never will be manifested. New combinations of properties are just that: new combinations, not new properties. (This is not to reject complex properties, but only to reaffirm that complex properties are nothing over and above their constituents suitably arranged.)

Does this mean that emergence, genuine emergence, the emergence of genuinely new properties (as distinct from new arrangements of old properties), is impossible? Not at all. If emergence occurs – and we have no reason to doubt that it does – it occurs at the basic level. At the basic level what is emergent cannot be reduced to anything more basic. Imagine, for instance, that the universe contained just two kinds of elementary particle, $\alpha$-particles and $\beta$-particles. Prior to some particular time, these particles never interact – owing, perhaps, to their occupying non-overlapping spatial regions. Eventually, however, an $\alpha$-particle and a $\beta$-particle collide. The result is the emergence of a new kind of elementary particle, a $\chi$-particle. Something like this might have occurred during, or immediately after, the Big Bang. And it may occur nowadays in particle accelerators.

The compositional picture obliges us to distinguish complex properties that are nothing more than (possibly novel) combinations of simple properties, from genuinely emergent simple properties. The possibility of simple emergent properties is written into (that is, is intrinsic to) the properties that serve as the vehicles of their emergence. In this regard, all the possibilities flow from the simple properties. These possibilities include the possibility of complex, non-emergent properties, and the possibility of simple, non-complex emergents.

## Ontological layers

Does the ontology I am recommending fly in the face of everyday experience or our ordinary take on reality? Not at all. It does, certainly, fly in the face of a popular philosophical refrain according to which the world is layered: the world contains levels of objects and properties. These levels are philosophical posits introduced as ingredients of philosophical theories. Such theories are, often enough, designed to account for our everyday experience. In rejecting a philosophical posit and the theory in which it is embedded, however, I am not recommending that you turn your back on everyday experience. On the contrary, I am offering a competing account of the basis of that experience, one that, with luck, meshes as well with what the sciences tell us about our world.

At this point, someone could dig in. The layered view of the world, it might be argued, comes not from everyday experience, but from science. The special sciences concern objects and properties occupying distinct ontological strata. Each level is autonomous with respect to those below it, in the sense that it cannot be reduced to lower levels. Laws governing higher-level objects are not replaceable by or derivable from lower-level laws. Nevertheless, objects and properties at higher levels are in some way grounded in objects and properties occupying lower levels. The favored account of this grounding relation is thought to be captured by the notion of "supervenience": higher-level items supervene on those at lower levels. This means, roughly, that lower-level objects and properties suffice for higher-level objects and properties, but that the higher-level supervening objects and properties are distinct from their lower-level grounds.[1] Their being distinct is reflected in (or perhaps is constituted by) their being governed by distinct laws of nature.

An evaluation of this approach will require a detour through the philosophy of language.

---

[1] Supervenience, as it is usually characterized, is consistent with, but does not imply, the second conjunct. I include it merely to make explicit one prominent motive for appeals to supervenience.

## Predicates and properties

Properties, as I have characterized them, are concrete features of the world: particularized ways objects are. Such features are to be distinguished from our representations of them. We distinguish the property of sphericity – being spherical – from the predicate "is spherical," a linguistic expression the role of which is to name or designate the property. Does every property have a linguistic designation? That seems unlikely. As we learn more about our world, we uncover new, as yet unnamed, properties. Laboratories and particle accelerators are designed to facilitate the creation of new properties, properties not previously encountered. When this happens, we are obliged to invent a new name or devise a descriptive predicate.

This much seems obvious. What is less obvious, however, is whether every predicate designates a property. To be sure, some predicates apparently designate nothing at all: the predicate "is a cure for the common cold," although perfectly meaningful, designates no property possessed by any object. Does that mean that it designates no property? Perhaps; unless one countenances the existence of properties that have no instances.

Other predicates present different challenges. Consider the predicate "is good." It is a matter of great controversy whether this predicate designates a property of objects, or whether it serves merely to signal a speaker's approval of objects. When you tell me that Brussels sprouts are good, are you saying that Brussels sprouts, in addition to being leafy, green, and pungent, possess the property of being good? Or are you rather commending Brussels sprouts (perhaps because they are leafy, green, and pungent)? We need not try to answer this question here. It is enough to recognize that it is at least a matter of dispute whether "is good" designates a genuine property.

What of a predicate like "is a stone"? Does this predicate designate a property possessed by objects, those qualifying as stones? There are stones, undeniably. But is there a property, the property of being a stone, possessed by certain objects and in virtue of which it is true that these objects are stones? This may strike you as an odd question, but bear with me. Perhaps we can see our way through at least one philosophical thicket, and begin to pull some of the lessons of this chapter together.

## Properties, realism, and anti-realism

Philosophers sometimes argue as follows.

> (A) Take a predicate, "$\phi$." Either "$\phi$" designates a property or it does not. If "$\phi$" designates a property, then to say that

something, *a*, is $\phi$ is to say something true (if *a* has $\phi$) or false (if *a* lacks $\phi$). We are realists about $\phi$'s insofar as we take "$\phi$" to express a property. Otherwise we are anti-realists about $\phi$'s.

Anti-realists about a given domain hold that entities in the domain are either non-existent or in some way mind-dependent. Most of us are anti-realists in the first sense about ghosts and unicorns. We deny that such things exist. Putting this into the philosophers' linguistic mode: we believe that the predicate "is a ghost" and the predicate "is a unicorn" designate nothing at all. (One qualification: any consistent predicate can hold true of agents' beliefs. It might be true of you that you believe in ghosts or unicorns.) Relative to believers in such things, we could be described as "eliminativists" about ghosts and unicorns. Where $\phi$'s are unicorns, we declare that there are no $\phi$'s.

Other anti-realists are more subtle – or devious. They hold that sentences apparently ascribing $\phi$'s to objects need to be understood, not as straightforward ascriptions, but as something else. "Expressivist" views in ethics are a familiar example. To say that *a* is good, for instance, is taken not to ascribe a property, goodness, to *a*, but to express the speaker's approval of *a*.

All this is well and good, but what are we to say about thesis (A)? My suggestion is that (A) mischaracterizes realism. One source of this mischaracterization is a failure to take seriously the distinction between predicates and properties. And one result of a tacit allegiance to (A), or something like (A), is that the kind of ontology introduced in this chapter is unjustifiably cast in an especially unflattering light.

To see what is wrong with (A), consider how a predicate might be thought to hold true of an object. The predicate "is spherical," we might say, holds true of a billiard ball in virtue of the ball's possessing the property of being spherical. Now consider the predicate "is a stone." Most of us would agree that this predicate holds true of many objects: many objects are stones. Does "is a stone" name or designate a property of objects, a property in virtue of which objects satisfy the predicate "is a stone"?

Do not say: well of course! If the predicate did not designate a property, then it would be false that it was satisfied by objects. But that is absurd – surely there are stones! This amounts to nothing more than a reaffirmation of (A).

Let us briefly reconsider properties. If, against my recommendation, you regard properties as universals, then every object possessing this property must be, in some respect, identical with, or at the very least exactly similar to, every other object possessing it. If you agree with me that a property is a way an object is, then you will agree that the sense in which two objects "share" a property, the sense in which they have "the same" property, is just that the two objects are exactly similar in some way. Although the sphericity of this billiard ball is numerically distinct from the sphericity of another billiard ball, the sphericity of the two balls is exactly similar. None of this implies that, if being spherical is a property, every spherical object must be exactly like every other. It does imply that every spherical object must be exactly like every other spherical object in some way.

In the case of sphericity, it appears obvious that this condition is often satisfied. Many different objects, many different kinds of object, are identical (or exactly similar) with respect to their sphericity. (If you are worried that no two objects could be exactly similar with respect to their sphericity, then replace sphericity with the mass of an electron. I use the example only to illustrate the point, not to make it.) What of being a stone? Again, many different things, many different kinds of thing, satisfy the predicate "is a stone." But do these things share a single property, are they identical (or exactly similar) in some one respect, a respect in virtue of which the predicate "is a stone" holds true of them? Suppose, as I think likely, they do not. Must we conclude that stones do not exist? Must we be anti-realists about stones?

No; not unless we cling to principle (A). The predicate "is a stone," like most predicates, is intended to apply indifferently to a wide range of objects with a wide range of complex properties. It does so, not because these objects are identical (or exactly similar) in some one respect. It does so because the objects are similar enough. How similar objects must be to satisfy a predicate depends on the predicate. This is something we learn when we learn to apply particular predicates to objects.

I do not think that there is anything new or startling about this idea. It has been advanced at various times by many different philosophers. Wittgenstein is only the most celebrated recent example of a philosopher who has harped on the point. But I do not think the idea includes much in the way of substantive philosophy. Every language user appreciates it quite directly.

Now, it is crucially important to see that a predicate that does not designate a property could nevertheless hold true (or fail to hold true) of an object in virtue of that object's properties. An object is spherical, perhaps, in virtue of possessing the property of sphericity. An object is a stone, however, not in virtue of possessing the property of being a stone, but in virtue of possessing certain other properties. It could well be the case that properties sufficing for the application of the predicate "is a stone" form an open-ended class. If this is so, then stones need have nothing in common beyond a certain family resemblance. Only a philosopher with an agenda would conclude from this that there are no stones, or that nothing really is a stone.

Let me summarize. Some predicates hold true of objects in virtue of properties possessed by those objects. Of these predicates, some designate properties possessed by the objects to which they apply. Others do not. (In putting the point this way, I am using expressions of the form " '$\phi$' designates (or 'expresses') a property" to characterize cases in which "$\phi$" functions as the name of a property – if properties are universals – or as the name of a class of exactly similar properties – if properties are my particularized "ways.") Realism about a given predicate, "$\phi$," realism about $\phi$'s, requires that "$\phi$" applies truly to objects in virtue of properties possessed by those objects. Realism does not require that "$\phi$" designates a property. If "$\phi$" does designate a property, then objects satisfying "$\phi$" must be identical (or exactly similar) in some one respect, a respect in virtue of which "$\phi$" holds true of them. And, we might add, objects that do not satisfy "$\phi$" differ from objects that do satisfy "$\phi$" in this respect. (I do not mean, of course, that objects sharing a property could not be identical – or exactly similar – in many respects, nor that objects lacking the property could not be different in many respects.)

All this, I submit, is just to take properties seriously. When we do, we must grant that it is unlikely that we could "read off" the properties from the predicates contained in ordinary language. Moreover, unless you regard (A) as unassailable, you should be happy to allow that predicates need not name properties in order to hold true of objects, and indeed to hold true of those objects in virtue of properties they possess.

I see this line of reasoning as a natural extension of the line taken on objects earlier. We can allow that statues exist – we can be realists about statues – without supposing that "being a statue" designates a single property shared by all statues. This fits smoothly with the compositional picture. A statue is nothing more than a collection of simpler objects bearing appropriate relations to one another and to other collections of objects. This in no way jeopardizes the standing of ordinary objects like statues, nor, I believe, would anyone other than a philosopher imagine that it does.

## Applying the view

The world comprises simple objects standing in endless relations to one another. Simple objects, although lacking in parts, exhibit a structure. We can consider an object as a bearer of properties, itself unborne. We can also consider an object by considering its properties, ways the object is. Complex objects are made up of (possibly dynamic) collections of simple objects. Complex objects possess complex properties, properties wholly constituted by properties of the object's simple constituents arranged as they are. Distinct objects "share" a property when there is some way in which the objects are exactly similar.

You need not agree with the details of this ontological blueprint to appreciate the lessons for the philosophy of mind I now hope to extract from it. An adequate defense of those details would require an extended excursion into hard-core metaphysics not appropriate in a volume of this sort. The same could be said for most of what follows. My intent is not to offer knock-down proofs, however, but merely to illustrate the benefits of a comprehensive ontology for the kinds of issues in the philosophy of mind that have occupied us throughout the preceding chapters.

## Multiple realizability

Philosophers of mind, particularly those of a functionalist bent, are fond of the idea that mental properties are "multiply realizable." I know of no clear account of multiple realizability, but the idea is roughly this:

> (MR) A property, $\phi$, is multiply realizable, when an object, $\alpha$'s, having $\phi$ depends on and is determined by $\alpha$'s possessing some property, $\sigma$, from a (possibly open-ended) class of properties, $\Sigma$. When a member of $\Sigma$ is possessed by some object, it realizes $\phi$.

I do not put much weight on the details of this characterization. What I have to say depends only on the idea that, when a property is multiply realized, objects possessing it possess both that property and the property that realizes it. This, I think, is a central feature of the notion of multiple realizability as most philosophers conceive of it.

Let us pretend that being in pain is a multiply realized property. It is a property possessed, as we suppose, by many very different kinds of creature. If the property is multiply realized, then each creature possessing it does so in virtue of possessing some distinct realizing property. This property realizes pain in that creature. The guiding idea is that a property like being in pain has endless and varied realizers. The neurological property that realizes your pain is to be distinguished from the very different neurological property that realizes pain in an octopus. If Alpha Centaurians experience pain, and if Alpha Centaurians have silicon-based nervous systems, then some utterly different property realizes pain in Alpha Centaurians.

One much-discussed problem facing those who, like functionalists, regard mental properties generally as multiply realizable, is the problem of mental causation. If a mental property is realized by a material property, then it looks as though its material realizer pre-empts any causal contribution on the part of the realized mental property.

The difficulty is illustrated in figure 6.2 (where $M_1$ and $M_2$ are mental properties, $P_1$ and $P_2$ are non-mental realizers, ⇑ represents the realizing relation, and → indicates the causal relation.) In this case, mental properties, $M_1$ and $M_2$, appear to be "epiphenomenal": $M_1$ has no causal part in bringing about either $P_2$ or $M_2$.

If you insist that mental properties make a causal difference, then you are obliged to say how this might work. Suppose, for instance, $M_1$ is the property of being in pain, $P_1$ is its neurological realizer, $M_2$ is the property of intending to take aspirin, and $P_2$ is $M_2$'s realizer. Now, it is natural to suppose that $M_1$ brings about $M_2$ (figure 6.3). Given the relation of $M_2$ to $P_2$, however, it is hard to see how $M_1$ could produce $M_2$, except by inducing $P_2$ (figure 6.4). What makes it the case – or so it would seem – that $M_2$ is on the scene, is not $M_1$, but $P_2$'s being on the scene. The difficulty now is that $P_2$ appears to be "causally overdetermined." $P_1$, by itself, provides sufficient causal grounds for $P_2$.

Worse, perhaps, in imagining that $M_1$ could play a role in the production of $P_2$, we seem to be flying in the face of a widely-held belief that the physical order is "causally closed" or autonomous. Whether this is a serious difficulty, or merely a prejudice that we could abandon without jeopardizing the autonomy of physics, is debatable. I shall argue, in any case, that we need not choose between epiphenomenalism (illustrated in figure 6.2), on the one hand, and, on the other hand, "downward causation" (figure 6.4).

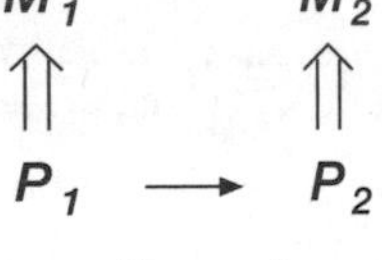

$$M_1 \qquad M_2$$
$$\Uparrow \qquad \Uparrow$$
$$P_1 \longrightarrow P_2$$

Figure 6.2

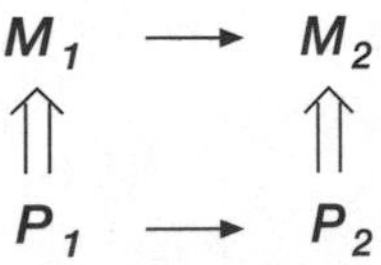

$$M_1 \longrightarrow M_2$$
$$\Uparrow \qquad \Uparrow$$
$$P_1 \longrightarrow P_2$$

Figure 6.3

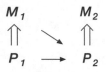

Figure 6.4

Suppose, first, that I am right about properties endowing objects possessing them with particular dispositionalities and qualitative characteristics: an object has the dispositions (or causal powers) and qualities it has in virtue of the properties it possesses. Further, every property makes a distinctive contribution to the dispositionality and qualitative character of objects to which it belongs. This supposition squares with the conception of properties advanced in the first section of this chapter. (And it squares, as well, with many other conceptions of properties.) Now imagine that being in pain is realized in you by your possessing a particular complex neurological configuration. When we consider your wiring, it looks as though it is this neurological configuration – the putative realizer of pain – and not the pain itself that brings about bodily changes we associate with pain.

You may find this last thought baffling. If a property realizes the property of being in pain, then why not say that pain is identifiable with its realizer? If the realizing property makes a causal contribution, then so does the realized property, being in pain. The difficulty (or rather one of the difficulties) with this suggestion is that proponents of multiple realizability regard it as vital to distinguish realized, higher-level properties from their lower-level realizers. Thus, when a higher-level property is realized by a lower-level property, both properties must somehow be present. The realized property, or its instance, cannot be absorbed by the realizing property, or its instance.

Attempts to reconcile multiple realizability and causal efficacy have included appeals to purely counterfactual accounts of causation, to the idea that any property that figures in a causal law (even a "hedged" *ceteris paribus* law) thereby possesses causal efficacy, and to assorted varieties of reductionism: mental properties are to be identified with their realizers or with disjunctions of their realizers. I think that we have a right to be suspicious of all these strategies. Rather than arguing the point here, however, I shall present an alternative picture of multiple realizability. This alternative picture takes seriously the ontology of properties, and applies my earlier observations about predicates and properties.

## Is pain a property?

Suppose, if you will, that the predicate "is in pain," like the predicate "is a stone," does not designate a property. True enough, the predicate "is in pain" is satisfied by objects, and it is satisfied by those objects in virtue of their properties. But the property in virtue of which an object satisfies the predicate "is in pain" is not the generic property of being in pain. There is no such property.

I hope I have said enough to make it clear that I am not advocating a form of eliminativism or anti-realism about pain. I am not denying that it is often true of creatures that they are in pain. The idea, rather, is that "is in pain" applies to creatures that are similar in certain salient respects: similar enough to merit application of the predicate. These similarities stem from creatures' possession of certain properties. But the properties need not be the same in every case: creatures are neither identical nor exactly similar in those respects in virtue of which it is true of them that they satisfy the predicate "is in pain."

This result would seem to offer us exactly what we want. It allows us to be realists about pain, but it does not lead to worries about pain's being causally insignificant, "epiphenomenal." Moreover, it accommodates the notion that what it is in virtue of which a creature is in pain could vary widely across species or even individuals. Pretend, for a moment, that pain is, at least in part, a functional notion. That is, a creature satisfies the predicate "is in pain" partly in virtue of being in a state that plays a particular sort of complex causal role. (This could be so even if pain has, as I believe it must have, an essential qualitative dimension.) As functionalists never tire of pointing out, many different kinds of state could play this role. (This is especially clear because any specification of the role will, of necessity, incorporate a measure of vagueness.) Very different kinds of creature, then, could be in pain. They are all in pain, however, not because they share (in whatever sense) a property – the putatively higher-level property of being in pain – but because they are similar in relevant ways. The ways are relevant because they are so counted by wielders of the predicate "is in pain." And their similarities stem from distinct but similar complex properties possessed by creatures satisfying this predicate.

## Pain as a second-order property

As we discovered in chapter four, mainstream functionalists contend that, by virtue of being functional properties, mental properties are second-order properties. Being in pain is, on this view, the second-order property of possessing some property (being in some state) that fills a particular functional role. (Differently put: pain is the role, not its occupant.) Although I have grave doubts about functionalism, let us imagine for the moment that all there is to a creature's being in pain is for the creature to possess an appropriate functional organization. Does it follow that being in pain is a second-order property?

It is not at all clear what there could be to an object's possessing a second-order property beyond its possessing some first-order realizing property. Suppose, as we have been supposing, that the predicate "is in pain" is satisfied by objects possessing a range of distinct, though similar, properties, properties similar with respect to the dispositionalities they bestow on their possessors. There is no obvious reason to postulate an additional second-order property to accompany each of these diverse first-order properties – and good reasons not to do so. If there is a second-order unifying element in the picture, it is supplied by our use of the predicate.

If I am right about this, then multiple realizability is not, as it is standardly thought to be, a relation among properties. It is simply the phenomenon of predicates applying to objects in virtue of distinct, though pertinently similar, properties possessed by those objects. And it would seem that this is something that holds of many of the predicates we deploy in everyday life and in the pursuit of science.

Someone might object that a view of this sort requires an excessively austere conception of properties. Why not allow that, when it is true of me that I am in pain, it is true in virtue of my possessing a distinctive property? This property may be complex, but no less a property for that. And if this much is conceded, then why not grant that the property in question is the property of being in pain?

This objection misses the point. Nothing I have said denigrates complex properties. Suppose you satisfy the predicate "is in pain" in virtue of possessing a certain complex property, $\pi$. Might creatures very different from you, creatures belonging to other species, satisfy the predicate "is in pain" in virtue of possessing $\pi$? That would seem unlikely. Remember: distinct objects that share a property must be, in some respect, exactly similar or even (on some views of properties as universals) identical. (And "identical" here means, not exactly similar, but "one and the same.") If we take seriously familiar functionalists' arguments for multiple realizability, however, we shall be strongly inclined to doubt that the requisite exact similarities (or identities) are in the cards.

This conclusion depends, not on some arcane conception of properties, but merely on an element common to many conceptions. I regard this as an important point in its favor. Equally important is its being based, not on a conception of properties tailored to some thesis in the philosophy of mind, but on an independently motivated ontological picture.

## Causality and *ceteris paribus* laws

A view of the kind I have sketched enables us to make sense of the significance of so-called *ceteris paribus* laws in the special sciences, including psychology (see chapter four). *Ceteris paribus* laws are taken to differ from allegedly "strict" exceptionless laws associated with physics. The behavior of every material object is governed by the laws of physics. Supposed higher-level objects, however, in virtue of their supposed higher-level properties, are thought to be governed by less strict *ceteris paribus* laws. Indeed, a predicate's figuring in formulations of such laws is sometimes taken as a criterion of its designating a genuine higher-level property. This is thought to account for the "projectability" of certain predicates. (A predicate is projectable when it can, for instance, be deployed successfully in inductive contexts – in reasoning, for instance, from all heretofore observed $\alpha$'s are $\beta$'s to all $\alpha$'s are $\beta$'s.)

On the view I am recommending, there are no higher-level objects or properties. There are, to be sure, complex objects, objects made up of parts that are themselves objects. Properties of complex objects – complex properties – owe their nature to properties of their constituent objects and relations these constituent objects bear to one another (and, in some cases, to external objects as well). We are supposing that an object's dispositional character is bestowed on it by its properties, and that properties are distinguished, in part, by the dispositionalities they bestow. Objects possessing similar properties can be counted on to behave similarly, then, at least insofar as their behavior is affected by their possession of those properties. This, I submit, is enough to ground lawlike generalizations holding – *ceteris paribus*, other things equal – of those objects.

This way of looking at matters locates causal powers squarely in the world and downplays causal laws as distinct external factors in causal relations. A causal law is expressed by a true statement that holds of the world in virtue of the properties present in the world. Worlds, indiscernible with respect to the properties present in them, would then be indiscernible with respect to their causal laws. Laws are contingent, if they are contingent, not because there could be worlds indiscernible from ours with respect to their objects and properties, but discernible with respect to their laws. Rather, laws are contingent if there could be worlds discernible with respect to properties present in those worlds.

## Levels of reality vs levels of description

Where does this leave us? My suggestion is that we should do well to dispense with the voguish "layered" conception of the world. It is one thing to accept the platitude that reality can be variously described, and then to notice that our descriptions can be ordered in a loose hierarchy. It is another matter to reify the hierarchy, imagining that it maps ontological strata.

I suspect that the tendency to read our descriptive practices into the world is abetted by our sometimes excessive reliance on formal techniques in addressing substantive metaphysical concerns. Abstract reasoning requires ontological grounding, however. This is easy to lose sight of so long as we persist in conceptualizing substantive issues by invoking purely modal notions like supervenience (a detailed discussion of which you have been mercifully spared) and relying on appeals to counterfactual and sub-junctive conditional analyses to capture substantive features of the world – like dispositionality and its cousin causality. We need not, perhaps, commit ourselves to a detailed ontological scheme, but we must at least have a grasp of the options and their implications. And this is a matter of taking up an attitude of ontological seriousness.

## Zombies

In assessing functionalism in chapter four, we encountered the distinct-ively philosophical notion of a zombie. A zombie, you may recall, is a being just like you or me with respect to its physical constitution, but lacking in conscious experience. Zombies are not detectable (so the story goes), because their nervous systems are, physically at least, exactly like ours. As a result, their behavior perfectly mirrors ours. When a zombie sits on a tack, its neural circuits are activated just as yours would be had you sat on a tack, and so it leaps up, yelping. What the zombie lacks is any conscious feeling of pain.

How could a zombie fail to notice this deficit, you might ask. Well, functionalism holds that mental properties are functional properties. Func-tional properties are possessed by objects in virtue of their dispositional makeup. And (we are assuming) a zombie's dispositional makeup, like yours or mine, is grounded in its nervous system. The zombie, then, will behave as you or I behave, and believe what you or I believe. The zombie will, just as you or I would, scoff at the suggestion that it lacks conscious experiences. And because the zombie believes that it has conscious experi-ences, its denial is, although false, perfectly sincere.

You may find all this quite beyond the pale. The thought that there could be a creature who is a molecule-for-molecule duplicate of you, yet lacks any conscious experiences is one only a philosopher could entertain. The idea, however, is that there is nothing in the intrinsic nature of our physical constitution that flat-out guarantees consciousness in the way three-sidedness guarantees triangularity. This is sometimes expressed by saying that it is "logically (or "conceptually") possible" that zombies exist. Of course (the thought continues), as a matter of fact the laws of nature ensure that any creature with your physical constitution (indeed, if David Chalmers is right, any system at all with the right kind of functional organization) will be conscious. In the same way, although there is no logical impossibility in the thought that pigs can fly, pigs cannot fly. The difference in these cases is that we can see why pigs cannot fly, we have an explanation of their inability to fly. We have no comparable explanation for the fact that certain neural configurations yield conscious experiences. Laws of nature are contingent; they hold in our world, but there is no further reason why they should hold: they just do. Thus, the connection between your physical nature and your conscious experiences, although predictable, is, in the final analysis, imponderable, an inexplicable brute fact. This is the deep mystery at the center of what Chalmers calls the "hard problem" of consciousness.

The first thing to notice about a view of this sort is that it presumes a particular ontology of properties. Properties are taken to be bearers of causal powers: a property contributes in a unique way to the dispositionalities of objects possessing it. The causal powers or dispositionality of a property are not intrinsic to it, however, not a part of its nature. It is at least "logically possible" that there could be a world consisting of objects bearing the same properties as objects in our world (and no others), yet in that world the properties would bestow entirely different dispositionalities on their bearers. Further, the relation between the dispositional and the qualitative is contingent. It is, at most, a matter of contingent natural law that objects possessing particular dispositionalities possess particular qualities.

We have seen that there is an alternative to this conception of properties. Every property exhibits a dual nature: it is both dispositional and qualitative. This means that every property contributes in a distinctive way to its possessor's qualities and to its possessor's dispositionalities. These contributions belong to the nature of the property. It would be impossible, flat-out impossible, for there to be a world containing the same properties as our world (and no more), but differing in respect to the causal powers or qualities possessible by its objects.

Every property makes a definite contribution to the qualities of objects possessing it. Philosophers sometimes speak as though qualities were unique to conscious experiences. These qualities – "qualia," so-called – are regarded as a special problem for the philosophy of mind. But, as we have seen, there is ample reason to think that every object has qualities. We are apt to lose sight of this seemingly obvious point if we follow the functionalists and fixate on causal powers. When we do that, qualities seem not to matter. If qualities do not matter, if they are "epiphenomenal," then they lack scientific standing. And, indeed, when we look at science, we find that qualities are, on the whole, ignored. In physics, for instance, laws and principles are formulated as ranging over numerical magnitudes that are presumably grounded in the dispositionalities of the fundamental constituents and states. It is a mistake, however, to interpret physics' silence about qualities as an outright denial that objects, even fundamental objects – quarks and electrons – have qualities.

Suppose I am right; suppose every property contributes in a distinctive way to its possessor's dispositionalities and qualities; and suppose that this is built into the nature of properties. Suppose, as well, that you are at bottom a complex object wholly constituted by simpler objects bearing appropriate relations to one another and to other objects that make up the world. Your experiences are states of and events involving this complex object. These states and events are manifestations and manifestings of finely-tuned dispositionalities, expressions of your dispositional nature. But you have, as well, a qualitative nature, one inseparable (except in thought) from your dispositionality. Your experiences have the qualities they have, not because these are tacked on by idiosyncratic laws of nature, but because they are built into the properties that constitute your mental life. Whatever exists has qualities, so it is no surprise that states of mind have qualities.

## Qualities of conscious experience

Now a new problem arises, however. The qualities of experiences evidently differ dramatically from qualities we discover when we inspect the nervous systems of conscious agents. How could the qualities of a conscious experience turn out to be the qualities of brains and neurological events?

You are looking at a ripe tomato in bright sunlight and having a characteristic kind of conscious experience. Simultaneously, a neuroscientist scans your brain. But the neuroscientist observes nothing at all resembling the qualities of your experience. The neuroscientist's observations reveal only assorted spongy, gray neurological qualities utterly foreign to your experience. And, in fact, the qualities of your experience appear to be found nowhere else; they seem not to be the sorts of quality that could conceivably occur outside your experiences – or the experiences of other conscious beings.

This way of formulating the problem, however, is founded on a confusion, one we first encountered in chapter three.

As a preliminary, let us be clear that the qualities we are concerned with are the qualities of your visual experience of a tomato and not qualities of the tomato. It should present no surprise that nothing red and roundish occurs inside your cranium when you look at a red and roundish tomato. To be sure, you are apt to describe your experience as of a red round object, but it is the tomato that is red and round, not your experience. So the first distinction to be made here is that between qualities of experiences and qualities of objects experienced.

A second distinction is related to the first. When a neuroscientist observes your brain (visually, let us suppose), the neuroscientist undergoes certain experiences with certain intrinsic qualities. There is no reason to think that the qualities of this experience ought in any way to resemble the qualities of your experience of a tomato (and in fact every reason to think that they ought not to resemble those qualities). Suppose that your visual experience of the tomato is constituted by a complex occurrence in your brain, and that this occurrence is observed by the neuroscientist. Then there is no particular mystery in the fact that the neuroscientist's experience differs qualitatively from your experience.

Now, however, we find ourselves face to face with a deeper mystery. The qualities of our experiences appear to differ utterly from the qualities of any imaginable material object. How then could we seriously entertain the hypothesis that conscious agents are nothing more than congeries of material objects, conscious experiences nothing more than manifestations of complex material dispositions?

I take the worry here to be two-fold. First, the qualities of conscious experience seem utterly different – qualitatively, if you like – from the qualities of material objects. Second, the qualities of conscious experience appear to be ineluctably tied to subjects of experience, experiencers. Without experiencers, these qualities could not exist. They are in this respect mind-dependent. Further, our "access" to these qualities is direct and privileged in a way that does not hold for our access to the qualities of any material object. The qualities of a conscious experience are necessarily "private," available only to the agent undergoing the experience; the qualities of material objects, in contrast, are "public," and necessarily so. Let me address these concerns in order.

I have advanced what many philosophers would describe as a "materialist" or "physicalist" conception of mind. I reject this description for reasons that will soon become clear. But, for the moment, let us suppose that the position I am advocating is a form of materialism. This means, I suppose, that every object, property, state, and event is a material object, property, state, or event.

As you read these words, you are undergoing a particular visual experience, you are visually experiencing the print on this page (and perhaps much else besides). Direct your attention to the qualities of this experience. This will require a shift of attention from the words on the page to your awareness of the words on the page. The qualities you encounter when you do so are not ones you can easily describe. This is not because these qualities are unfamiliar or elusive. They are the most familiar qualities of all. If they seem difficult to describe, this is because you have learned to ignore them, to treat them as transparent indicators of the qualities of perceived objects. Your description of them, then, would likely be framed in terms of the objects your experience is an experience of: the qualities of your current visual experience are qualities of the sort you have when you look at a book in conditions like those under which you are now looking at this book.

In becoming aware of the qualities of your experience, then, assuming materialism, you become aware of material qualities, presumably qualities of your brain. The qualities of your experiences are the only material qualities with which you are acquainted in this immediate way. Your acquaintance with the qualities of the book is causally indirect. (It is causally indirect even if it is not "epistemically indirect," even if it does not require an inference on your part.) It is a matter of your undergoing an experience as a result of your perceptual contact with the book. This experience is a mutual manifestation of neurological dispositions and those of the book and the intervening light radiation.

Your visual awareness of the print on this page is a matter of your having experiences with particular qualities. A neuroscientist's simultaneous visual awareness of goings-on in your brain is a matter of the neuroscientist's having experiences with particular qualities. In each case, the qualities are qualities of neurological activities. The qualities constituting the neuroscientist's awareness differ from the qualities constituting your awareness. This is not because the qualities belong to radically distinct kinds of substance – yours belonging to a mental substance, the neuroscientist's to a material substance. On the contrary, the qualities of both experiences belong to brains.

It would seem, then, that we have a direct line to some material qualities, qualities of our brains. The puzzle (presupposed by philosophers who regard "qualia" as mysterious) of how the qualities of conscious experiences could possibly be qualities of material objects is undercut. If we are serious materialists, then it is hard to see how this result could be avoided.

Ah, but I have denied that the view sketched in this chapter is materialist. Am I an idealist? Not at all. I reject the "materialist" label only because it carries with it the implication that there is a bifurcation between the mental and the material. On the view I am recommending, there is no such bifurcation. If you insist on a label, I prefer one used by Bertrand Russell – and, more recently, by Michael Lockwood – in making many of the points I have been making here: "neutral monism." Neutral monism is just the denial that there is a mental–material chasm to be bridged. One advantage of such a position is that it sidesteps questions as to what exactly counts as a material – as opposed to mental – object, property, state, or event. These are questions that a conventional materialist cannot avoid. And they are notoriously difficult to answer in a satisfying way.

Are we left with a deep mystery? Does what I have said threaten to burden physics and neuroscience with a range of unexpected qualities?

Not at all. Physics and neuroscience are advised to proceed exactly as they now do. I am simply indicating how it could be possible for neurological goings-on to possess the kinds of quality associated with conscious experience. Bear in mind that any neuroscientist who denies that qualities of conscious experience could be neurological qualities must first convince us that this denial is not based on the kind of confusion scouted earlier: a confusion between the qualities of different kinds of experience. A visual experience of a brain will itself be qualitatively different from a visual experience of a ripe tomato. The experience had by a neuroscientist observing your experiencing a ripe tomato need be nothing at all like the neuroscientist's experience of a ripe tomato.

## "Privileged access"

We can dispense, then, with the idea that "qualia," the qualities of conscious experience, are an embarrassment, or that such things are artifacts of old-fashioned philosophical theories to be banished with those theories. Such ideas are founded on ontologies that have little to be said in their favor.

Still, we are left with a formidable problem as regards the qualities of conscious experience. Experiences evidently depend on us for their existence; an experience is always the experience of some conscious agent. Further, agents are conscious of their experiences (and their qualities) – insofar as they can be conscious of them – in a way that apparently precludes error. You can misdescribe or mislabel an experience, but it is hard to see how you could be mistaken about your experiences – how you might, for instance, take yourself to be in pain when you are not in pain. According to a long tradition that includes Hume (and, more recently, John Searle), when it comes to your own experiences, there can be no distinction between appearance and reality: the appearance is the reality. If experiences are neurological goings-on, however, if the qualities of our experiences are neurological qualities, then how could we begin to account for the intimate relation we evidently bear to them?

Once again, it is vital to recognize that your awareness of your own conscious experience is not a matter of your having two experiences: one, the original experience, and another, an experience of the original experience. Your awareness of your experience is constituted by your having it. For this reason, talk of "access" to the character of conscious experiences is misleading. It conjures an inappropriate model, that of object and observer. Your sensation of pain is not an object that you inwardly experience – or sense. Your having it is your sensing it.

We have seen (in chapters three and four) that it is important to distinguish an agent's undergoing some process or being in some state, from observations of that agent's undergoing a process or being in a state. To hearken back to an example used in chapter three, your refrigerator's defrosting unproblematically differs from your observing its defrosting. In just the same way, your undergoing a pain is altogether different from my observing your undergoing it. Now, if "directly observing a pain" involves having that pain, it is unsurprising that only you can "directly observe" your pains. This is just to say that only you can have your pains. And that is no more mysterious than the thought that only my refrigerator can undergo its defrosting.

None of this implies that we could not be wrong about our sensory states. Error, like truth, presupposes judgment. Judgments you make about your conscious states are distinct from those states. This leaves room for error.

But wait. Common experience, buttressed by philosophical tradition, suggests that, when it comes to your own conscious states of mind, your judgments are "incorrigible": error about such things is impossible. Is there some way we can honor this conviction – or what lies behind it – without a commitment to incorrigibility? I believe that we can.

Think for a moment about ordinary perceptual error. You easily mistake a stick in your path for a snake. Sticks, after all, can look very like snakes. Expectation can have an important role here. You are more likely, perhaps, to mistake a stick for a snake when you are on the lookout for snakes. It is less easy to see how you could mistake a stick for a billiard ball – or, for that matter, a hawk for a handsaw. This does not mean that such mistakes are impossible. But to make sense of them, we should have to tell a complicated story. (In desperation we might appeal to the philosopher's catch-all error-producer, the evil scientist who interferes directly with your brain.)

When it comes to your own sensory states, it is relatively easy to see how you could err in judging a state to be of a particular sort when it is in fact a state of a different, though similar, sort. (Is the feeling in the pit of your stomach hunger or nausea? You may find it difficult to say.) And, as in cases of ordinary perceptual error, expectation can lead you astray. Further, neurological disorder, or a hypnotist, or an evil scientist might bring it about that you err more egregiously: you judge that you are in pain when you are not, or that you are not in pain when you are.

One source of the conviction that we cannot be wrong about our own conscious sensory states, then, is the difficulty in imagining how a sensory episode could be mistaken for something else. A second source stems from the recognition that error in judgment is unlikely when, to paraphrase Locke, the content or object of a judgment (or a belief) and the proximal cause of the judgment (or belief) are one and the same. Your being in pain

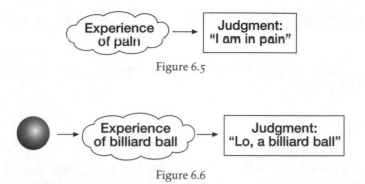

Figure 6.5

Figure 6.6

leads you "directly" to judge that you are in pain (or to form the belief that you are in pain). (See figure 6.5.)

In contrast, the proximate cause of your judgment that a billiard ball lies in your path is not the billiard ball, but your experience of the billiard ball (figure 6.6). We can imagine cases in which a "billiard-ballish" experience occurs, and so leads you to judge that a billiard ball is present, when no billiard ball is present. Hallucination, perceptual illusion, dreaming, and of course the machinations of an evil scientist could result in such non-veridical experiences. And, of course, post-hypnotic suggestion or neuro-logical disorder could result in your judging that a billiard ball is present when neither a billiard ball nor a billiard-ball experience is present.

We can make sense, then, of our impression that we could not be wrong about our own conscious experiences without supposing that judgments about such things are incorrigible. We can see, as well, how it might seem to us that, although we could be wrong about the presence of billiard balls, we could not be wrong about the occurrence of "billiard-ballish" experi-ences. In all such cases, error is possible, albeit unlikely.

What of the ego – the "I" – the subject of experiences? Where do we locate subjects on my conception? Not, I think, in anything like an inner observer or spectator, an entity that monitors experiential goings-on. You do not observe your experiences, you undergo them. You are, it would seem, partly constituted by those experiences.

I conclude that the approach to mind that I am recommending – an approach based on work by C. B. Martin – provides an appealing account of conscious experience. Much of its attraction stems from its being grounded in a sensible ontology. That ontology was introduced, not *ad hoc* because it promised to solve particular problems in the philosophy of mind, but because it offers an independently plausible picture of the world. Although I am partial to this picture, I admit that many of the conclusions I have drawn out of it are individually consistent with other ontologies. The question is whether competitors can comfortably accommodate the range of phenomena discussed here. An ontology cannot be assessed piecemeal. Nor is it advisable to pursue ontology by looking at problems in isolation. The measure of an ontology is its power, its capacity to make sense of a broad assortment of disparate puzzles, and to do so in a natural way. On this measure, the ontology sketched here has a good deal to be said for it.

## Mental imagery

Thus far I have ignored a topic that, in recent years, has dominated mainstream work in the philosophy of mind: intentionality. Intentional states of mind are those that are in some respect representational. Your thinking of a Whopper is a matter of your having a thought with a particular content. Your thought concerns, it is of or about, a Whopper.

In chapter five, we examined two influential approaches to the propositional attitudes (beliefs, desires, intentions, and the like). These form an important class of intentional states of mind. Do they exhaust the class? Some philosophers and psychologists seem to have thought so. Surely this is a distortion. Consider, for instance, the phenomenon of mental imagery. On the face of it, imagery represents an important species of "non-propositional" intentionality. Your believing that Whoppers are delectable is perhaps not imagistic. But I would wager that the bulk of your Whopper-related thoughts are exclusively imagistic.

Around the turn of the century (nineteenth to twentieth) psychologists engaged in a lively debate over the possibility of "imageless thought." At the time, the radicals were those who contended that thought is not invariably "imagistic." We find ourselves now at the turn of another century, and the roles are reversed: the radicals are those who deny that thought is wholly non-imagistic.

Why should anyone doubt the occurrence of mental imagery? In part, perhaps, because of an ongoing worry about "qualia," the qualities of conscious experiences that come to the fore when we investigate imagery. If you are a functionalist, there appears to be no room for such things. As a result, functionalists and materialists who fancy that qualities, generally, are metaphysically or scientifically dubious, have deployed various analytical techniques designed to boil qualities down into something non-qualitative. We have seen that there is no need to do this, however, no need to fear that the qualities of conscious experience are scientifically dodgy.

A second worry about imagery stems from a tendency to suppose that having a mental image is a matter of observing (with the mind's eye, if the image is visual) a picture inside the head. A fierce debate has raged between proponents of "pictorial" conceptions of imagery (like Stephen Kosslyn) and those who take imagery to be "propositional" (Zenon

Pylyshyn, for instance). My belief is that both parties to the debate mis-
conceive the nature of imagery. Having an image (a visual image, let us suppose) of a red squirrel is not like having a picture of a red squirrel (in your
head, or your pocket, or anywhere else). Having an image of a red squirrel is
like perceiving a red squirrel. And perceiving, even perceiving a picture, is
not picture-like. The entities – and qualities – involved in imagery are no
more (nor less) remarkable than those implicated in ordinary perception.

Once we recognize this, we are free to admit what is obvious anyway,
that mental imagery plays a central role in our intelligent commerce with
the world. How central a role? Philosophers are perhaps by nature inclined
to play down the significance of imagery. This may be due, in part, to
philosophers' fixation on arguments and theses expressed in language.
When we turn our thoughts to such things, we typically do so in a linguistic frame of mind. We rehearse arguments, try out theses, and formulate replies, all in language. I suspect that this longstanding practice has
contributed to the widespread belief that the mind is largely – even
exclusively – a consumer of propositional attitudes.

A moment's thought, however, reveals that nothing of the sort follows.
When you rehearse an argument in your head, you are engaged in an
important form of mental imagery: verbal imagery. You hear words in
your head, or, more likely, you both feel and hear yourself uttering words.
This is, if anything is, a robust species of imagery.

How exactly are we to fit imagery into the picture of mind that has
emerged in this chapter? Recall our discussion of your visually apprehend-
ing a ripe tomato in bright sunlight. The visual experience you undergo
when this happens exhibits certain qualities. Now imagine what a ripe
tomato in bright sunlight looks like: form a visual image of the tomato.
When you do this successfully, you pass into a state that resembles the
state you are in when you actually see the tomato. Your imagining the
tomato resembles your visually perceiving the tomato – though of course
not the tomato. This is just to say that the qualities of the two states are
similar. Talking silently to yourself yields the same kind of phenomenon.
In talking to yourself, your experience resembles, qualitatively, the
experience you have when you talk aloud.

I blush to admit that these points seem so obvious I scarcely know how
to argue for them. Even so, they are often denied. In discussions of mental
imagery, it is common for discussants to proclaim that their imagery is
dramatically attenuated, or even altogether absent. (In some quarters a
professed lack of imagery is worn as a badge of honor.) My suspicion is
that these assertions are founded on what psychologists call a criterion
difference, a difference in what we take to constitute imagery.

I have said that imagining a ripe tomato illuminated in bright sunlight
resembles perceiving a ripe tomato illuminated in bright sunlight. Bear in

mind that the qualities of your perceptual experience are manifestly not the qualities of the tomato. The tomato is red and round, but your visual experience is neither red nor round. Bear in mind, as well, that the occurrence of visual imagery of this kind is not a matter of scrutinizing (with an inward-looking mind's eye) a private interior object or a picture on an interior television screen. If you ask yourself whether you encounter such objects and suppose that a negative answer implies that you lack imagery (or that your imagery is severely attenuated), you are misconstruing the nature of imagery.

## Uses of imagery

What use is mental imagery? Well, consider that any conscious thinking will be imagistic. (Here I align myself with the early twentieth-century foes of imageless thought.) If you are like me, then much of the pertinent imagery will be verbal imagery. But all of us rely endlessly on imagery of other sorts in negotiating our world. Imagery is a fundamental ingredient in our capacity for anticipatory action. Intelligent creatures do not merely react to stimuli from the outside. Intelligence – or mindfulness – includes the ability to anticipate environmental vicissitudes and the effects of prospective actions. We can "see" that we have room to pass the car ahead of us on a narrow road, that the cereal box is too tall to be placed upright on the shelf. Carpenters employ images in constructing cabinets, and athletes rely on imagery to maneuver past opponents. Imagery, I claim, plays a fundamental, and almost certainly ineliminable, role in the exercise of such abilities.

Perhaps because cognitive psychology has been dominated by the computer paradigm, imagistic thinking has received little attention. Attempts to study imagery using computational models too often miss the point altogether by seeking to reduce images to descriptions easily capturable in lines of code. Neither imagery nor perception can be so reduced, however – and indeed, as I have suggested, imagery and perception are intimately connected. The qualities of perceptual experiences are what survive in imagery. When we engage in functional abstraction, however, we risk losing sight of these qualities. The point of functionalism (and its close relative, the computational model of mind) is to settle on a level of description that factors out qualities of states of mind altogether. Against this background, it is no wonder that imagery has been underappreciated.

Suppose I am right. Suppose that mental imagery is fundamental to minds regarded as systems of representations. And suppose that imagery is a matter of our undergoing experiences qualitatively resembling perceptual experiences. Then we can see why computational models of the mind are so often unpromising. Imagining an object is akin to perceiving an object, not to describing it. The aim of many computational models, however, is the construction of descriptions. We take ourselves to have modeled perceiving or imagining if we can envision a device that, in response to appropriate inputs, produces descriptions of things seen or imagined. That psychologists – egged on by philosophers, it has to be said – have taken such models as their guiding inspiration perhaps explains the disappointing one-dimensional character of so much mainstream cognitive psychology. Ironically, although thought is indeed often linguistic in character, it is no less imagistic for that.

## Intentionality

Even if these ideas are on the right track, we are still a long way from anything approximating an account of intentionality – the "ofness" and "aboutness" of thought. The prevailing "externalist" line on intentionality regards intentional states of mind as owing their content (what they are of or about) to causal relations agents bear to the world. The inspiration for this view stems chiefly from a handful of clever thought experiments. Here is one example made famous by Hilary Putnam.

The term "water," as we use it, designates a particular kind of colorless liquid that, as we now know, is $H_2O$. When we entertain thoughts we should express (in English) by means of the word "water," our thoughts concern this substance. Now imagine a distant planet, Twin-Earth, a planet that is, in all ways save one, a precise duplicate of Earth, containing inhabitants that are (except in one respect) precise duplicates of the inhabitants of Earth. Were you miraculously transported to Twin-Earth, you would not detect the slightest difference, and were your twin on Twin-Earth transported to Earth, that twin would likewise be oblivious to the change. There is, however, one important difference between Earth and Twin-Earth. The colorless, tasteless, transparent stuff that fills rivers and lakes, is used in making tea, falls from the sky, and is called (by Twin-English speakers) "water," is not $H_2O$, but a different chemical compound: XYZ.

Now, while the English word "water" means water (that is, $H_2O$) and thoughts we should express using the word "water" are thoughts about water, the Twin-English word "water" does not mean water (does not mean what "water" in English means). Nor do inhabitants of Twin-Earth who think thoughts they would express (in Twin-English) using the word "water" entertain thoughts of water. No, the meanings and thoughts associated with your twin's utterances of "water" mean, not water, but XYZ – which we could call "twater."

Of course, I am describing the case from my perspective as an English speaker on Earth. My Twin-Earth counterpart would use words indistinguishable from mine. But we on Earth should translate his references to (what he calls) "water" as references to twater, his references to (what he calls) "Earth" as references to Twin-Earth, and so on. Similarly, my twin would describe my references to (what I call) "water" as references to (what he calls) "twater," and – well, you get the idea.

Putnam invites us to conclude from such thought experiments that "meanings just ain't in the head." What words mean, and similarly what thoughts those words express, depends on whatever it is with which speakers and thinkers causally interact. "Water" in your mouth means water (and not twater) because you are causally related to water (and not twater). The same sounds produced by your twin mean twater (not water) because your twin stands in causal relations to twater (XYZ) and not water ($H_2O$). Applying this theme more broadly, we can say that the meanings of the words we use and the contents of our thoughts (what our thoughts concern) depend on causal relations we bear to our surroundings. Still more broadly, intentionality depends on context. Context must include appropriate causal relations, but it might include assorted social relations as well. The meanings of your utterances might depend, for instance, on your occupying a place in a particular community of speakers, a community with various linguistic norms and standards.

Let us focus briefly on the causal requirement. The idea, put in its simplest terms, is that thoughts concern their causes. We have encountered this idea already (in chapter five) in our discussion of Davidson. But now let us consider it as a component in a general theory of intentionality. A causal view, like Putnam's, competes with views that try to explain intentionality "from the inside out." The Twin-Earth case might be taken to show that no "inside-out" account of thoughts could work. After all, you and your twin are identical on the inside; yet your thoughts differ in content: yours concern water, your twin's concern twater. Do Twin-Earth cases support a causal account of intentionality as against an "inside-out" account? Let us imagine a competitor theory and see.

Pretend for a moment that the directedness of your thoughts resembles the aiming and tossing of a dart. Gravitational influences aside, the direction a dart takes depends wholly on agent-centered factors: how you grip it, the character of your arm motion, the timing of the release, and the like. However, although a dart's trajectory depends wholly on the agent, what the dart hits depends on features of the world, features over which an agent might have no control. When you toss a dart aimed at the center of a target, it will not hit the center if I move the target while the dart is in flight. We might sum this up by saying that what a dart hits depends on two factors: how it is tossed – its agent-determined trajectory – and how the world is.

Imagine that the directedness of thoughts were like the aiming of a tossed dart. Imagine, that is, that a thought's "aim" were a wholly internal affair. (Never mind for now what it would be for a thought to be "aimed.") This is the kind of view that Twin-Earth cases and their many cousins are designed to refute. But consider: your thought of water on Earth "hits" water, $H_2O$; your twin's intrinsically indiscernible thought on Twin-Earth "hits" twater, XYZ. We can say that your thought is about water, your twin's thought is about twater, without supposing that the explanation of this difference is to be found in an incoming causal chain. But if both the "inside-out" model and the causal model yield the same judgments in Twin-Earth cases, these cases can scarcely be used to support causal accounts of intentionality against internalist, "inside-out" competitors.

You may be skeptical of the hokey internalist dart-tossing model to which I have appealed. How, you might reasonably ask, are thoughts supposed to project outward – like darts?

Think first of dispositionality. I have argued that properties have a dual nature: every property contributes in a distinctive way to the qualities and dispositionalities of objects possessing it. Now, a disposition is intrinsically "projective"; it is for a particular kind of manifestation with a particular kind of reciprocal disposition partner. A disposition may fail ever to be manifested – if, for instance, an appropriate reciprocal partner is absent or non-existent. Nevertheless, the disposition is projective for this manifestation with this kind of reciprocal partner.

My first suggestion, then, is that a central ingredient of intentionality, projectability, is built into every property. I do not mean that every object thinks or is endowed with intentionality. I mean only that every object possesses projective dispositionalities. And these, I submit, are apt building blocks for complex intentional states.

Second, consider an intelligent creature navigating its environment. The creature entertains imagistic thoughts. These enable the creature to test "hypotheses" and, in general, serve to guide its actions in a way that we should describe as intelligent. What accounts for the contents of the creature's imagistic thoughts? What makes a creature's image of a tree branch an image of a tree branch? The creature is in causal contact with its surroundings, to be sure. But is it this causal contact that is responsible for the creature's thoughts' projective, intentional character? I say that it is not. The thoughts' projectivity comes from the distinctive anticipatory and reflective role they have in the life of the creature. This role is founded in complex, focused dispositionalities that constitute the creature's states of mind.

Suppose, for instance, that your visually perceiving a ripe tomato in bright sunlight is a matter of your undergoing a particular sort of conscious experience. This conscious experience is the mutual manifesting of a complex disposition intrinsic to your visual system and dispositions of the tomato and the intervening light radiation. What makes this manifesting a visual perceiving of the tomato is its being a mutual manifesting with dispositions of the tomato. (This is simply to acknowledge the causal requirement included in our concept of perception.) But, I contend, what makes the experience projective for the tomato (what gives it its intentional "trajectory") is intrinsic to you.

Consider a case in which you hallucinate a tomato. Here, your dispositional condition is manifested as in the first case, but with other reciprocal partners – internal partners, presumably. The result is an experience that qualitatively resembles the experience you have when you visually apprehend a tomato. The intentionality of this experience, what makes it an hallucination of a tomato, is not grounded in causal connections you might bear to tomatoes. Nor, incidentally, is it based on the resemblance of your experience to a tomato: experiences of tomatoes do not resemble tomatoes. The "ofness" of your experience is grounded rather in the fact that it is a manifesting of a disposition apt for visual experiences of tomatoes. This aptness, like any dispositional aptness, is built in, intrinsic to your visual system. It does not depend on your being in causal contact with tomatoes, nor, for that matter, on there being any tomatoes at all. In this respect it is no different from the disposition of a salt crystal to dissolve in water. The salt possesses this disposition even in circumstances (or imagined worlds) in which there is no water.

Context plays a role in such cases, but not the role ascribed to it by the causal theorist. Your "tomato thoughts" are, as I have put it, "apt" for tomatoes because your environment includes tomatoes and not twin-tomatoes. But this is no more than a reflection of a point made earlier. What a thought concerns depends on two factors: how the thought projects, its "aim," and the character of the world on which it projects, its "target."

It may sound as though I am endorsing a vaguely functionalist conception of intentionality, but I am not. It is essential to an imagistic thought that it possess certain qualities. These qualities are what suit it to play the role it plays. Functionalism abstracts from the qualities possessed by items that play particular roles. These items have qualities perhaps (though even this is doubted in some quarters), but the qualities are incidental to the items' roles in the system. I disagree. The qualitative similarity of imagistic thought to perceptual experience fits that thought for its role in the life of the creature.

Although perceptual experience undoubtedly precedes (and has a causal bearing on) subsequent reflective imagistic thought, it is not this causal linkage that accounts for thoughts' projective character. Projectivity is built into the thought. A thought "fits" a state of affairs by virtue of endowing its possessor with a capacity to anticipate and interact with states of affairs of that kind. Of course, which state of affairs a creature interacts with depends on the creature's circumstances. We interact with water, our twins on Twin-Earth interact with XYZ.

I am not denying that some mental concepts are causally loaded. What you remember or perceive, for instance, depends in part on the causal source of your thoughts about the past or your current perceptual state. Nor am I denying that we rely heavily on observations of causal connections in ascribing thoughts to others. What I am denying is that any of this explains the projectivity, the fundamental intentionality, of states of mind. The projectivity of thought is dispositionally grounded, and the pertinent dispositions, even those with external causes, are intrinsic to thinkers.

I am not suggesting, either, that a thought's hitting a target – a thought's being about a particular individual, for instance – is explicable solely on the basis of the intrinsic features of the agent. What target a thought hits depends on factors that may be largely outside the agent's control. Your thoughts are about water, in part because of their intrinsic character, and in part because of your circumstances. Your twin's thoughts, on Twin-Earth, concern twater, not water, because your twin's circumstances differ from yours.

These sketchy remarks are not meant to encompass a complete theory of intentionality. I intend them only as antidotes to prevailing doctrines. This may seem thin stuff. I might feel more guilty were it the case that those wedded to causal accounts of intentionality possessed detailed theories. But they do not. They offer examples designed to convince us that intentionality requires an incoming causal component of some kind. I admit that there is often an incoming causal component, but I deny that this is the basis of intentionality.

## Dénouement

At the outset of this chapter, I indicated that an advantage of the conception of mind to be discussed was that it accounted for a range of plausible ingredients of its competitors. I have said enough now to make the conception clear, at least in its broad outlines. It is time to look again at the competition.

## Dualism

Mind–body dualism focuses on what appear to be dramatic differences between the mental and the material: states of mind are private, our "access" to them privileged, and the mental realm exhibits a range of distinctive qualities seemingly absent from the material domain. In contrast, material states of affairs are public, our access to them is indirect and fallible, and they are apparently bereft of anything like the qualities exhibited in conscious experience. On some views, material objects lack qualities altogether; their properties are exclusively dispositional.

What of the essentially "subjective" character of states of mind? The dualists' mistake is to imagine that this is to be explained by taking minds to be windowless containers housing objects only observable from the inside. (Images on an internal television monitor purporting to represent the "external world.") Those on the outside can only guess at the mind's contents. This is the wrong model. I have suggested that the privacy and privilege apparently enjoyed by states of mind is to be explained, in part, by reference to a distinction between being in a state and observing a state. Your awareness of your conscious states of mind is constituted by your being in those states. Judgments you form about those states, while not incorrigible, are nevertheless eminently trustworthy. I am aware of your conscious states of mind, if at all, not by being in those states, but by being in a distinct state, one that constitutes my awareness of you and your antics. This, I might add, is not a comment on neurological mechanisms, but a reflection on the basis of a much-discussed epistemological asymmetry.

What of distinctive mental qualities? We have seen that it is by no means always clear what these qualities are. When you savor the aroma of a Whopper, your enjoyment is founded on qualities of your olfactory experience. Before you deny that these qualities could conceivably be qualities of your brain, you should be clear on their precise nature. And, I have suggested, this is not something we have an especially good grip on.

In any case, if we take seriously the kind of compositional ontology I have defended in this chapter, and we honor the minimal requirements of a causal account of perception, then we should be prepared to recognize that the qualities of our conscious experiences are in fact qualities of our brains. If you think of a brain as a material object, then these qualities are material qualities. Moreover, these are the material qualities with which we have what could be called direct acquaintance. We have no such direct acquaintance with the qualities of material objects we observe in the world around us, or in the laboratory. I am not suggesting that there is an unbridgeable epistemological gap here. I am only pointing out one consequence of a position that takes the denial of dualism seriously. Philosophers who oppose dualism, while harping on vast differences between mental and material qualities, seem to have hold of the wrong end of the stick.

All this leads me to characterize the account of the mind defended in this chapter as a version of neutral monism. Mental and material properties are not distinctive kinds of property. Certainly we label some properties mental and some material. But the idea that this practice has momentous ontological significance is largely a prejudice inherited from dualism. One symptom of this is the difficulty philosophers have in making the mental–material distinction precise. My advice is to abandon the distinction and turn instead to serious ontology.

## The identity theory

The identity theory holds that mental properties are identical with material properties. In one respect, the thesis I have defended in this chapter is in agreement: there are no mental properties distinct from material properties. In another respect, however, the identity theory evidently misfires. Identity theorists identify being in pain, for instance, with a particular neural condition. In so doing, they tacitly suppose that being in pain is a property. Being in pain is a property that, as it happens, is identical with a certain neurological property.

We have seen, however, that it is a mistake to imagine that every predicate used truly to ascribe a state of mind to a creature designates a property possessed by that creature and by any other creature (or entity) to which it applies. The predicate holds of assorted creatures, and it holds of them in virtue of properties they possess, but it does not follow that it holds of them in virtue of their possessing the very same (or an exactly resembling) property. This is the lesson of functionalism. The functionalist critique of the identity theory makes it clear that it is unlikely that there is a single neurological property answering to the predicate "is in pain." The appropriate response, however, is not to suppose that "is in pain" must therefore designate a higher-level or second-order property. Rather, we must simply recognize that the properties in virtue of which it is true that very different kinds of creature are in pain are just different – although similar – properties.

If we eliminate this confusion, however, I am happy to call the neutral monist thesis sketched in this chapter a kind of identity theory.

## Functionalism

One way to understand functionalism is to reflect that functionalists fixate on the dispositional nature of properties that gives minds their distinctive character. This is perfectly appropriate. What is not appropriate, however, is the further thought that minds are nothing more than systems of pure dispositions.

I hold that there are good ontological reasons to suppose that every property has a dual nature: every property is both dispositional and qualitative. Moreover, this dispositionality and (if I may) qualitativity are inseparable – except in thought. States of mind are, at the same time, qualitative and dispositional. But there is no special mystery here: every state is simultaneously qualitative and dispositional. If we regard the mind as a broadly functional system, then we can still say that some components in this system occupy the roles they occupy, in part, because of their qualities. But as soon as we say this, we have turned our backs on a central tenet of functionalism.

By and large the most basic sciences are in the business of exposing the dispositional structure of the world. As I have suggested in a number of places, however, it would be a mistake to infer from the silence of physics on the world's qualitative nature that physics shows that the world lacks such a nature. This mistake – the mistake of the functionalist – becomes crippling when we set out to understand the mind and its operations. A scientist can pass the buck on qualities by assigning them to minds. The current crisis over consciousness, the so-called "hard problem" of consciousness, stems from an implicit recognition that the buck stops here. But the crisis is of our own making. If everything has qualities, then it cannot be a mystery that states of mind have qualities. If states of mind are states of the brain, then the qualities of those states are qualities of brain states. I hope that I have done enough in this chapter to make this conclusion less counterintuitive than it is customarily taken to be.

## Interpretationism

Nothing I have said here is obviously inconsistent with a Davidson-style account of the propositional attitudes. I am prepared to accept the broad outlines of Davidson's account of interpretation, and even the idea that in ascribing beliefs, desires, intentions, and the like we are deploying a "metric." This metric is apt for plotting – what? It is apt for plotting the dispositional system that constitutes the minds of language users.

Davidson insists that only an interpreter can be interpreted, only a language user can be correctly described as believing, for instance, that a Whopper is a culinary *tour de force*. This is not because beliefs are sentences inside the head that depend somehow on believers' linguistic abilities. Consider: only a language user is in a position to accept this description of his own state of mind as apt. Only a language user sees, or might see, himself in this light.

Why should this matter? Recall that it is the possession of propositional attitudes that is supposed to explain rational choice. Rational choice, however, is essentially reflective. It is not enough that a rational agent has beliefs and desires. A rational agent is capable of reflecting on those beliefs and desires and subsequently acting on those reflections. In ascribing propositional attitudes to an agent, then, we ascribe states of mind in a way that aligns with the agent's own assessment of those states of mind.

All this is perfectly fine. It would be wrong, however, to conclude that there is nothing more to the mind. It would not just be wrong, it would be crazy. Our mental lives are much richer than anything included in the output of theories of interpretation, what I have called *I*-theories. Such theories capture a facet of our mentality, perhaps, but they are silent on imagistic thinking – which, I have suggested, is utterly fundamental. Such theories provide no help at all with the minds of non-linguistic creatures. And, finally, an agent's capacity to deploy such theories – a capacity that must be present if the agent is to answer to an *I*-theory – rests on a range of mental abilities that fall outside any Davidson-style theory of interpretation. To deploy an *I*-theory, you must have the ability to reflect on your world and its contents. This ability is grounded in your dispositional (and, of course, qualitative) makeup.

## Concluding note

Perhaps I have said enough to provide an inkling of a way of approaching minds and their place in nature that addresses longstanding puzzles in the philosophy of mind. I claim that the approach promises to solve problems its competitors purport to solve, and that it does so without their attendant liabilities. This is a large claim. It would be immodest were it not for the fact that I do not represent the view as original; I trace it to the work of C. B. Martin.

I do not pretend that this sketch is enough to persuade confirmed proponents of alternative views. I hope, however, that I have managed at least to lend plausibility to the approach, and thereby to attract fence-sitters and neutral bystanders. Readers wanting more are invited to consult the readings set out in the section that follows.

# Suggested reading

C. B. Martin defends aspects of the approach to mind discussed in this chapter in "Substance Substantiated" (1980), "Power for Realists" (1992), "The Need for Ontology: Some Choices" (1993), "On the Need for Properties: The Road to Pythagoreanism and Back" (1997). See also C. B. Martin and John Heil, "Rules and Powers" (forthcoming). Readers seeking enlightenment on the account of intentionality introduced here should consult Martin's "Proto-Language" (1987).

Michael Lockwood, in *Mind, Brain, and Quantum* (1989), chap. 10, advances a view of mental qualities – "qualia" – similar to that discussed in this chapter. See also "The Grain Problem" (1993). Lockwood draws on Bertrand Russell's *Analysis of Matter* (1927), and in an historical appendix cites Schopenhauer, W. K. Clifford, Wilhelm Wundt, and Immanuel Kant as promoting related views. The position I advance, however, differs from Lockwood's in a number of important respects. Lockwood takes dispositions to be grounded in what he calls "intrinsic qualities," for instance. Following Martin, I regard every property as intrinsically dispositional and qualitative. Lockwood distinguishes qualities of conscious experiences from our awareness of those qualities. I take conscious experiences to be manifestations of neurological dispositions. The qualities of these are conscious qualities. The awareness of those qualities is partly constituted by their being possessed by our experiences.

Daniel Dennett is one philosopher who argues for the replacement of metaphysics by empirical science when it comes to questions about the nature of mind. For a readable introduction to Dennett's views, see *Kinds of Minds: Toward an Understanding of Consciousness* (1996).

The thesis that, if there are objects, there are simple objects, is discussed by E. J. Lowe in "Primitive Substances" (1994). For an account of objects as fields, see Steven Weinberg, "Before the Big Bang" (1997). Weinberg says (p. 17): "In the modern theory of elementary particles known as the Standard Model, a theory that has been well-verified experimentally, the fundamental components of nature are a few dozen different kinds of field." (I owe the citation to Michael Lockwood.)

Locke's conception of substance is spelled out in *An Essay Concerning Human Understanding*, ed. P. H. Nidditch (1690/1978), see especially book II, chap. 23. See also Martin's "Substance Substantiated" (1980) and E. J. Lowe's *Locke on Human Understanding* (1995), chap. 4.

Plato discusses universals – what he calls the Forms – in the *Phaedo*, in the *Republic* (books 6 and 7) and in a more critical mode, in the *Parmenides*. David Armstrong provides a deft introduction to the topic in *Universals: An Opinionated Introduction* (1989).

Hugh Mellor and Sydney Shoemaker both depict properties as fundamentally dispositional. See Mellor's "In Defense of Dispositions" (1974), and Shoemaker's "Causality and Properties" (1980).

The notion that dispositions are categorically grounded is defended by David Armstrong in many places, including *A Materialist Theory of the Mind* (1968), pp. 85–8. See also Frank Jackson's "Mental Causation" (1996). I call this view into question, although it is widely regarded as so obvious as not to require defense – and so deserves to be called the default view.

Jeffrey Poland's *Physicalism: The Philosophical Foundations* (1994) nicely articulates a layered ontology of the kind attacked in this chapter. See also my *The Nature of True Minds* (1992), especially chap. 3 where I argue (mistakenly, as I now think) for the layered picture.

Readers seeking an example of an argument in which realism about predicates is linked to those predicates designating properties might consult Paul A. Boghossian, "The Status of Content" (1990). In explicating "non-factualist" (that is, anti-realist) accounts of a predicate, "*P*," Boghossian says that what such conceptions have in common is "(1) [t]he claim that the predicate '*P*' does not denote a property and (hence) (2) the claim that the overall (atomic) declarative sentence in which it appears does not express a truth condition" (p. 161). Note the parenthetical "hence."

Poland (in *Physicalism: The Philosophical Foundations*, chap. 4) advances an account of the realizing relation according to which realizing properties (1) suffice ("nomologically," that is, as a matter of natural law) for realized properties and (2) instances of realizing properties constitute instances of realized properties. I produce a similar conception in *The Nature of True Minds*, pp. 135–9.

For an enthusiastic discussion of *ceteris paribus* laws, and their significance for the special sciences, see Jerry Fodor's "You Can Fool Some of the People All of the Time, Everything Else Being Equal: Hedged Laws and Psychological Explanation" (1991). An application of this kind of view to the problem of mental causation can be found in Ernest Lepore and Barry Loewer, "Mind Matters" (1987).

Readers hankering for more information on supervenience should consult Jaegwon Kim's "Supervenience as a Philosophical Concept" (1990) and Terence Horgan's "From Supervenience to Superdupervenience" (1993). I provide an overview of the topic and discuss its implications for the philosophy of mind in *The Nature of True Minds*, chap. 3.

David Chalmers discusses zombies at great length (and defends their possibility) in his *The Conscious Mind: In Search of a Fundamental Theory* (1996), chap. 3.

Nigel J. T. Thomas's "Are Theories of Imagery Theories of Imagination" (forthcoming) contains an excellent historical and philosophical discussion of theories of imagery. Thomas's "Experience and Theory as Determinants of Attitudes toward Mental Representation: The Case of Knight Dunlap and the Vanishing Images of J. B. Watson" (1989) contains a fascinating discussion of what I call "criterion differences" in reports of imagery (or the lack of it). Michael Tye discusses the rather dreary debate between proponents of "pictorial" and "propositional" conceptions of imagery in *The Imagery Debate* (1991). Zenon Pylyshyn depicts imagery "propositionally" in "What the Mind's Eye Tells the Mind's Brain: A Critique of Mental Imagery" (1973). The "imageless thought" controversy raged early in the twentieth century. For a useful summary and discussion, see Kurt Danziger, "The History of Introspection Reconsidered" (1980).

Causal theories of content in the philosophy of mind and the philosophy of language (roughly, the view that meaning or content depends on agents' causal histories) are all the rage. Without endorsing them, I attempt to motivate such views in *The Nature of True Minds*, chap. 2. Interested readers should consult Hilary Putnam, "The Meaning of 'Meaning'" (1975a), and *Reason, Truth, and History* (1981), chaps 1 and 2; Tyler Burge, "Individualism and the Mental" (1979), and "Individualism and Psychology" (1986); Lynne Rudder Baker, *Saving Belief: A Critique of Physicalism* (1987); and Donald Davidson, "Radical Interpretation" (1973).

# Bibliography

Anderson, A. R. (ed.) (1964) *Minds and Machines*, Englewood Cliffs: Prentice-Hall.

Armstrong, D. M. (1968) *A Materialist Theory of the Mind*, London: Routledge and Kegan Paul.

Armstrong, D. M. (1989) *Universals: An Opinionated Introduction*, Boulder: Westview Press.

Bacon, J., Campbell, K., and Reinhardt, L. (eds) (1992) *Ontology, Causality, and Mind*, Cambridge: Cambridge University Press.

Baker, Lynne Rudder (1987) *Saving Belief: A Critique of Physicalism*, Princeton: Princeton University Press.

Barnes, J. (1987) *Early Greek Philosophy*, London: Penguin.

Berkeley, George (1710/1979) *Three Dialogues between Hylas and Philonous*, ed. Robert M. Adams, Indianapolis: Hackett Publishing Co.

Berkeley, George (1713/1983) *Treatise Concerning the Principles of Human Knowledge*, ed. Kenneth Winkler, Indianapolis: Hackett Publishing Co.

Blackburn, Simon (1990) "Filling in Space," *Analysis* 50: 62–5.

Blakeslee, Sandra (1996) "The Brain in the Gut," *New York Times* (*Science Times*), Tuesday, 23 January, B5 and B10.

Block, Ned (1978) "Troubles with Functionalism," in C. W. Savage (ed.), *Perception and Cognition: Issues in the Foundations of Psychology* (*Minnesota Studies in the Philosophy of Science* 9), Minneapolis: University of Minnesota Press: 261–325. Reprinted in Block (1980a): 268–305; and in Rosenthal (1991): 211–28.

Block, Ned (ed.) (1980a) *Readings in Philosophy of Psychology*, vol. 1, Cambridge, Mass.: Harvard University Press.

Block, Ned (1980b) "What is Functionalism," in Block (1980a): 171–84.

Boghossian, Paul A. (1990) "The Status of Content," *The Philosophical Review* 99: 157–84.

Broad, C. D. (1925) *The Mind and Its Place in Nature*, London: Routledge and Kegan Paul.

Burge, Tyler (1979) "Individualism and the Mental," *Midwest Studies in Philosophy* 4: 73–121.

Burge, Tyler (1986) "Individualism and Psychology," *Philosophical Review* 45: 3–45. Reprinted in Rosenthal (1991): 536–67.

Chalmers, David (1996) *The Conscious Mind: In Search of a Fundamental Theory*, New York: Oxford University Press.

Chalmers, David and Searle, John (1997) "Consciousness and the Philosophers: An Exchange," *New York Review of Books*, 15 May: 60–1.

Cheney, D. L. and Seyfarth, R. M. (1990) *How Monkeys See the World: Inside the Mind of Another Species*, Chicago: University of Chicago Press.

Cheney, D. L. and Seyfarth, R. M. (1992) "Précis of *How Monkeys See the World: Inside the Mind of Another Species*," *Behavioral and Brain Sciences* 15: 135–82.

Chomsky, Noam (1959) "Review of *Verbal Behavior*," *Language* 35: 26–58.

Chomsky, Noam (1966) *Cartesian Linguistics: A Chapter in the History of Rationalist Thought*, New York: Harper and Row.

Churchland, Patricia (1986) *Neurophilosophy*, Cambridge, Mass.: MIT Press.

Churchland, Paul (1979) *Scientific Realism and the Plasticity of Mind*, Cambridge: Cambridge University Press.

Churchland, Paul (1981) "Eliminative Materialism and the Propositional Attitudes," *Journal of Philosophy* 78: 67–90. Reprinted in Rosenthal (1991): 601–12.

Coren, Stanley (1994) *The Intelligence of Dogs: Canine Consciousness and Capabilities*, New York: Scribner.

Crick, Francis (1994) *The Astonishing Hypothesis: The Scientific Search for the Soul*, New York: Scribner.

Danziger, Kurt (1980) "The History of Introspection Reconsidered," *Journal of the History of the Behavioral Sciences* 16: 241–62.

Davidson, Donald (1967) "Truth and Meaning," *Synthese* 17: 304–23. Reprinted in Davidson (1984): 17–36.

Davidson, Donald (1973) "Radical Interpretation," *Dialectica* 27: 313–28. Reprinted in Davidson (1984): 125–39.

Davidson, Donald (1974a) "Belief and the Basis of Meaning," *Synthese* 27: 309–23. Reprinted in Davidson (1984): 141–54.

Davidson, Donald (1974b) "Psychology as Philosophy," in S. C. Brown (ed.), *Philosophy of Psychology*, New York: Barnes and Noble Books: 41–52. Reprinted in Davidson (1980): 231–9.

Davidson, Donald (1975) "Thought and Talk," in Samuel Guttenplan (ed.), *Mind and Language: Wolfson College Lectures 1974*, Oxford: Clarendon Press: 7–23. Reprinted in Davidson (1984): 155–70.

Davidson, Donald (1977) "Reality without Reference," *Dialectica* 31: 247–53. Reprinted in Davidson (1984): 215–25.

Davidson, Donald (1980) *Essays on Actions and Events*, Oxford: Clarendon Press.

Davidson, Donald (1984) *Inquiries into Truth and Interpretation*, Oxford: Clarendon Press.

Davidson, Donald (1986) "A Coherence Theory of Truth and Knowledge," in Lepore (1986): 307–19.

Dennett, Daniel (1987) *The Intentional Stance*, Cambridge, Mass.: MIT Press.

Dennett, Daniel (1991a) *Consciousness Explained*, Boston, Mass.: Little, Brown.

Dennett, Daniel (1991b) "Real Patterns," *Journal of Philosophy* 89: 27–51.

Dennett, Daniel (1996) *Kinds of Minds: Toward an Understanding of Consciousness*, New York: Basic Books.

Dennett, Daniel and Hofstadter, Douglas (eds) (1981) *The Mind's I*, New York: Basic Books.

Descartes, René (1641/1986) *Meditations on First Philosophy*, trans. John Cottingham, Cambridge: Cambridge University Press.

Dretske, Fred (1988) *Explaining Behavior: Reasons in a World of Causes*, Cambridge, Mass.: MIT Press.

Dretske, Fred (1995) *Naturalizing the Mind*, Cambridge, Mass.: MIT Press.

Evnine, Simon (1991) *Donald Davidson*, Stanford: Stanford University Press.

Feigl, Herbert (1958) "The 'Mental' and the 'Physical'," in H. Feigl, M. Scriven, and G. Maxwell (eds) *Concepts, Theories, and the Mind–Body Problem* (*Minnesota Studies in the Philosophy of Science* 2), Minneapolis: University of Minnesota Press: 370–497. Reissued in 1967 as a monograph, *The "Mental" and the "Physical"*, Minneapolis: University of Minnesota Press.

Fodor, Jerry (1975) *The Language of Thought*, New York: T. Y. Crowell.

Fodor, Jerry (1988) *Psychosemantics*, Cambridge, Mass.: MIT Press.

Fodor, Jerry (1991) "You Can Fool Some of the People All of the Time, Everything Else Being Equal: Hedged Laws and Psychological Explanation," *Mind* 100: 19–34.

Fodor, Jerry (1994) *The Elm and the Expert: Mentalese and its Semantics*, Cambridge, Mass.: MIT Press.

Foster, John (1991) *The Immaterial Self*, London: Routledge.

Gopnik, Alison and Astington, J. W. (1988) "Children's Understanding of Representational Change and its Relation to the Understanding of False Belief and the Appearance–Reality Distinction," *Child Development* 59: 26–37.

Harman, Gilbert (1990) "The Intrinsic Quality of Experience," *Philosophical Perspectives* 4: 31–52.

Haugeland, John (ed.) (1981a) *Mind Design*, Cambridge, Mass.: MIT Press.

Haugeland, John (1981b) "Semantic Engines: An Introduction to Mind Design," in Haugeland (1981a): 1–34.

Haugeland, John (1985) *Artificial Intelligence: The Very Idea*, Cambridge, Mass.: MIT Press.

Heil, John (1983) *Perception and Cognition*, Berkeley: University of California Press.

Heil, John (1992) *The Nature of True Minds*, Cambridge: Cambridge University Press.

Hobbes, Thomas (1651/1994) *Leviathan*, ed. Edwin Curley, Indianapolis: Hackett Publishing Co.

Horgan, T. (1993) "From Supervenience to Superdupervenience: Meeting the Demands of a Material World," *Mind* 102: 555–86.

Hume, David (1739/1978) *A Treatise of Human Nature*, ed. L. A. Selby-Bigge and P. H. Nidditch, Oxford: Clarendon Press.

Hume, David (1748/1975) *Enquiry Concerning Human Understanding*, ed. L. A. Selby-Bigge, Oxford: Clarendon Press.

Huxley, T. H. (1901) *Methods and Results: Essays*, New York: D. Appleton.

Jackson, Frank (1982) "Epiphenomenal Qualia," *The Philosophical Quarterly* 32: 127–36.

Jackson, Frank (1996) "Mental Causation," *Mind* 105: 377–41.

Kant, Immanuel (1787/1964) *The Critique of Pure Reason*, trans. Norman Kemp Smith, London: Macmillan.

Kim, Jaegwon (1990) "Supervenience as a Philosophical Concept," *Metaphilosophy* 12: 1–27. Reprinted in Kim (1993): 131–60.

Kim, Jaegwon (1993) *Supervenience and Mind: Selected Philosophical Essays*, Cambridge: Cambridge University Press.

Kirk, G. S., Raven, J. E., and Schofield, M. (1983) *The Presocratic Philosophers*, 2nd ed., Cambridge: Cambridge University Press.

Kirk, Robert (1974) "Zombies vs. Materialists," *Proceedings of the Aristotelian Society*, Supplementary vol. 48: 135–52.

Kirk, Robert (1996) *Raw Feeling*, Oxford: Clarendon Press.

La Mettrie, Julien Offraye de (1747 and 1748/1994) *Man a Machine*, trans. R. Watson and M. Rybalka, Indianapolis: Hackett Publishing Co.

Leibniz, Gottfried Wilhelm (1787/1973) *Monadology*, in Mary Morris and G. H. R. Parkinson (trans.) and G. H. R. Parkinson (ed.), *Leibniz: Philosophical Writings*, London: J. M. Dent and Sons: 179–94.

Lepore, Ernest (ed.) (1986) *Truth and Interpretation: Perspectives on the Philosophy of Donald Davidson*, Oxford: Basil Blackwell.

Lepore, Ernest and Loewer, Barry (1987) "Mind Matters," *Journal of Philosophy* 84: 630–42.

Levine, Joseph (1983) "Materialism and Qualia: The Explanatory Gap," *Pacific Philosophical Quarterly* 64: 354–61.

Lewis, David (1966) "An Argument for the Identity Theory," *Journal of Philosophy* 63: 17–25. Reprinted in Lewis (1983): 99–107.

Lewis, David (1972) "Psychophysical and Theoretical Identifications," *Australasian Journal of Philosophy* 50: 249–58. Reprinted in Block (1980a): 207–15; and in Rosenthal (1991): 204–10.

Lewis, David (1980) "Mad Pain and Martian Pain," in Block (1980a): 216–22. Reprinted in Lewis (1983): 122–9; and in Rosenthal (1991): 229–35.

Lewis, David (1983) *Philosophical Papers*, vol. 1, New York: Oxford University Press.

Lewis, David (1994) "Reduction of Mind," in Samuel Guttenplan (ed.), *A Companion to the Philosophy of Mind*, Oxford: Basil Blackwell: 412–31.

Locke, John (1690/1978) *An Essay Concerning Human Understanding*, ed. P. H. Nidditch, Oxford: Clarendon Press.

Lockwood, Michael (1989) *Mind, Brain, and Quantum*, Oxford: Basil Blackwell.

Lockwood, Michael (1993) "The Grain Problem," in H. Robinson (ed.), *Objections to Physicalism*, Oxford: Clarendon Press: 271–91.

Lowe, E. J. (1988) "Substance," in G. H. R. Parkinson (ed.), *An Encyclopedia of Philosophy*, London: Routledge: 255–78.

Lowe, E. J. (1994) "Primitive Substances," *Philosophy and Phenomenological Research* 54: 531–52.

Lowe, E. J. (1995) *Locke on Human Understanding*, London: Routledge.

Lowe, E. J. (1996) *Subjects of Experience*, Cambridge: Cambridge University Press.

Lycan, W. G. (1987) *Consciousness*, Cambridge, Mass.: MIT Press.

McKirahan, R. (1994) *Philosophy Before Socrates: An Introduction with Texts and Commentary*, Indianapolis: Hackett Publishing Co.

Malebranche, Nicholas (1688/1997) *Dialogues on Metaphysics and Religion*, trans. Nicholas Jolley and David Scott, Cambridge: Cambridge University Press.

Martin, C. B. (1980) "Substance Substantiated," *Australasian Journal of Philosophy* 58: 3–10.

Martin, C. B. (1987) "Proto-Language," *Australasian Journal of Philosophy* 65: 277–89.

Martin, C. B. (1992) "Power for Realists," in Bacon *et al.* (1992): 175–86.

Martin, C. B. (1993) "The Need for Ontology: Some Choices," *Philosophy* 68: 505–22.

Martin, C. B. (1994) "Dispositions and Conditionals," *The Philosophical Quarterly* 44: 1–8.

Martin, C. B. (1997) "On the Need for Properties: The Road to Pythagoreanism and Back," *Synthese* 112: 193–231.

Martin, C. B. and Heil, John (forthcoming) "Rules and Powers," *Philosophical Perspectives*.

Mele, Alfred R. (1987) *Irrationality: An Essay on Akrasia, Self-Deception, and Self-Control*, New York: Oxford University Press.

Mellor, Hugh (1974) "In Defense of Dispositions," *Philosophical Review* 83: 157–81. Reprinted in Mellor (1991): 104–22.

Mellor, Hugh (1991) *Matters of Metaphysics*, Cambridge: Cambridge University Press.

Millikan, Ruth (1984) *Language, Thought, and Other Biological Categories: New Foundations for Realism*, Cambridge, Mass.: MIT Press.

Millikan, Ruth (1989) "Biosemantics," *Journal of Philosophy* 86: 281–97.

Moses, Louis J. and Flavell, J. H. (1990) "Inferring False Beliefs from Actions and Reactions," *Child Development* 61: 929–45.

Nagel, Thomas (1974) "What is it Like to be a Bat?" *Philosophical Review* 83: 435–50. Reprinted in Nagel (1979): 165–80. Also reprinted in Block (1980a): 159–68; and in Rosenthal (1991): 422–8.

Nagel, Thomas (1979) *Mortal Questions*, Cambridge: Cambridge University Press.

Perner, Josef (1991) *Understanding the Representational Mind*, Cambridge, Mass.: MIT Press.

Place, U. T. (1956) "Is Consciousness A Brain Process?" *The British Journal of Psychology* 47: 44–50.

Plato, *Parmenides*, in B. Jowett (trans.), *The Dialogues of Plato*, 4th ed., vol. 2, Oxford: Clarendon Press, 1953.

Plato, *Phaedo*, in B. Jowett (trans.), *The Dialogues of Plato*, 4th ed., vol. 1, Oxford: Clarendon Press, 1953.

Plato, *Republic*, in B. Jowett (trans.), *The Dialogues of Plato*, 4th ed., vol. 2, Oxford: Clarendon Press, 1953.

Poland, Jeffrey (1994) *Physicalism: The Philosophical Foundations*, Oxford: Clarendon Press.

Putnam, Hilary. (1975a) "The Meaning of 'Meaning,'" in Keith Gunderson (ed.), *Language, Mind, and Knowledge* (*Minnesota Studies in the Philosophy of Science 7*), Minneapolis: University of Minnesota Press: 131–93. Reprinted in Putnam (1975b): 215–71.

Putnam, Hilary (1975b) *Mind, Language, and Reality: Philosophical Papers*, vol. 2, Cambridge: Cambridge University Press.

Putnam, Hilary (1981) *Reason, Truth, and History*, Cambridge: Cambridge University Press.

Pylyshyn, Zenon (1973) "What then Mind's Eye Tells the Mind's Brain: A Critique of Mental Imagery," *Psychological Bulletin* 80: 1–25.

Quine, W. V. O. (1961) *Word and Object*, Cambridge, Mass.: MIT Press.

Rosenthal, David (ed.) (1991) *The Nature of Mind*, New York: Oxford University Press.

Russell, Bertrand (1927) *Analysis of Matter*, London: Kegan Paul.

Ryder, D. T. (1996) "Evaluating Theories of Consciousness Using the Autonomic Nervous System for Comparison," unpublished MA thesis, University of Calgary.

Ryle, Gilbert (1949) *The Concept of Mind*, London: Hutchinson.

Searle, John (1980) "Minds, Brains, and Programs," *Behavioral and Brain Sciences* 3: 417–24. Reprinted in Haugeland (1981a): 282–306; in Dennett and Hofstadter (1981): 353–82; and in Rosenthal (1991): 509–23.

Searle, John (1992) *The Rediscovery of the Mind*, Cambridge, Mass.: MIT Press.

Searle, John (1997) "Consciousness and the Philosophers," *New York Review of Books*, 6 March: 43–50.

Shoemaker, Sydney (1975) "Functionalism and Qualia," *Philosophical Studies* 27: 291–315. Reprinted in Block (1980a): 251–67; in Shoemaker (1984a): 184–205; and in Rosenthal (1991): 395–407.

Shoemaker, Sydney (1980) "Causality and Properties," in Peter van Inwagen (ed.), *Time and Cause*, Dordrecht: Reidel Publishing Co.: 109–35. Reprinted in Shoemaker (1984a): 206–33.

Shoemaker, Sydney (1981) "Some Varieties of Functionalism," *Philosophical Topics* 12: 83–118. Reprinted in Shoemaker (1984a): 261–86.

Shoemaker, Sydney (1984a) *Identity, Cause, and Mind: Philosophical Essays*, Cambridge: Cambridge University Press.

Shoemaker, Sydney (1984b) "Absent Qualia are Impossible–A Reply to Block," in Shoemaker (1984a): 309–26.

Skinner, B. F. (1953) *Science and Human Behavior*, New York: Macmillan.

Skinner, B. F. (1957) *Verbal Behavior*, New York: Appleton–Century–Crofts.

Skinner, B. F. (1963) "Behaviorism at Fifty," *Science* 140: 951–8. Reprinted with commentaries and Skinner's responses in *Behavioral and Brain Sciences* 7 (1984): 615–57.

Smart, J. J. C. (1959) "Sensations and Brain Processes," *Philosophical Review* 68: 141–56. Reprinted in Rosenthal (1991): 169–76.

Sterelny, Kim (1990) *The Representational Theory of Mind: An Introduction*, Oxford: Blackwell Publishers.

Stich, Stephen (1983) *From Folk Psychology to Cognitive Science: The Case Against Belief*, Cambridge, Mass.: MIT Press.

Strawson, P. F. (1959) *Individuals: An Essay in Descriptive Metaphysics*, London: Methuen.

Tarski, Alfred (1956) "The Concept of Truth in Formalized Languages," in *Logic, Semantics, and Metamathematics*, Oxford: Clarendon Press: 152–278.

Thomas, Elizabeth Marshall (1993) *The Hidden Life of Dogs*, New York: Houghton-Mifflin.

Thomas, Elizabeth Marshall (1994) *The Tribe of the Tiger*, New York: Simon and Schuster.

Thomas, Nigel J. T. (1989) "Experience and Theory as Determinants of Attitudes toward Mental Representation: The Case of Knight Dunlap and the Vanishing Images of J. B. Watson," *American Journal of Psychology* 102: 395–412.

Thomas, Nigel J. T. (forthcoming) "Are Theories of Imagery Theories of Imagination?" *Cognitive Science*.

Tolman, E. C. (1948) "Cognitive Maps in Rats and Men," *Psychological Review* 55: 189–208.

Turing, Alan (1950) "Computing Machinery and Intelligence," *Mind* 59: 434–60. Reprinted in Dennett and Hofstadter (1981): 53–68; and in Anderson (1964): 4–30.

Tye, Michael (1991) *The Imagery Debate*, Cambridge, Mass.: MIT Press.

van Inwagen, Peter (1993) *Metaphysics*, Boulder: Westview Press.

Waal, F. B. M. de (1982) *Chimpanzee Politics*, New York: Harper and Row.

Watson, J. B. (1913) "Psychology as the Behaviorist Views It," *Psychological Review* 20: 158–77.

Weinberg, Steven (1997) "Before the Big Bang," *New York Review of Books*, 12 June: 16–20.

Wimmer, Heinz and Perner, Josef (1983) "Beliefs about Beliefs: Representation and Constraining Function of Wrong Beliefs in Young Children's Understanding of Deception," *Cognition* 13: 103–28.

Wittgenstein, Ludwig (1922/1961) *Tractatus Logico-Philosophicus*, trans. D. F. Pears and B. F. McGuinness, London: Routledge and Kegan Paul.

Wittgenstein, Ludwig (1953/1968) *Philosophical Investigations*, trans. G. E. M. Anscombe, Oxford: Basil Blackwell.

Wittgenstein, Ludwig (1969) *On Certainty*, eds G. E. M. Anscombe and G. H. von Wright, trans. Denis Paul and G. E. M. Anscombe, Oxford: Basil Blackwell.

# Index

Numbers in bold type refer to pages where key terms are explained.